British Studies Series

General Editor JEREMY BLACK

Published

John Charmley **A History of Conservative** ₊₀
David Childs **Britain since 1939**
David Eastwood **Government and Commun₍ ₋₎ne English Provinces,
1700–1870**
Brian Hill **The Early Parties and Politics in Britain, 1688–1832**
Kevin Jeffreys **Retreat from New Jerusalem: British Politics, 1951–1964**
T. A. Jenkins **The Liberal Ascendancy, 1830–1886**
David Loades **Power in Tudor England**
Murray G. H. Pittock **Inventing and Resisting Britain: Cultural Identities
in Britain and Ireland, 1685–1789**
Andrew Thorpe **A History of the British Labour Party**

Forthcoming

D. G. Boyce **Britain and Decolonisation**
Glenn Burgess **British Political Thought from Reformation to
Revolution**
J. B. Christoph **The Twentieth-Century British State**
Gary De Krey **Restoration and Revolution in Britain**
W. H. Fraser **The Rise and Fall of British Trade Unionism**
Jeremy Gregory **The Long Reformation: Religion and Society in England
c. 1530–1870**
Katrina Honeyman **Women and Industrialization**
Jon Lawrence **Britain and the First World War**

(List continued overleaf)

F. J. Levy **Politics and Culture in Tudor England**
Diarmaid MacCulloch **The Reformation in Britain, 1480–1680**
Allan Macinnes **The British Revolution**
G. I. T. Machin **The Rise of British Democracy**
Thomas Mayer **Britain, 1450–1603**
Michael Mendle **The English Civil War and Political Thought**
Alexander Murdoch **British History, 1660–1832**
W. Rubinstein **History of Britain in the Twentieth Century**
Howard Temperley **Britain and America**

British Studies Series
Series Standing Order ISBN 978-0-333-69332-2

You can receive future titles in this series as they are published by placing a standing order. Please contact your bookseller or, in case of difficulty, write to us at the address below with your name and address, the title of the series and the ISBN quoted above.

Customer Services Department, Macmillan Distribution Ltd
Houndmills, Basingstoke, Hampshire RG21 6XS, England

Inventing and Resisting Britain

Cultural Identities in Britain and Ireland, 1685–1789

Murray G. H. Pittock

© Murray G. H. Pittock 1997

All rights reserved. No reproduction, copy or transmission of
this publication may be made without written permission.

No paragraph of this publication may be reproduced, copied or
transmitted save with written permission or in accordance with
the provisions of the Copyright, Designs and Patents Act 1988,
or under the terms of any licence permitting limited copying
issued by the Copyright Licensing Agency, 90 Tottenham Court
Road, London W1P 9HE.

Any person who does any unauthorised act in relation to this
publication may be liable to criminal prosecution and civil
claims for damages.

The author has asserted his rights to be identified as the author of this
work in accordance with the Copyright, Designs and Patents Act 1988.

First published 1997 by
MACMILLAN PRESS LTD
Houndmills, Basingstoke, Hampshire RG21 6XS
and London
Companies and representatives
throughout the world

ISBN 978-0-333-65061-5   ISBN 978-1-349-25619-8 (eBook)
DOI 10.1007/978-1-349-25619-8

A catalogue record for this book is available
from the British Library.

This book is printed on paper suitable
for recycling and made from fully
managed and sustained forest sources.

10   9   8   7   6   5   4   3   2   1
06   05   04   03   02   01   00   99   98   97

Typeset by EXPO Holdings, Malaysia

Published in the United States of America 1997 by
ST. MARTIN'S PRESS, INC.,
Scholarly and Reference Division
175 Fifth Avenue, New York, N.Y. 10010

ISBN 978-0-312-16576-5

For Anne

Contents

Acknowledgements

This book is one of the many things owed in whole or in part to the support of the University of Edinburgh, having been developed as an idea and partly written during two periods of research support in 1994–5, the first taken as a Visiting Fellow in the Thomas Reid Institute of the University of Aberdeen. If these allowed the time to plan and begin, a good deal of the texture of the book has come out in debate with colleagues and students over the years, in particular in discussions with Colin Nicholson on the Financial Revolution.

The idea of 'Britishness' itself, its fluidity, rhetoric and vulnerability, was something I first worked on in detail in preparation for giving the Royal Society of Edinburgh BP Prize Lecture in 1993, on 'Inventing and Resisting Britain: Successes and Failures of the British Idea'. In its specific application here, I must acknowledge the influence and help of many friends and supportive colleagues, notably Jeremy Black, Eveline Cruickshanks, Harry Dickinson, Owen Dudley Edwards and Frank McLynn.

In the longer term, this book clearly owes much to a range of distinguished writers, and to the redevelopment of 'four nations' history in the post-colonial era, spurred on by J. G. A. Pocock's influential essays. However, as is argued in the pages that follow, this approach has not yet matured enough to be multifocal rather than merely multinational.

My wife, Anne, has as ever contributed both patience and an unfailing supply of wit and good humour: it was family holidays to the countryside of her childhood and to Ludlow which first set me thinking on the culture of the Welsh Marches. Any errors which follow are my own.

Murray G. H. Pittock
Edinburgh

1 Inventing and Resisting Britain

England, Scotland, Ireland and Wales 1685–8

This book is an examination of the cultural and political diversity of Britain and Ireland in the eighteenth century, and the extent to which we can speak of 'Britain' as a unified country at all at times of crisis during this period. In the ensuing discussion, it is inevitable that minorities within the British Isles will receive a high degree of attention, but this is relevant not only because many of the histories of eighteenth-century Britain are written from a centralizing 'core' perspective, but also because a multiplicity of minorities in the period may well constitute a majority. In the early eighteenth century, for example, the population of England was little more than that of Scotland, Wales and Ireland combined. Today, it is four times this: such a demographic shift has obvious cultural effects. Large-scale alterations in political authority, allegiance and religious or cultural practice have also taken place. In this process, the eighteenth century was crucial: it is the historic battleground of the formation of Great Britain, and subsequent historians have viewed it as such. In the conclusion to this book, their position and the principles underlying definitions of identity in general will be further scrutinized. Traditional historiographical practice has, sometimes overtly, sometimes unconsciously, often chosen the narrative which leads to the status quo of its own day. Like an interviewing panel which selects its own likeness for corporate preferment, the history of the century covered here has often (especially and continuingly on a textbook level) promoted the political and high cultural life of the English heartland, and in particular of London. This book cannot be altogether free of the bias of conscious selection, still less that of inevitably partial knowledge, but in presenting the diversity of the

1

stories of the four nations and many regions which make up these islands, it aims to minimize any bias. Viewing different groups in their own terms should allow the uncertainty and provisionality of British identity in the period to emerge – as they appeared to contemporaries. Such cultural variety will also give a perspective on the different qualities of London and 'core' English culture, and inform us as to the means by which selected features of this culture became the landmarks of historical narrative by which the century is visible, as well as tracing the ways in which other elements of Britain were alienized as 'provincial', 'barbarous' or 'other'. This narrative concentrates on the perceived drift to modernity at the core of the British state, whether in the old Whig historiographic guise of liberties broadening from precedent to precedent, or the more muted versions of 'the growth of stability', 'a polite and commercial people' and so on. It has had a powerful and prolonged appeal, rooted not only in inherited ideological value, but also in the strong evidence from some parts of the British Isles on which it has been able to draw.

In 1685, London and the English south-east and east midlands formed, as they still do, the core of British political culture. This bore about it, at least to the casual observer, the marks of a world not too dissimilar from our own in structure if not in appearance (as Macaulay wrote, 'could the England of 1685 be ... set before our eyes, we should not know one landscape in a hundred or one building in ten thousand'). Improvement was still largely a matter of theory rather than practice: after all the Stuarts were still on the throne. If this picture was true of the south, it seems for Macaulay most thoroughly the case in the supposedly uncultivated and broken-down provinces: Cumberland, where 'no traveller ventured ... without making his will', the 'state of barbarism' north of Trent, 'constantly desolated by bands of Scottish marauders' and so on. Though Macaulay's cruder strictures have long vanished, this is not so true of his focus, which does have a certain plausibility to it, given the special development of London as a metropolis of far greater comparative and absolute size than was common in Europe. At the top of the political tree was a monarchy, which, despite or because of its disastrous shipwreck in the war of three kingdoms forty years earlier, stood apparently far removed from the jurisprudential brigandage which had seen Henry I chop off the right hands of all the moneyers in England, or the ferocity of religious and political persecution under Henry VIII and Mary only 130 years before. The Earl of Rochester's court skit, reputedly 'posted on Whitehall gate', was surely indicative of a freer, more modern world:

> God bless our good and gracious King,
>   Whose promise none relies on;
> Who never said a foolish thing,
>   Nor ever did a wise one.

Charles was supposed to have answered, 'My words are my own, my acts those of my ministers.' Such a public satire and such a response might have seemed inconceivable in the world before 1638. The King's reply itself casts a sidelong glance at the criticism or excuse of moderate Parliamentarians and their Royalist equivalents in the 1640s: that Charles I was badly advised rather than ill-intentioned. London, the south-east and east midlands had not been fertile territory for the king in 1642: more proof, if proof were needed, that the Stuarts were not 'modern'.[1]

If the condition of post-Cromwellian monarchy seemed to render it newly vulnerable to irony, this would be in no small measure the achievement of Parliament. The Exclusion Crisis of 1679–82 was in this context arguably the most serious constitutional challenge which the hereditary monarchy had yet faced. Northumberland's Protestant coup of 1553 was, by comparison, only a traditionally crude and illegitimate use of magnate power, and it collapsed within days. The sustained and largely constitutional challenge posed to a Catholic successor towards the end of Charles II's life was surely a sign that the modern political nation was bent on resisting the threat of continental absolutism, and that, to borrow Trevelyan's comment on the situation in 1680, 'Slowly, through blood and tears, justice and freedom had been advancing.' A few years later, the Trial of the Seven Bishops was to show that the leaders of the constitutional political nation included those ancient props of monarchy, the leaders of the Church of England: while the bloodless Revolution which followed displayed the moderation of true liberty, as it asserted itself in the face of what was, in English terms, an anachronistic drift back to 'the more barbarous methods of Elizabeth and the mediaeval kings'.[2]

In the cultural realm too, architecture, literature and science seemed to be emerging in a relatively modern dress. The rebuilding of London after the Great Fire of 1666, which destroyed 89 churches and 13 000 houses (itself an apocalyptic overthrow of the symbolically pre-modern plague of the preceding year) is also a token of modernity, the complete alteration in the capital's skyline revealing a shift into a new world under the guidance of architects such as Christopher Wren and Nicholas Hawksmoor. St Paul's Cathedral can be seen as an icon of a self-confident Anglican polity, whose special status was reinforced by the monument claiming that Catholics started the Great Fire, the 'tall bully' of Pope's *Epistle to Bathurst*: statements of cultural identity from an England discarding a superstitious past in its move to the imperial phase and creation of the British state.[3]

Amid all this many have found a consciousness of a new age and new cultural responsibilities. The Royal Society of London, founded in 1660, marked a formalization of moves towards scientific enquiry, hitherto more or less the preserve of isolated gentleman amateurs. In the context of the Plague and Fire, the Society can also be seen working for social improvement (again, something on which Macaulay comments in his process of alienizing the remoter provinces from central British development). The Royal Society also enshrined the superiority of the Plain Style which had been defended by those critical of baroque and Ciceronian tendencies in the Royalist and particularly Laudian rhetoric of the 1630s and 1640s. Although the direct brevity of plainer Senecan prose had its scientific antecedents in Bacon, Plain Style's adoption had nonetheless powerful political echoes of the conflicts of a generation before, which had led to war in all three kingdoms and the principality of Wales, with casualty levels proportionately unmatched until the First World War. Awareness of language as a definer of modernity was strongly present in literature also. Pope's fear that 'Our sons their fathers' failing language see/And such as Chaucer is, shall Dryden be', displayed a new awareness of sociolinguistic change, already present at the end of the seventeenth century in Dryden's translations of Chaucer. The horizons of national culture were altering, and with them the horizons of language, as demonstrated in the newfound imperialist and orientalist rhetoric of the tragedies of Dryden, Poet Laureate since 1670 and the figurehead of late Stuart literature.[4]

A growing sense of distance from the past could also be seen as compounded by the growth of scholarship in the modern sense, whether that of classical scholars like Richard Bentley or, a little later, Shakespearean editors such as Theobald, some of whose emendations can still be said to stand the test of time. In their turn, these new practices flourished in a world where the book trade was increasing in volume, with dictionaries and reference works slowly becoming available (a shrewd move for booksellers, as it turned out, because they needed regular modernizing and upgrading, thus providing a steady stream of sales). The wars of the 1640s had already sparked off a massive increase in the volume of publications, and the intimate links between the political climate and printing were soon to expand further. A more informed public was, surely, a public more conscious of its right to liberty, and thus more vigilant towards any attempt to undermine such a right. A hundred years later, the vast circulations of Thomas Paine's *Common Sense* and *The Rights of Man* could be held to support this argument; twenty-five years after Charles II's death, the similarly huge sale of Dr Sacheverell's *The Perils of False Brethren* presents a more equivocal example.[5]

It is such equivocations which beset the above manifestly incomplete account of cultural identity in Britain and Ireland in the eighteenth century. To take as an example only the fashionable view (best articulated by Linda Colley in her 1992 book, *Britons*) of Protestant solidarity as the basis for unitary British identity, it is surely strange in such a context that the High Anglican concerns of a quasi-Jacobite like Sacheverell could touch a raw nerve on such a scale: many in the High Church grouping displayed a considerably more antagonistic attitude to Dissenters than they could be brought to show for Catholics, Dean Swift being a prominent exemplar of this attitude. Nor were such concerns directed either from or towards an unrepresentative minority. Recalling the different population balance between the 'Celtic fringe' and southeast England that then obtained, it can readily be seen that almost half the population in the British Isles did not conform to jurant Anglicanism (that is, those Anglicans who tacitly or actively accepted the overthrow of James II and VII, and the establishment of a Protestant succession), and that even within the juring Anglican ranks, many suspected government religious policy (Sacheverell's tract sold up to 100 000). Such facts have the potential to alter considerably our view of the Britain which pre-saged our own. The widespread perception of metropolitan insen-sitivity and self-absorption in today's media, common not only in the non-English countries of Britain but in many English regions, is only one sign in our own day of the persisting quality of a sim-plistic historical view of British selfhood. Whether in the context of the bloodlessness of the 'Glorious' Revolution (so identified first in 1689, when the killing associated with it was still going on), the characterization of rural Britain in terms of the rolling coun-tryside of the south, or the prophecy of imperial victory on the playing fields of Eton, Britain is the inheritor in cultural, histori-cal and political terms of the English state's historic achievement of early centralization. The very high proportion of BBC pro-grammes made in the London area in 1995, for example, (as compared with Scotland's c. 2 per cent), is the outcome of a string of policy decisions linked through time to the narrative of how Britain was constructed historically and culturally relayed to the decision-makers of our own day. Because even now what we experience as 'British' in the narrative of cultural comment has been created through a selective adoption of the central English politico-cultural concerns of the past three hundred years, it is all the more important to investigate questions of cultural complex-ity which lie behind the building of Britain, and which cannot be answered by seductive appeals to single motivating historical forces, be they religious or economic. Teleology explores time in order to appropriate it; it is not so much at its ease with space, which it must colonize rather than integrate. The decolonization of British space in the eighteenth century will allow us a clearer vision of differences than that permitted by teleological narratives of religious or economic integration through time.[6]

This chapter examines both the invention of the modern British state in the 1685–1714 period, and the nature of resistance to it. Returning to where I began, at the close of the reign of Charles II, it is instructive to see how the proto-modernity which can be read into cultural developments in south-east England appeared elsewhere. A limited and ironized royal authority was considerably less apparent in the Scotland of Lauderdale and the Killing Times or the Ireland of the vice-royalty than it may have been to certain privileged members or associates of the governing class in London. Scotland was ruled with autocratic force through the king's representative and a largely compliant parliament: yet it was not as marginal to royal concerns as it later became. The decoration and redevelopment of Holyrood Palace in Edinburgh during Charles II's reign may have been part of a royal plan to bolster the country's status as a separate kingdom, both perhaps to minimize the complaints of Anglicization which had led to the explosion of 1638, and also to reinforce Stuart authority and legitimacy as kings of Scotland. The series of portraits of the Scottish royal line dating back to Fergus, commissioned for De Wet to paint at Holyrood in 1684–6, both linked the Stuarts to a distinctively Scottish monarchy, and aligned them with heroic predecessors such as Robert I, as well as foregrounding them in the context of a designed 'perpetual contemporaneity'. The vandalizing of these portraits by Hawley's dragoons during the Jacobite Rising of 1745–6 was thus symbolically apt, for they were a visual endorsement of the legitimacy of Stuart power in Scotland.[7]

As Keith Brown has pointed out, in some respects Stuart kingship was better suited to thrive outside London. The viceregal court in Dublin had shown the potential for a strong court culture as early as the 1630s, and while James held court at Holyrood as Duke of Albany during the Exclusion Crisis, 'there was an explosion of enthusiasm for the royal family and a renewed determination to underline its Scottish origins':

> Scottish noblemen deserted London – 'I do not hear of one that stays', wrote Lord Wharton – and Edinburgh became the centre of a thriving court with an unmistakably Scottish flavour.

The enormous potential appeal of a Scottish court to such Scots was doubtless underlined by the declining influence of Scotsmen in London, where 'after 1660 no Scot held a major court office', in contrast to the position under James I and VI, when over two-fifths of important offices at the London court were in Scottish hands. At the same time, this process of Anglicization may have had a positive effect on Stuart relations with Scotland, for Charles I's unwise measures may have been due to his belief that, as a Scotsman born, he knew more of his countrymen's inclinations than was in fact the case. James's commission from his brother, 'to work "for the general settlement of the peace of that our ancient kingdom"', was by contrast carried out with relative success: while remaining ideologically interested in Scotland, the later Stuarts had lost the personal links which had earlier served to confuse matters.[8]

Moreover, James did not merely succeed in conferring a degree of peace on a country which had recently seen its Primate, Archbishop Sharp, murdered, and two significant engagements with the Covenanting dissenters of the West in a rising finally defeated by the Duke of Monmouth at Bothwell Brig. James also 'determined to make Edinburgh an intellectual centre for Stuart royalism'. Disaffection in the capital had been the beginning of the end for the Stuart regime in the 1630s, and no doubt James wished to prevent a repetition of this. If so, he achieved his aim in fine style. In 1681, the Scots Parliament endorsed him fulsomely against the pretensions of Exclusion:

> the Kings of this Realme deryving their Royall power from God almightie alone, doe succeid lineallie therto according to the known decrees of Proximitie in blood, which cannot be interrupted suspended or diverted by any Act or Statute whatsoever.

Nor was this formal gesture the only sign of enthusiasm. The important figures of Edinburgh society talked 'with delight of the gaiety and brilliancy of the court of Holyroodhouse', where James patronized the arts, especially drama (Dryden's *Indian Emperor* may have been performed there), and the intellectual infrastructure of the city was developed significantly. In the 1680s, James helped to extend the mission of the university, instituted the Advocates' Library and the Royal College of Physicians and founded chivalrous organizations such as the Royal Company of Archers (a Jacobite hotbed until the middle of the eighteenth century) and the revivified Order of the Thistle. The range of royal action was wide, showing Edinburgh clearly in the light of a secondary capital in a multi-kingdom monarchy:

> New charters were provided for both the City of Edinburgh and its College. Patronage was provided for surgery, cartography, mathematics and engineering, and individuals who benefited from the royalist regime were involved in the full range of seventeenth century intellectual activities, from the medicine of

Harvey and the philosophy of Newton to numismatics and weather recording.[9]

In responding to the intellectual demands of the Scottish aristocracy and professional classes, James 'constructed a dominant position in Scottish politics', one which was vitiated only by the Catholicizing policies pursued by his Chancellor, the Earl of Perth, in the later 1680s. Nevertheless, whatever was to happen later, James's actions can be seen as serving to lay the foundations for that 'hotbed of genius' which became the Scottish Enlightenment. A city of 30 000 people (50 000 by 1750), Edinburgh was larger than any mainland British town outside London. Concentrated as it was into a small space, its intense intellectual activity and the status of a capital, more fully granted it by the cultural developments of the 1680s, all served to nourish an intimate atmosphere of intellectual exchange. In this context it is an irony that one of the achievements of the Enlightenment was to alter the nature of the urban environment which had made it possible. The 'heavenly city of the Enlightenment philosophers', the Edinburgh New Town, was a remaking of a national capital which, a century later, echoes that of London after the Great Fire: it was a plan first mooted under James's administration.[10]

Could Edinburgh then in 1685 also appear a city of modernity, with its developing intellectual establishments and a growing interest in scientific enquiry? There remained very important differences in the Scottish polity, even leaving aside the more autocratic nature of Stuart rule there. In England, it might be possible to believe (just) in a political culture chiefly united and denominated through anti-Catholicism: in Scotland, tensions over the nature of the Church of Scotland itself made this much more difficult.

Edinburgh under James was being developed as an Episcopalian royal capital, just as London was an Anglican one, but only fifty miles from Holyrood a band of Protestant extremists had shot at, stabbed, slashed and hacked to death the Episcopalian Archbishop of St Andrews two miles from his city, at midday on 3 May 1679, and in full view of his daughter. Episcopalian apologists such as William Thoirs likened Archbishop Sharp's murder to that of Cardinal Beaton, killed by reformers in 1546: Catholic and Episcopalian archbishops alike slain by fanatics. Sharp's murder was not, however, to be taken as a sign of a disorderly and barbarous country. The treatment of his murderers was, in the words of Julia Buckroyd, 'a tribute to the sophistication and respect for law of seventeenth-century Scotland'. Rather, Sharp's death was a sign of the presence in Scottish society of deep-seated hostility between two rival reformed positions, and of the profound irreconcilability of a significant group of Covenanting zealots (whose culture survived and arguably survives among its descendants in Ulster). The division between Episcopalian and Covenanter was as profound in the late seventeenth and early eighteenth centuries as that between Catholic and Protestant at the time of Beaton's death. Nor was (as sometimes has been suggested) Archbishop Sharp the representative of a tiny oppressing minority in a Presbyterian country: evidence from the 1708 Synod lists and other sources show Scotland as between one-third and one-half Episcopalian. Religious divisions over forms of church government and what they symbolized were so deep and bitter north of the Border as to make a mockery of any united Protestant front.[11]

In Ireland, Charles II's reign had seen the restoration, on a limited scale, of Catholic lands lost in the War of the Three Kingdoms, with the passing of Acts of Settlement (1662) and Explanation (1665), the net effect of which 'was to increase the Catholic share of profitable land to around 20 per cent' (from 8–9 per cent in 1660); but the royal administration did not favour Catholics with political influence to the same extent, though moves to extend English anti-Catholic legislation to Ireland were blocked by Ormonde on Charles's orders in 1663. The effects of the Cromwellian settlement continued to a significant degree, both in Ireland and abroad. Montserrat, to which some 50 000 Irish were transported in the late 1650s, reportedly remained Irish-speaking until the end of the eighteenth century. It was not, however, Catholicism and its native language alone which divided Ireland from mainland British society. In the early years of the king's reign, Ormonde's regime 'savagely harried the dissenters … and confused, demoralized, and divided Protestant opinion', while by contrast the Viceroy was less inclined to take alarm at the Catholic 'threat', even during the Popish Plot hysteria – a position not uncharacteristic of High Church Irishmen into the following century. In 1670, under Lord Berkeley's Lord Lieutenancy, there

was general Catholic tolerance: the Anglican archbishop even permitted his Catholic counterpart 'to set up Catholic grammar
schools in the diocese'. By the early 1670s, agents agitated openly
for a revised land settlement in the Catholic interest, and a Royal
Commission was set up to examine its injustices. In 1672, a
'Declaration of Indulgence' suspended 'all penal laws against
Catholics and Dissenters'. The anti-Catholic reaction of 1673 and
the years that followed initiated a campaign of repression 'to
appease English opinion', but 'went no further than was necessary
for that purpose'. Even in the Popish Plot period itself, 'the
Catholic archbishop of Cashel reported to Rome that "the government here is far more moderate ... has not oppressed us at all so
much as in England"'. In the aftermath of the Plot's 'exposure',
royal policy intensified its attacks on Protestant dissent in both
Scotland and Ireland. Throughout Ireland, 'ministers were bound
over and meeting-houses closed, while units of the army were
quartered in Presbyterian strongholds in Ulster'. By early 1685,
the implicit bias towards the Catholic interest inherent in such
proceedings was made clear, when 'power to give army commis-
sions was taken away from the Lord-Lieutenant into the direct gift
of the king', with a resulting increase in the number of commis-
sions given to Catholic Royalists.[12]

Ireland was a country dominated (as it was to be throughout
the following century) by an Anglican élite, divided from both the
Catholic majority and the Dissenters, whose own political agenda
was to surface strongly in the later eighteenth century. Socially
and culturally, the country was split four ways: the native Irish and
the old English Catholic settlers, who were being steadily driven
together by issues of religion and landownership; the Anglican
community of largely English origin and the substantially Scottish
Dissenters (in 1695, Lord Chancellor Porter argued 'that it might
at some time be necessary to arm Irish Catholics in order to
subdue the Scots of Ulster'). Differences in national origin
increased the cultural and religious divisions between these communities. The Anglican governing classes usually disowned their
Irishness: the 4th Earl of Orrery for example, although he took
considerable part in Irish affairs, was, according to his most recent
biographer, entirely devoid of any self-identification as Irish, while
Swift, for all his sympathies, viewed himself as a stranger in a
strange land. There were those from this group who argued that

Ireland was an 'enlarged part of England ... to be reputed no more separate from the care of the monarch of Great Britain than Yorkshire, Cheshire or any other part of England'. By contrast, a kind of Irish difference (though strongly separated from Catholic Ireland) is visible at a relatively early stage in the dissenting community, descending to us today in the very marked features of Ulster Protestant self-definition. Even in this group, however, there was a dislike of the term 'Irish': though Glasgow University students from Ulster seemed happy enough to be described as 'Scotus Hibernus' (Scots-Irish) in the eighteenth century, 'in 1722 there were bitter protests when the lord-advocate [of Scotland] referred disparagingly to two such students who had appeared before him as "Irishmen"'. Despite this, unified Irish Protestant acceptance of a 'British' identity, occasionally glimpsed in references in 1689–91, does not seem to have survived effectively for long (for one thing, the Protestant groups' claims to ascendancy depended on the view that Ireland was a separate kingdom which they were entitled to govern, and not a colony governed from England). In any case it was clear that its definition was sectarian rather than ethnic, for the old English Catholics do not seem to have seen themselves this way at all. As early as 1663, Henry Bennet remarked that

> the English that have been some time here hate as much that anyone should come amongst them as the Creolians of Mexico and Peru do the natives of Spain that go every year to the Indies.

The implication was plain: this group had already 'gone native'.[13]

Like Scotland, Ireland also had lost a Primate in the last few years of Charles's reign. St Oliver Plunket, Archbishop of Armagh, was not, however, murdered by extremist Presbyterians, but convicted in London in 1681 in a sham trial brought about by the fever surrounding the Popish Plot and its supposed Irish counterpart: 'an utterly harmless man caught up in the wheels of politics and crushed'. Given the minimalist repression carried on by the royal authorities in Ireland, the fact that the Archbishop had to be brought to London for martyrdom is significant. If the death of Sharp could be blamed on the supposed incivility and intolerance of Scottish society, that of Armagh shows up the deep limitations on any notions of proto-modernity which we might be tempted to apply to late seventeenth-century England. Interestingly enough, it was the Archbishop's own view that anti-Catholicism in England was more ferocious and bigoted than in Ireland itself:

> In his speech from the scaffold he reiterated his conviction that the charges against him would have been rejected out of hand by any Protestant jury in Ireland.

Controversy over the sacred and its nature dogged all three kingdoms, and in some ways the most 'modern', England, was the most bigoted of the three.[14]

Wales, 'the fag-end of Creation' as it was unkindly called by Ned Ward, 'was a remote and inaccessible federation of small communities' in this period: there was a widespread view that it was 'a backwater "of popery and paganism"'. Compared with Scotland or Ireland, it was markedly under-urbanized (Dublin had a population of 45 000 in 1685, and Ireland as a whole eight times the number of people in Wales, while Scotland had four or five times as many). Its gentry, especially in counties such as Montgomery, Flint and Caernarfonshire, were notoriously poor, though, like their Scots counterparts, intensely proud of their ancestry: 'poor as a church mouse but ready to rattle off his pedigree to the ninth generation or even back to Brutus and Adam', as English caricaturists presented it. From the late fifteenth century there had been pressure on them to learn English, and by the eighteenth century the richer gentlemen were largely Anglicized. The Council of Wales, 'primarily a court of law', in effect 'represented a remarkable experiment in regional government'. It sat at Ludlow, and was normally convened by a major Welsh magnate. Because of its status as the original British nation (being the remnant of the Celtic Britons driven out of England by the Saxons, and chief setting for the stories of King Arthur), the idea of the Britishness of Wales was by no means an alien one, and indeed among the Anglophone political classes it is hard to discern the notion of Welsh national difference at all. The Henrician incorporating Union of 1536, emanating as it did from a quasi-Welsh dynasty, had no serious political opposition in Stuart times, while by the 1690s there was 'very little protest' at the abolition of the Welsh Council by the centralizing Williamite administration, although to support it could admittedly be seen as endorsing the overthrown Stuart power-structures. Anti-Catholic hysteria was not noticeably less pronounced in the Principality than it was in England: the Marquis of Worcester (later Duke of Beaufort), who was from 1672 President of the Council of Wales, was 'widely suspected of being a crypto-papist' and was on the receiving end of a campaign of anti-Catholic hatred led by the Welsh and Herefordshire landowners, John Arnold MP and John Scudamore.[15]

Wales was nonetheless a different society from England, and at local and linguistic levels, this sense of difference was preserved. In a striking anticipation of modern resentment of incomers and holiday cottages, there was widespread opposition to 'speculation' by 'strangers' in Flintshire land under Charles II, which was believed to be 'undoing the county' by 'making land dear to the natives', while in foreign policy there were independent attempts to found a Welsh colony, such as the grant of Cambriol in Newfoundland to William Vaughan of Llangyndeyrn under Charles I (the colony failed within twenty years). Under Elizabeth and James I and VI the Council at Ludlow had almost become a national court for Wales. Among other commentators, Richard Baxter 'was to learn from experience how the swarms of flunkeys, hangers-on and minor functionaries that came in its train could give the town some of the darker aspects of a metropolis'. Technically peripatetic, the Council, which had informally met at Ludlow since 1471, had statutory powers settled on it by the 1536 Act of Union, and gradually confirmed its base in the town. When the Welsh-speaking Earl of Pembroke succeeded to the Lord Presidency of the 'Council of the Dominion and Principality of Wales and the Marches' in the 1580s, 'the courts ... at Ludlow' became 'brilliant social occasions'; in 1587, Thomas Churchyard called Ludlow 'the capital of Wales' with 'the air of a metropolis'. After 1603, James I and VI tried to check the tendency to call Welsh cases to London, and the political power of the Council of Wales (and indeed of the North at York) strengthened, despite the development of an alternative power base in Wales by the largely Catholic Earls of Worcester. Welsh-speakers found it easier to have their cases heard at Ludlow. John Milton's pastoral masque *Comus*, performed on Michaelmas night to Lawes' music,

was perhaps the leading example of the many courtly entertain-
ments held at the Shropshire town. Under the Earl of
Bridgewater, the Welsh Council included up to twenty-four peers
and eleven bishops, a major regional power base which the
Stuarts were keen to develop in order to limit the power of
London. In the 1630s, Charles I cherished the 'true affections' of
the 'ancient Brittaines' of Wales, and it was rumoured in 1642
that the Prince of Wales was to be sent to hold court at Ludlow.
Welsh royalism and local autonomy were anathema to the
Parliamentary authorities, and in 1641 the Council was abolished,
despite an interesting scheme from Richard Lloyd of Eschius
(near Wrexham) to incorporate Ludlow into Wales as its formal
metropolis. Restored under Charles II (though perhaps not to all
its former glories), the Council continued to represent a degree
of Welsh localism which the Stuarts nurtured. The Welsh gentry
were heavily opposed to Exclusion, while James II and VII (whose
Lord Chancellor, Judge Jeffreys, was a Welshman, and many of
whose advisers came from Wales or the Marches) toured the
Welsh border in 1687, though that autumn the Lord President
could get little satisfaction from the magistrates and deputy lieu-
tenants at Ludlow that they would implement the king's pro-
Catholic policies (in 1686, James had made the last royal
pilgrimage to date to St Winifred's Well at Holywell, Flintshire).
Some Dissenters were more optimistic. 'King James, God keep
him, is an instrument in God's hand to give us a likeable freedom'
sang one Baptist miller, though the general reaction to James's
1687 suspension of the earlier Test Acts was far from being so
optimistic. After the overthrow of the Stuart regime in 1688, the
Council was finally wound up by the Earl of Macclesfield, an
English peer, though Wales (excluding Monmouthshire) retained
a distinctive system of courts of law up until 1830. As the relevant
Act (I William & Mary sess. i.c.2) put it, 'the powers of the Lord
President had been much abused, and ... the institution had
become a great grievance to the subject'.[16]

One of the chief areas of sacramentalism in late seventeenth-
and early eighteenth-century Britain was that attached to the
monarchy. Traditional patriarchal sacramentality survived and
indeed prospered in a contemporary atmosphere of religious hysteria. The monarchy might be ironized by a select crowd, but it
still had enormous reserves of popular veneration on which to

draw. Charles II used the sacramental power of the Royal Touch to treat 100 000 people for scrofula and similar complaints, the peaks in such activity not infrequently coming at times of religious or political crisis. Medieval addresses to kings as 'Holy Father' and 'Your Holiness' exemplified the sacramental status of monarchy against which popes such as Gregory VII had inveighed, and which Henry VIII had taken supreme advantage of in the 1530s. This status was still accepted to a considerable degree in the late seventeenth century (it was indeed one of the reasons why executing Charles I had been a political mistake), and touchpieces continued to be used long after the fall of the Stuarts, even into the twentieth century in Ireland. So closely linked was sacramental authority to legitimacy that the Duke of Monmouth touched 'at least once' during the Exclusion Crisis, and also in the year when he rebelled (1685), as part of a vain attempt to demonstrate his legitimacy. Subsequently the Touch was used by the Stuarts in exile as a sign of their *de jure* right.[17]

Lest the Touch be thought a medieval survival which progressive constitutionalism rightly discarded ('God send you better health, and more sense' said William III and II to one who desired it of him), it is instructive to note that Charles II, despite being deeply committed to such sacramental display, showed far less of the hysteria which greeted Oates's allegations than did his more constitutionally 'progressive' House of Commons. Absurd levels of anti-Catholic furore were the preserve of the supposedly more 'modern' elements of government in the 1680s: Shaftesbury even fomented the 'Irish plot' in order to revive the flagging fortunes of anti-Catholicism on the mainland. It was not only on the peripheries that odd and superstitious practices continued: they existed at the core of English society. In 1685, 'as the law then stood, the person who admitted a proselyte into the Roman Catholic Church was guilty of a capital crime'. The time was surely inauspicious for the accession of a Catholic heir.[18]

Yet James came to the throne amid considerable popular acclaim. The probity which had impressed the Scottish court now had the chance to shine on a larger stage. James certainly did his best to reassure the Anglican establishment:

I have been reputed to be a man for arbitrary power, but that is not the only story that has been made of me: and I shall make it my endeavour to preserve the government in Church and State as it is now by law established ... I shall never depart from the just rights and prerogative of the Crown, so I shall never invade any man's property.

As the many histories of his reign make clear in their different ways, few can accept that James kept these promises. Yet at the time, both the English and Scottish parliaments fulsomely welcomed the new monarch, the latter proclaiming with satisfaction that 'this nation hath continued now upwards of two thousand years in the unaltered form of our monarchical government'. A strong re-emphasis on the Stuarts' place in the Scottish foundation myth had borne fruit, as it had in Ireland, where James's descent from Irish roots (via Scotland) was a powerful boost to his legitimacy, were his religion alone not sufficient.[19]

As James's government developed, so this enthusiasm waned: his relatively limited concessions to Catholics were simply too much for the climate of opinion to bear. Events such as a stay of punishment on all loyal recusants (February 1686), the presence of five Catholics on the Privy Council by that autumn, or the public reception of the Papal Nuncio in the following July, quite outweighed in the minds of many the mass release of Quakers from prison or the conditional relief given, albeit grudgingly, to Huguenots fleeing Louis XIV's persecution. Although James's Declarations of Indulgence ran counter to the trend of events in France, many chose to believe that they were a prelude to similar moves.[20]

In the English provinces, the threat of limited Catholic intrusion into the coveted prizes of local authority, lieutenancies, magistracies and the like, was arguably even more damaging. In a similar context, the King's attempt to grant the presidency of Magdalen College, Oxford, to a Catholic was a symbolic focal point for local opposition, and succeeded in creating a year's conflict over a matter of utterly marginal importance to the state. At Oxford in September 1687, James resorted to the Touch to underline his authority, administering it 700–800 times in two days. But sacramentality was not enough in the face of the Three Questions and the repeal of the Test Act and Penal Laws: though it should be noted that James was perhaps not entirely unsuccessful in gaining tacit dissenting support in the early stages of Toleration.

Among the Anglican establishment it was a different matter: despite the accompanying threats, only 26 per cent of respondents in England and 22 per cent in Wales expressed support for Toleration and increased opportunity in civil life for Catholics. There were, it is true, many ambivalent answers: but on the whole positive support in England for James's measures was low (though rising above the average in counties like Lancashire, with a strong Roman Catholic tradition. Monmouthshire also had many Catholics). It could be argued, however, that this lack of enthusiasm was the result of a rather bifurcated response as much as it was evidence of the King's being out of touch. Royal policy would have increased opportunities for Catholic gentry, and early eighteenth-century evidence suggests that where there were large numbers of such Catholics (as in the north of England), they integrated well into county society, and were treated as the social equals of their Anglican brethren who alone had access to office; who despite this, may well have believed in the Catholic menace. In English county society, the fact that 'some of my best friends are Papists' did not necessarily abrogate their abstract status as a threat.[21]

There were riots in Coventry, Worcester and Bristol, while in Scotland, Toleration was rejected by a majority of nearly two to one. Nevertheless, James possessed a bulwark of support north of the border in the shape of the Episcopal Church, which commanded majority or near-majority adherence north of the Tay, where more than half the population of Scotland then lived. The Royalist culture James sought to foster in Edinburgh was one which the Episcopalian community were best placed to take advantage of. Its leading clergy and laity saw themselves as the inheritors of pre-Reformation Scotland in a manner which was closed to their Presbyterian rivals, who often had difficulty coming to terms with the achievements of Scotland's medieval Catholic past. Though Episcopalianism had by no means a monopoly on learning and culture, it benefited not only from the situation in Edinburgh, but also from the distinctive local culture of its heartland in north-east Scotland: the core zone of what Gordon Donaldson termed 'the conservative north' of the country, whose castles were one of the last outposts of court culture in Scotland after 1603. Many of the prominent figures in the Scottish Church and Scottish letters came from this area:

figures like Archbishop Sharp, Robert Fergusson, Thomas Ruddiman, James Macpherson, even by origin Robert Burns himself. The north-east, and the universities of Aberdeen in particular (notably King's College), were at the heart of a distinctive Scoto-Latinist culture which lasted until the death of Dr James Melvin in 1853 – a man who still taught in a mixture of Latin and Scots a century after the campaigns to eradicate Scotticisms from educated writing and speech north of the border had begun. From the Aberdeen doctors who resisted the Covenant in the 1630s, through a number of distinguished theologians to the writers and Jacobites of a century later, the north-east was the home of the moderate reformed party in the Church.[22]

As was apparently the case with many Anglican clergy, Episcopalian priests could possess a deep interest in the folklore of the places where they ministered, as well as in more conventional scholarship represented by Archbishop Leighton's library at Dunblane. The Reverend Robert Kirk of Aberfoyle's *History of the Secret Commonwealth of the Elves and Fairies* (1690) was reputed to have led to its author's abduction by the Little People for exposing their secrets.

A safer kind of interest in oral tradition was evident in the work of Episcopalian Royalism's leading ideologue, Sir George Mackenzie.[23] In his *Defence of the Antiquity of the Royal Line of Scotland* (1685), Sir George defends Stuart right as proceeding from the immemorial antiquity of the Scottish foundation myth as well as the Stuarts' senior status among all the dynasties with a claim on the English throne. James was the senior heir of the houses of Tudor, Plantagenet and Wessex as well as that of Stuart, and the arguments along these lines made by Mackenzie go some way to showing how the dethronement of the main Stuart line, heavy as it was with centuries of cultural and dynastic baggage, was to deeply affect political life and cultural ideology for at least a century after it occurred. In a religious age, the Stuart family's steady accretion of dynastic rights must have seemed providential: the first kings of Britain, they were also virtually the first English monarchs to rule with unchallenged title. In the context of such magnificent and comprehensive fittingness, Sir George also appeals to tradition, including the oral tradition of the people, to justify the status of the Royal House of Stuart: it is 'probable Tradition' and 'the general belief' which underpin its dynastic

antiquity. When it comes to the remote past, it is tradition
Mackenzie trusts and not documents: 'the best Records', he says,
'were then faithfull Remembrance of things past', and Sir George
points out that the bardic seannachies, who recited the genealogy
of the incoming monarch, were in use up to the coronation of
'King *Charles* the *Martyr*'. In other words, poetic tradition and the
voice of the people confirm the antiquity and (implicitly) the
indefeasibility of Stuart power, which even makes the King
'undoubted Successor of the *Blood-Royal* of *Wales*'. Sir George concludes that

> God has, from an extraordinary kindness ... lodged in the
> person of our present Sovereign King *James* the 7th (whom
> GOD *Almighty* long preserve) all those opposite and different
> rights, by which our peace might have been formerly
> disturb'd.[24]

Such ultramontane Episcopalian royalism met with rebuffs from
the other side of the Cheviots from Dr Stillingfleet and the Bishop
of St Asaph, who criticized the 'old and fabulous beginnings' celebrated by Mackenzie. In response, Sir George wrote *The Antiquity
of the Royal Line of Scotland Farther Cleared and Defended* (1686), in
which his repeated appeal to tradition renders his apologia very
close in spirit to what may be called Catholic history (this without
prejudice to the fact that it was a Catholic writer, Fr Innes, who
exploded the legend of the antiquity of Scotland's royal line):
general beliefs of long standing are treated as if their authority
matched or indeed replaced that of documents. For a leading
lawyer, this is perhaps quite a remarkable view: it interestingly
foreshadows the division between an 'old' Scotland of customary
rights and a 'new' one of legislative formalities so ably depicted by
Sir Walter Scott and reputedly at issue in the Highland
Clearances.[25]

Reverence paid to customary value had important political connotations too, not least in contrast to the Covenanters, whose declaration of 27 May 1681 rejected '*Pipings, Sportings, Dancings,
Laughings, singing profane and lustfull songs and ballads*' and who
were opposed to 'story-books ... Romances and Pamphlets,
Comedy-Books, Cards and Dice'. In the earlier seventeenth
century the Book of Sports had arguably shown some of the bias

to the poor evident in respect for their traditions, as had the concerns of the Book of Order and Archbishop Laud's opposition to enclosures, a scourge of the poor in the 150 years that followed. The kind of position represented by Mackenzie thus had powerful implications in political belief and action, despite its apparent obscurantism. In Scotland in particular, the depth of the appeal to tradition, especially pre-Reformation tradition, gave James a cultural heartland of support, which it continued to offer him and his successors for a century after he was thrust from the throne, the Episcopalian Bishop Rose having declined to support William except 'insofar as law or conscience will allow'.[26]

In England too, there were still links between high culture and popular tradition. There is some evidence that the Anglican Church returned to the earlier Stuart practice of championing folkways in the aftermath of the Restoration: it was not until the eighteenth century that the Church 'lost command over the "leisure" of the poor, their feasts and festivals, and, with this, over a large area of plebeian culture'. Daniel Defoe's assertion that 6325 maypoles were erected in the five years after 1660 is an example of the anecdotal evidence which links Stuart culture to the preservation and development of festival practices in the localities. This link was later demonstrated in the nature of pro-Stuart celebration in the eighteenth century, and the suspicion expressed towards folkways by Whigs such as Henry Fielding. As the Marquis of Newcastle advised at the Restoration:

> may-games, morris-dancers, the Lords of the May and Lady of the May, the fool – and the hobby-horse must not be forgotten. also the Whitsun Lord and Lady, thrashing of hens at Shrovetide, carols and wassails at Christmas, with good plum porridge and pies which are now forbidden as profane ungodly things – and after evening prayer every Sunday and holy day – the country people with their fresher lasses to trip on the town green about the May-pole to the louder bagpipe there to be refreshed with ale and cakes.

Whatever the success of such measures, it seems to be the case that the later Stuart regime at least relaxed the policing of popular practice by high cultural ideology, with the result that 'there was a general and sometimes exuberant revival of popular sports, wakes, rush bearings and rituals'. These were also celebrated in high culture: in 1669 Shadwell's *The Royal Shepherdesse* included 'a list of genuine English rural games'. The preservation of such practices after 1688 was sometimes conjoined with Stuart loyalism: Jacobites could celebrate spring via commemorations of the Restoration (29 May: Oak Apple Day) and the birthday of James III and VIII (10 June: White Rose Day). Oak Apple Day, which survived until at least the 1930s as a festive occasion, was a relatively safe way of displaying popular Jacobitism due to the uncontroversial nature of what it celebrated. Displays of Stuart sympathy which offered 'no handle to the law officers of the Crown', as the *Norwich Gazette* put it in May 1723, were understandably popular.[27]

It was not only the culture of the people which used spring ritual in Stuart celebration: just as Sir George Mackenzie lauded popular tradition in Scotland, so in England a writer like John Dryden not only drew on chapbook and popular literature for his religious apologia, *The Hind and the Panther*, but also delved into Stuart associations with May festivities in his widely circulated May Queen poem, 'The Lady's Song' (which exists in various versions):

A choir of bright beauties in spring did appear
To choose a May-lady to govern the year:
All the nymphs were in white, and the shepherds in green,
The garland was given, and Phyllis was queen;
But Phyllis refused it, and sighing did say,
I'll not wear a garland while Pan is away.[28]

Pan and Syrinx, as coded names for James and Mary of Modena, passed, possibly from this song, into the classical ciphers of Jacobite culture. It can also be argued that even the more overtly high cultural classicism evident in Dryden's taking on the role of Vergil to the Stuart Augusti (a role crowned in his jacobitical translation of the *Aeneid*) had its popular parallels. Public celebration in the late seventeenth century was itself drawing on 'two different iconographical and mythological traditions, learned and popular respectively'. Just as on one level the exile of the Stuarts was linked by Dryden and others to the wandering of Aeneas, so on another it partook of popular mythology concerning the fertility of good kings and the famine attending their loss (a belief particularly strong in both Scotland and Ireland). Both these interpretations converged into a vision of the exile of the Stuarts as the exile of justice and the topoi of defeat and banishment present in Dryden's heroic stage after 1688. Likewise the popular symbol of the oak (once the Stuart clan badge) was linked to royal Stuart iconography in a positive reading of James's administration which even extended its symbolism to Judge Jeffreys:

> The Root of Monarchy is fixt more sure;
> More wide the lovely Branches spread;
> And up to Heaven advance their awful Head:
> Nor can the Thunders ere their hurt procure;
> Since they the Thund'rers Glory do secure;
> Nor shall they fear the touch of Lightning's Blast;
> Gainst Rebell Winds and Storms they shall endure,
> And an adored Oak of Trophies, last:
> Till Jeffreys' Fame's asleep, and
> Time itself be past.

This, of course, was markedly optimistic: within three years the medallic iconography of William's regime was to show Aenean and Stuart oak overturned and blasted by the very thunders whose touch Barnes here scorns. Themselves alert to the ascendancy of the Stuart cause and its imagery in both high and more popular artforms, the Williamites and their successors sought to turn the popular tradition against the Stuarts, and undermine by mockery what they could not overcome in contest. As Lois Potter puts it:

> Whig writers attack the Stuart cause with the low humour of the popular tradition, in which the fallen man is always ridiculous, never an 'archangel ruined'. They borrowed the form of 'low culture' in order, first, to prove that the accession of William and Mary had been accepted by *all* classes of English society, and, second, to discredit Jacobite authors by opposing to their 'wit' the plain common sense of the freedom-loving Englishman.[29]

Various strategies were used to this end in the 1680s and 90s. The archetypal expression of Williamite popular culture was probably the song 'Lilliburlero', 'once in the mouths of all the people', which in its various sets expressed Protestant English vigour in the face of a putative Scottish or Irish threat, which is alienized by emphasizing its poverty, squalor and brutality. In the 1680s set, the caricature Irish speaker looks forward to the cutting of 'all de English throat'; in the 1740s one, the Scots are an 'army ... without any shoes', the mocked thieves and rogues of the margins: 'Court country and city, against a banditti/ Lilliburlero, bullen a la'.[30]

Elsewhere, xenophobic and racist traits in popular society developed in both anti-Jacobite and Jacobite culture, as for example in a broadside of August 1689, addressed 'to the Brave Apprentices, journey-men and ... Porters, Labourers, and others', which advised such to 'send these Damn'd Dutch Tubs out of the nation'. On the Williamite side there was an intention, typified by 'Lilliburlero', to blacken the reputation of the Jacobite localities and to exaggerate the Catholic threat from which what John Hampden called 'this glorious revolution' had delivered England. In this context, Reresby's 'sour remark' that there were more Catholics in William's army than James's (c. 10 per cent of the officer corps were Catholic in 1687) was not without foundation:

> Some of the Exeter magistrates wondered what religion, if any, many of the soldiers belonged to. According to Robert Ferguson, who was with them, there were twice as many Roman Catholics in William's army as in James's, though others put the number in each as equal.

Just as the level of James's Catholicizing was exaggerated, so also was the nationality of his dynasty; the Prince of Wales (who was, of course, also accused of being illegitimate) being characterized either as a Welshman or a Gaelic-speaking buffoon in some anti-Jacobite writing. Attacks on the Celtic fringe were strong, but remote parts of England were also targets, as in the case of one chapbook which told a story of cannibalism in Devonshire not unlike the Scottish legend or 'urban myth' of Sawney Bean (there were Jacobite riots in Exeter as late as 1752). In cultural terms, Williamite and Whig writing marked a shift towards the core of the nascent British state: the Whig heartland of London and the south-east was to be the English heartland too. Party helped to manufacture identity.[31]

The very poor were, like the marginal localities, also stigmatized as politically unreliable by the new regime: hence the quite unreasonable paranoia felt about the supposedly rampant Jacobitism of the Newcastle keelmen in 1715, which in the event proved grossly exaggerated. A Whig propaganda song, which parodies an optimistic report from a Jacobite spy to James III and VIII, emphasizes the perceived outcast quality of Stuart support:

'Great news I've to tell you, dread sovereign', he cried...
'The sweepers of chimneys, and men that cry coals,
'The carmen and dustmen, in their fine array,
'With stink and black faces will fright Whigs away.
'Of strollers and beggars a regiment or two,
'Who swear what they're worth they'll spend all for you;
'Pickpockets, housebreakers, and highwaymen too,
'With bullies and sharpers, they all are for you.

What truth there was in such assertions, I hope to show. Certainly, if Macaulay had fully followed up his observation concerning the common people that 'a great part of their history is to be learned only from their ballads' (a sentiment which perhaps consciously echoed a statement made by Fletcher of Saltoun at the time of the Union), a very different view of the role of the margins in seventeenth- and eighteenth-century Britain might emerge. But in 1688, Britain was not yet the state it was to become. Such a development required Union with Scotland, a subject to which I now turn.[32]

Scotland and Britain 1688–1707

As P. W. J. Riley tells us, 'most Scots ... represented the entire episode of 1689 as a piece of sharp practice whereby the English secured a Scottish settlement on the cheap without concessions'. Whereas it is very difficult to say with certainty what 'most Scots' indeed thought, it remains true that the 1689 Claim of Right and the Scottish rejection of James (who promised to be present in person 'in a Parliament of our antient kingdom' (Scotland) as part of his offer to the Estates in 1689) had only the appearance rather than the reality of a joint settlement with England display-

ing common British intent. Although the Scottish Estates had
lent their imprimatur to the actions of the English Parliament,
the underlying differences were profound, as was to become clear
when the 1701 Act of Settlement was rejected by the Estates. Not
only did the controllers of England's political machinery begin
to take Scotland more for granted; English propagandists were
also busy reviving traditional ideas of English suzerainty over
Scotland, which 'increasingly suggested that Scottish co-operation
was only the legitimate development of Scottish subjection'. In
such a context, and given William's own repeated interest in
Anglo-Scottish union, it is little wonder that Scottish responses
such as the Acts of Security and Anent Peace and War (attempt-
ing to guarantee an independent succession and foreign policy)
cocked a snook at the increasing weight of English expectation of
Scottish complicity. To cap it all, 'King William's lean years', the
1690s, had been a time of terrible famine in Scotland, and
Scottish merchants had suffered damage through the loss of
French trade in Williamite wars. The Revolution had seen
Scotland confined to a British political context as never before,
and attempts to break out through independent ventures like the
Darien scheme proved disastrous. The attempt to found a
Scottish East India Company, first made by James VI in 1618, was
symptomatic: in 1695 a renewed Scottish company met with
English opposition 'on the very dubious grounds that English
investment and involvement had given succour to a foreign
power!'[33]

Nor did the new political situation damage Scotland's *amour
propre* or its pocket alone. Population attrition due to famine
reached between 5 and 33 per cent, the higher figure probably
including the thousands who emigrated to Ireland. While supporters of the Stuarts could see such economic disaster as divine
retribution for the exiling of their lawful king, Covenanting and
Presbyterian patriots might also be disaffected, as they looked
back half a century to when Scotland had been dictating a British
agenda, rather than being dragged along by it. The experiences
of the 1690s did much to concentrate Scottish opposition to the
idea of union when it was again seriously advanced, for they were
a decade which showed Scotland increasingly confined within
the bounds of the English polity as it strode across the world
stage:

European war from 1688 created a massive trade slump, and in 1702 the resurgence of war brought further contraction of markets and a rise in piracy, all of which damaged Scotland's tenuous trade in raw materials.

Thus, although the economic stresses brought about by William's accession and the resulting warfare affected both England and Scotland, they clearly weighed more heavily on the latter country, any efforts on whose part to develop a separate identity in foreign policy were viewed askance by its larger neighbour. In the years after 1688, Scotland and England grew further apart.[34]

The nature of internal political change in Scotland was also more radical and divisive than in the south. The packed General Assembly of 1690 effectively overthrew the Episcopalian establishment, and in the process implicitly endorsed the 'rabbling' of the priests in the west carried out by Covenanters in the aftermath of James's fall. Henceforward, Episcopal clergy survived best in pockets where local magnates were strong enough to protect them, though they gained a measure of toleration from the British Parliament in 1712 (only for those who prayed for the reigning family, though in fact the measure was largely sponsored by Jacobite MPs). The establishment of full-blown Presbyterianism was a major change which alienated most of Scotland outside the central belt and the Borders. Society was also disrupted by the rising on behalf of James VII led first by Viscount Dundee and then by Generals Buchan and Cannon, which although it spent much of its threat at the ineffective siege of Dunkeld in 1689, remained in the field two years longer. Isolated Scottish islands held out for James until 1691–3 (one, the Bass Rock, only twenty miles from Edinburgh), and the uncertainty and unease caused by such persisting activity contributed significantly to the Massacre of Glencoe in February 1692, an event which rapidly achieved symbolic importance as an example of treachery.[35]

Scottish society therefore suffered six-fold from religious controversy, military disturbance, confined trade, famine, mass emigration and the triumphalist assumptions of English suzerainty revived in the shadow of William's accession, assumptions which could only be reinforced by the increasingly divergent material wealth of Scotland and England. Savaged by half a century of religious conflict, tagged at the tail of William's ambition on the battlefields of Europe, unable to act autonomously to any effect, Scotland in the fifteen years before Union was in a parlous condition. Its economic decline and newly endemic conflicts underlined the irreconcilable duality of national aspiration and British policy. Whereas the evidence points to Charles II and James II and VII seeking to rule their Scottish and Irish realms as separate kingdoms with distinct establishments (though in the case of Ireland without truly native authority), William's accession had reversed this feature of the political process, brutally imposing conformity in Ireland and expecting it of Scotland: its centralizing agenda had been early visible in the final withdrawal of Welsh business to London in 1694.[36]

The agitated period leading up to Union bears witness to national tension through the pamphlet war carried on between the upholders of English and native rights to authority in Scotland. One of the curious features of this controversy to modern eyes is the way in which the contemporary difficulties in Scotland's constitutional position caused by the 1603 regal union are seldom addressed. Instead, the debate focused on historic claims and counterclaims dating back to the medieval period, itself a heartland of arguments for dynastic legitimacy centring on the Stuarts and iconized in the Holyrood portraits in the Stuarts' 'antient kingdom'. As Roger Mason puts it:

> the ancient line of kings supplied a vital counterweight to an English historiographical tradition which insisted that Scotland was and always had been a dependency of England.

This was one of the reasons why it was so vital (politically, as much as in terms of historical scholarship) for English writers to pour scorn on the arguments of Sir George Mackenzie and his ilk. Another was that these apologists themselves had to deal with the problem of frequent changes of dynasty in England. As Colin Kidd has pointed out, the vulnerability of England in its early development to external conquest and interference provided fodder for a Scottish critique of the beginnings of Whig historiography among Anglocentric apologists following 1688. Rather than face this degree of discontinuity in their own history, English controversialists appear to find refuge in the idea of England's historic overlordship of Britain: 'the English appropriated to themselves the heroic exploits of a British race whose Welsh descendants they were less inclined to honour'. The Brut myth, famously propounded by Geoffrey of Monmouth in the days of the Angevin Empire (doubtless a significant cultural context), implied English primacy through the partition of Britain among the sons of Brutus, the great-grandson of Aeneas, who was used as the ultimate symbol of legitimacy by Jacobite apologists for just this reason. Arthur, 'the Matter of Britain' of medieval times, was a more recent mythic pan-British overlord of Aenean descent: and the cult of Arthur revived by Henry II after 1170 dovetailed rather neatly with his assumption of the overlordship of Scotland in the Treaty of Falaise (1174), a position later abrogated by his son in return for money for the Crusades. Throughout the Middle Ages, English monarchs had renewed these claims: Edward I did so in 1301, Henry IV attempted it a century later, Henry V and VI were advised to do so, and Henry VIII made a suzerainty claim in 1542. It was normal in such circumstances to invoke the idea of Britain in political conflation with England: as long ago as the fourteenth century, English political rhetoric was using the term 'Britain' 'applied ... indiscriminately to mean either England or the whole island'.[37]

Scottish resistance to such claims centred on the greater dynastic integrity of their monarchy and the counterclaims made against Brut by the domestic Graeco-Egyptian-Irish foundation myth. The Stuarts on the English throne had accepted the Brut myth in London, but also continued to foster (as the Holyrood portraits show) the ancestral Scottish account in their northern capital, an account whose Irish element was highly significant for Stuart legitimism in Ireland. It is often forgotten that the Stuarts were the only British dynasty to rule Ireland who could claim descent from its ancient kings. In England, there was an emphasis on the Germanic roots of Englishness, which on occasion included the claim that 'the Scots were English in origin', a claim which (as far as the Lowlands were concerned at least), would be developed in the eighteenth century.[38]

In the tense pamphlet wars which preceded the Union, pro-English writers such as James Drake and William Nicolson attacked the integrity of the Scottish royal line and Anglo-Scottish relations: they were answered by Scottish controversialists such as James Anderson and James Dalrymple. The magnitude of the struggle is perhaps indicated in the publication of Sir Thomas Craig's century-old tract, *Scottish Soveraignty Asserted*, as ammunition in what was a vital propaganda war. The controversy's concentration on the monarchical and medieval past reflected the strong dynastic subtext in questions of national identity, which in the Scottish context played into the hands of the Jacobites, who could thus assume the nationalist mantle almost effortlessly after 1707, when 'Whiggish Scots patriots like the 10th Earl Marischal and the Master of Sinclair were left nowhere else to go ... if they wished to free Scotland from English domination'. In the end, this process may have entailed the gradual supersession of the foundation myth by the articulation of a national struggle, so it was perhaps no damage to Jacobitism that one of its scholars, Fr Thomas Innes, was centrally instrumental in undermining the credibility of the descent of the ancient Scottish line in his *Critical Essay* of 1729. Such a process had been implicit in the developments of thirty years before:

> British-based Stuart Arthurianism appears to begin to wither in Scotland in the 1690s, for the Stuart cause was in the process of hardening into the patriotic cause. With this came a slow shift in Scottish Stuart typology, which distorted the pan-British imagery and interests of the dynasty in eventual favour of a more democratic and localized view. The icon of the Highlander as patriot ... suggested the deliberately partialized view that all Lowlanders favoured the Union, while the image of Stuart king as Highland cateran suggested that he was a folkloric type of social bandit rather than the rightful head of the British state.

The shift in representation of Scottish royal and national identity towards the localized and vernacular during the Jacobite century helped demonstrate national difference in the face of the triumph of the Anglocentric case in the pamphlet war, a triumph which at the time culminated in Union and subsequently had longstanding consequences for British historiography. As late as 1923, Cassell's highly respectable *History of the British People* was reiterating pamphlet-war material from a quarter of a millennium before.[39]

This intensification of national differences and conflicts further fed a xenophobia already present in the 1690s in anti-

Dutch feeling in England and growing anti-English feeling in Scotland. The compliment was returned in the Alien Act of 1705, which threatened Scots with being categorized as foreigners south of the border. Queen Anne, a monarch in general quite enthusiastically supported by the jacobitically inclined in England, made no secret of her 'entirely English' identity. Though present at her father James's court in Edinburgh (Edward Gregg has called this 'one of the most profound formative experiences' for the future Queen), she was as much a British centralist as were George and William. Of the Irish, 'she understood they had a mind to be independent, if they could; but they should not', though in fact the Irish parliament (not a representative body) had petitioned the Queen for union in 1703. During the period of the Scottish Union, however, Anne re-emphasized one inherited Stuart practice: in 1706–7, 1877 touchpieces were ordered, the Royal Touch again being in demand as a charismatic pacifier in times of potential political turbulence. Occasions at which the Touch was to be given were oversubscribed with requests for admission.[40]

Scottish fears of being alienized and marooned on the periphery of Britain were stoked by Daniel Defoe (an English government agent at the time), with an additionally insulting suggestion that the Scots were already indistinguishable from the English abroad, lacking only their privileges, which would be accessible only through union:

SCOT, ... a Name that Foreigners can't find
While mixt with English het'rogeneous kind,
But now by Trade, inform the distant Poles,
That Britain is the World of Gallant Souls.

Such propaganda put the best face on strong anti-Scottish and anti-Irish feeling in England. It also attempted to minimize 'the vicious tide' of hatred against foreigners found on both sides, but particularly in the anti-Dutch, anti-German and anti-Saxon feelings of many Jacobites. Instead, Britain was to be united and the true foreign enemy, 'French bondage and King James VIII' kept at bay for ever. How far the enemy was truly external in eighteenth-century Britain is a question which will be answered as this book progresses: certainly, the years of British centralization were key years of imperial formation:

> in the years from 1689 to 1709 competing economic and political forces in English society fought over gaining access to the maximum profits to be had from trade in the Orient.[41]

The Union itself remains in Scotland, as it was in 1707, a matter of interest and debate. To this day 'it endlessly reproduces itself in a typological paradigm of vice or virtue, loyalty or corruption'. The accusations of bribery which still haunt its reputation became emplaced in its mythology at the time, while opposition to it was seen by its sympathizers and agents (such as Defoe), as a stalking-horse for Jacobitism, the more so in that 'many anti-Union addresses were signed by people who had refused the oaths, thus equating them with disaffection'. There was rioting throughout Scotland; of the burghs, only intensely Presbyterian Ayr supported Union, and for two years (culminating in the Jacobite attempt of 1708), armed bands swilled around the country looking for a leader, a role pretended to and avoided by the Duke of Hamilton. The alternative proposal of a federal union (mostly supported by Jacobites, with the notable exception of Andrew Fletcher of Saltoun, who, however, George Lockhart claims had an 'aversion to the English and the Union ... so great ... he would have sided with the royal family') was defeated. 'Sure I am', wrote one disconsolate opponent, 'the Advantage that Nation [England] has, is not equally sensible to them, as our loss is to us.' This opinion was implicitly borne out in Speaker Bromley's words to a Scots MP in 1713 (in the context of a struggle to repeal Union, bolstered by an unsuccessful Scottish petition in 1714–15, the failure of which culminated in a major armed insurrection): 'he [Bromley] was not very fond of the Union in all respects, but since there were some advantages to England from it, and that they had catcht hold of Scotland, they would keep her fast'.[42]

A propaganda war continued in Scotland after the Union in cultural terms which prioritized the past over the present (particularly in the view of history as a struggle for liberty), and concentrated on antiquarian and vernacular elements in Scottish identity. High cultural patriots who rejected the drift towards metropolitan norms expressed themselves increasingly in terms of folk cultural topoi: Jacobite nationalism drove cultural registers together in a process which conflated the legitimate inheritor of two millennia of dynastic history with the fertility king or Highland lover of the folk tradition. The view of royalty held in both Scottish and Irish culture, which conjoined rightful rule and fertile land, was strongly reinforced within the mainstream of patriotic cultural articulation in the half-century following 1707. In the localities, where 'Jacobites operated as a clearly identifiable group within the framework of the Scottish political system', their distinctive cultural networking may have at least partly made up for the Scottish parliament's failure as an instrument of effective opposition. The cultural symbolism through which such networking took place, both within and outside Scotland, deserves a separate account.[43]

Political Symbolism in Literature and Religion

Keep to the Church, while yet you may,
　　New Sects are still a growing,
And Popery that buds today,
To Morrow will be blowing.

The Muses Farewel to Popery & Slavery

'Relate at large, my godlike guest', she said,
'The Grecian stratagems, the town betray'd:
The fatal issue of so long a war,
Your flight, your wand'ring, and your woes, declare;
For, since on ev'ry sea, on ev'ry coast,
Your men have been distress'd, your navy toss'd,
Sev'n times the sun has either tropic view'd,
The winter banish'd, and the spring renew'd.'

Dido to Aeneas, *Aeneid* I (tr. Dryden)[44]

The major political symbols which had characterized the Stuart monarchy suffered a blow from the alteration of the succession in 1688 from which they arguably never recovered. What Paul Korshin has called 'the tumid enthusiasm of the seventeenth-century paean' enters a long diminuendo, being on occasion replaced by images of a 'King, Divine by Law and Sense' which owe more to contract theory than sacramentalism. Indeed, the superseded sacred monarch is stigmatized as a 'Goblin & Witchcraft, Priestcraft-Prince'. Supernaturalism, with its Catholic overtones, was under suspicion.[45]

Among the chief of the images of the old order was that of Astraea, the embodiment of justice, whose symbolism had strong links to both the caesaropapist ideology of Anglicanism (the monarch as church leader as type of eternal justice) and the image of the king as an agent of fertility: Astraea was *virgo spicifera*. This peculiarly effective icon was in turn significant through the conflation of the Blessed Virgin Mary, Queen of Heaven, with the virgin Astraea of Vergil's Fourth Eclogue, who heralds the arrival of Augustan justice to the troubled Roman world. Since at least the medieval period, this prophecy had been seen as referring to the Mother and birth of Christ. By the Reformation, in so far as 'Elizabethan Protestantism ... restored a golden age of pure imperial religion', the Queen herself was strongly associated both with Astraea and the Blessed Virgin, with Astraean symbolism increasing after the defeat of the Armada in 1588. Subsequently, Britannia also increased in importance in her role as iconographic usurper of the Blessed Virgin's place as mother of a particularly English Church: 'the garden precinct and the rose, symbols which had been used in connection with England, were also Mary's symbols' and Britannia was depicted 'as Mary Dolorosa'. Although Britannia survived the Revolution and its successor regime with more composure than Astraea, she seems to have gradually become emptied of supernatural symbolism.[46]

If Astraea/Britannia could be seen as representing the sacramental portion of monarchical patriotism in the paradigm of the King's Two Bodies, the monarchy's central mainly secular symbol was Aeneas, the founder of the British race and also of Rome. Vergil was the chief poet of both Astraea and Aeneas, who in turn were both foreshadowers of Augustus. Hence the Stuart idea of the monarch as Augustus, and John Dryden's self-conscious adoption of the role of Vergil to the Stuart Augusti, evident in poems such as *Astraea Redux, Threnodia Augustalis* or *Britannia Rediviva*, arguably the best poems ever written about monarchy by a poet laureate. The crowning achievement of Dryden's Vergilianism (that he was also sensitive to more native English typology is shown in his *King Arthur* (1691)) was his 1697 translation of the Aeneid, which is riddled with jacobitical expansion and allusion. As the poet himself wrote:

My Translation of Virgil is already in the Press ... I have
hinder'd it thus long in hopes of his return, for whom, and for
my conscience I have suffered, that I might have layd my
Authour at his feet.[47]

Even before Dryden published, writers such as James Philp
and Richard Maitland, fourth Earl of Lauderdale (whose translation Dryden saw in MS), had begun to exploit the powerful symbolic impetus given to identification of the Stuarts with Aeneas
by the exile of James from his Trojan/British kingdom in 1688.
In this, all were building on an established tradition of Royalist
Aenean code dating at least to the Civil War period: indeed,
Dryden re-used the plates from John Ogilby's 1654 Vergil, a
work in its day 'visibly the property of the beleaguered upper
class'. Ogilby was later entrusted with the 'poetical part' of
Charles II's coronation ritual. Although Williamite apologists
did make use of Vergilian imagery, the king himself was more
strongly associated with Hercules, other Greek heroes and Julius
Caesar. Such comparisons had also been made in the case of the
Stuart monarchs, but there is an apparent shift in emphasis,
partly no doubt consequent on the move away from supernaturalism: Aeneas had been 'a pre-Christian type of Christ' for the
Stuarts; 'pius Aeneas', the sacred monarch. Williamite iconography, on the other hand, arguably began to reflect the shift from
sacred typological history to one of progress and development,
the move from the oral traditions of Sir George Mackenzie to
the broadening precedent of Saxon liberty. In this shift the
monarch was not characterized so much by typological
definition as by the degree to which he exemplified and sur-
passed it. James might be a type of Aeneas/Augustus: but
William's forerunners only foreshadow his own crowning
achievement:

Vespasian, whose Imperial Name
Triumphant rides upon the Wings of Fame ...
No more Illustrious Shade shall mention'd be,
      But as the Type of Thee.

As the 'King divine by law and sense', William represented the
monarchical manifestation of more popular aspirations to liberty.

As Hercules (e.g. in the 1689 mezzotint by J. Broedelet), William is the heroic labourer, whose use of force to attain his ends is covertly justified. In medallic iconography, the Williamite orange tree springs freshly from the ruined Stuart oak: this image of William as the ultimate Orangeman served to distance his iconography from that of Aeneas, since it is by the magical bough of the oak, Druid tree and Stuart clan badge, that Aeneas enters the underworld in Book VI of Vergil's epic. The orange tree image also seems to mark a shift away from earlier tree depictions, such as 'Charles I Defending the Tree of Religion' (1645), a version of the common portrayal of the true church as a tree (cf. also the 1733 print 'The goodly CEDAR of Apostolick & Catholick EPISCOPACY'). It was not until the era of the Patriot Whigs in the 1730s that the Druidic and Stuart oak was formally recaptured from Jacobite iconography, though its appearance on the *Revirescit* medal of the Oak Society displayed as late as 1750 the tree's strong Stuart connotations. In May 1737, the Jacobite William King, whose 'REDEAT' oration in the 1740s was to show the continuing power of Stuart Augustan typology, displayed in a letter to Swift a typical example of Jacobite 'oak' allusion. The letter, ostensibly about the planning of a new government for Corsica (implicit Jacobite/Corsican nationalist analogies also occur in the work of Dr Johnson's biographer James Boswell), suggests that it should be 'headed by a king fashioned of oak ... I would have such a King as *Jupiter* first gave to the Frogs; who, by the way, possessed his Empire by Divine Right' (Jupiter subsequently sent a stork, who devoured the frogs as the Hanoverian regime is inferentially accused of doing). In such a manner did Jacobites discuss their worldview and hopes for the return of 'Astraea nostra' until well into the eighteenth century.[48]

The Jacobite use of Aeneas as the central figure of non-specifically sacred high cultural code continued for at least as long: 'Æneas & his two Sons' was a common cipher for James, Charles and Henry, both in Jacobite correspondence and elsewhere (as in the widespread tract *Ascanius, or the Young Adventurer*). The coded phrase 'Fuimus Troes', used to express both Jacobite loss and hopes of a restoration, is found repeatedly throughout British Jacobite writing: Sir Walter Scott was to put it, with symbolic aptness, in the mouth of the Baron of Bradwardine in *Waverley*. The theme continues in Jacobite artifacts: the most common mottoes on Jacobite glass come from the *Aeneid*, including one which identifies the Duke of Cumberland as Turnus. All this was part of a broader ambiguity in the nature of 'Augustanism', hinted at in Howard Erskine-Hill's interpretation of Francis Atterbury's Preface to the Second Part of Waller's Poems in 1690, intended 'to bid farewell to Augustan achievement with the end of the Stuart era': the image of Augustus was powerfully connected for sacred, secular and circumstantial reasons to the Stuart monarchy. The struggle over the literary and political possession of Augustan iconography was not finally resolved in favour of the successor regime until 1760, with the result that much writing from the so-called 'Augustan' age is more politically ambivalent, or at least conscious of political ambivalence, than might at first appear. Goldsmith's 'Threnodia Augustalis' of 1772 may cast only an innocent glance back to Dryden, but much before this there is a tension in Augustan and other Roman symbolism born of ambiguity: even so staunch a supporter of the Revolution settlement as Joseph Addison found his *Cato* (1713) picked over for hints of coded Toryism.[49]

Besides the Augustan/Aenean/Astraean symbolic nexus, Arthurianism was also a battleground for supporters and opponents of the events of 1688. During the 1690s, Dryden's Arthur was counterweighted by Sir Richard Blackmore, who adapted

> Geoffrey's [of Monmouth] story of Arthur to the Revolution in order to show William as the Christian hero overcoming the pagan Saxons, whom he identifies with the Catholics.

Blackmore also tried, less successfully, to link William to Aeneas: but his Williamite Arthurianism was very popular at the time.[50]

Another major Jacobite theme was found in the idea of ruralism and retreat, which had been popularly attached to the Stuart cause since the 1640s (Ogilby makes a thematic connection between '*sequestration*' as 'a chosen seclusion or withdrawal' and the seizure of Royalist estates). As a theme, it reflected real political circumstance and its sad necessity, and after 1688 was used by writers such as Pope in *Windsor Forest* and the *Epistle to Burlington*, and others as diverse as Major-General Alexander Robertson of Struan and the Countess of Winchilsea, to show both the fertility of Stuart monarchy and the moral purity of ruralism, an ideologi-

cal claim also reflected in the depth of hostility felt towards both
cities in general and the City in particular as hotbeds of Whig corruption. Pope's *Dunciad* and Dr Johnson's 'London' are among
the best-known poetic examples.[51]

Beyond the emplaced use of biblical and classical high cultural
topoi in the presentation of the traditional iconography of monarchy, there was also a lively conflict on the public stage of the
theatre, an area of symbolic interchange between high cultural
art and its audience. William Congreve, the leading dramatist of
his day, used the stage as a medium to express Lockean-style contract theory, the Whig view that sovereigns owed their right of
rule to popular consent. In both *Love for Love* (1695) and *The Way
of the World* (1700), Congreve seeks to make clear the extent to
which contracts are an essential foundation of civil society, the
antithesis to the seduction of power practised by his rakes and the
absolutist heroes of Stuart patriarchy such as Dorimant (a character based on the Earl of Rochester) in Etherege's 1675 play, *The
Man of Mode*. The Jacobite and Nonjuring priest (later bishop)
Jeremy Collier's 1698 attack on the contemporary stage was
doubtless a sign of concern not wholly unconnected to the fact
that 'dramatists after 1688 overwhelmingly supported the
Revolution Settlement'. The drama was becoming a vehicle for
Williamite propaganda: one sign of this is found in Collier's
objection to the treatment of country squires on stage, attacking
'playwrights who exhibited country gentlemen as ignorant ...
undermining respect for authority'. The country squirearchy,
popularly associated with Toryism and Jacobitism, were long
depicted by Whig writers as primitive, marginal and second-rate
anachronisms, and in this way were stigmatized as unworthy opponents. This propagandistic portrayal, to which Collier objects, was
long-lived: it can be found in Henry Fielding's characterization
of Squire Western in *Tom Jones* in the 1740s and Macaulay's
extended discussion of the provincialism and intellectual clumsi-
ness of the Tory gentry in his *History of England* in the 1850s. Whig
stereotypes had great staying power.[52]

If Jacobitism had (with the exception of Dryden's later plays
and interesting cases such as Thomas Otway's *Venice Preserved*)
little grip on the stage, it nevertheless appears to have had the
ability to exploit street theatre. By the early 1690s, Jacobite street
performers were having a significant impact in London: the 'car-

nival culture of popular protest' they represented 'was based on improvised oral communication'. In addition, the appearance of 'disaffected aristocrats, gentlemen and merchants' in a street carnival context was one of the early earnests of a crossclass alliance in displays of Jacobite culture in England. Although 'the new regime was adept at mounting public spectacles', the Jacobites retorted, 'commenting directly on Whig dominance of the official stage, by creating their own theatre of the streets', as is found in the presence of 'popular singing men' at the 10 June 1695 Dog Tavern riot, only 'a few feet from Drury Lane theatre'. 'The Jacobite press ... kept a large readership informed of the politics of the theatre and the street', and the 'rebirth of popular culture', which Paul Monod has linked to 'the spread of Jacobite sentiment'. Such cultural developments offstage kept a degree of pressure on the theatres: just as at the time of Essex's rebellion against Elizabeth *Richard II* was regarded as inflammatory, so were *Richard III* in 1700 and *Venice Preserved* at the time of the Sacheverell trial. John Ford's *Perkin Warbeck* was used by both sides, but particularly anti-Stuart propagandists, to identify the opposing claimant as an empty pretender (Ford's play was surely particularly useful to the government in that it emphasized the help the Scots gave to Perkin: clearly a rebellious lot who could not be trusted).[53]

The Sacheverell affair of 1709–10 was in many respects the literary and cultural high watermark of another strand in popular activity and paranoia, the theme of the Church in Danger. The measures taken to ameliorate the position of the Dissenters in England and Wales had irritated many Anglicans, who became convinced that the drift towards such Whig values would undermine their ascendancy. As Geoffrey Holmes says:

> One must appreciate that by 1709, the apogee of the Whigs in the reigns of William III and Anne, at least four-fifths of the parish clergy in England and Wales were convinced that the ruling party, given half a chance, would sell out the Anglican inheritance to dissenters and latitude-men, if not to the enemies of Christianity itself.

This fear was particularly marked among High Church Anglicans of caesaropapist tendencies, and the traditionalist Royalist mobs who were prepared to support their view that the integrity and special status of the Church of England were under threat. Accompanying this was a hostility towards and fear of Dissent as in practice a greater enemy than Rome, unsurprising in view of Dissent's role in the civil broils of the seventeenth century, but in contrast to the supposition of some historians that all 'Protestants' had common interests. In fact the Anglican mob cry of 'High Church and Ormond' was explicitly Jacobite in the aftermath of that Duke's flight to be James's Captain-General: some at least of the High Church party expected better protection for Anglicanism from a Catholic than a Lutheran king. Dr Henry Sacheverell, by all accounts a rather irritable and inflammatory Oxford don, was one of their number. Having first in 1705 preached a jacobitical sermon on *The Perils of False Brethren* (the text, 'In peril among false brethren', came from 2 Corinthians xi: 26) which nobody took much notice of, he caused a furore by repeating it on 5 November 1709 (an obviously inflammatory date) in St Paul's, and printing 40 000 copies. Eventually the sermon sold up to 100 000, a massive sale in a country of 5 million, still heavily illiterate. Today it is calculated that four people read a book or magazine for every purchase (more in the case of library copies): if the situation was the same in 1710, up to one English person in ten (including the illiterate and children) would have read Sacheverell's tract. It may be also, that in the days when books were few and many read aloud as a matter of course, that the numbers reading or hearing any single text would be higher than they are today. Sacheverell also found strong support in Wales, where he 'was a popular hero' among the clergy.[54]

In any event, Sacheverell's sales both ensured his impeachment (he was found guilty with a token penalty, owing to political pressure) and bore witness to the enormous political resonance of the question of the Church of England's status, which in turn led to a surge in both Tory and Jacobite support in the 1710 election:

> In the General Election of 1710, Tories still found it worth using slogans like 'No Rump Parliament', 'No Forty Eight', 'No Presbyterian Rebellion', 'Save the Queen's White Neck', to link Whiggery with regicide.

In the long view, the Sacheverell affair was to prove no more than the proverbial storm in a teacup; but in the highly charged political atmosphere of Anne's last years, it compared in impact to the debate over the French Revolution. *The Perils of False Brethren* far outsold Edmund Burke's *Reflections on the Revolution in France* and was not so far off matching Thomas Paine's *Rights of Man* in popularity, and this in a country of fewer people and probably poorer literacy than was to be the case in the 1790s.[55]

In this context, it is important to understand the mentality of the High Church position. The seven bishops who stood trial in 1688 could be heroicized as Protestant champions: yet a majority of them refused the oaths to William. In all, eight bishops, including the Archbishop of Canterbury, and 400 clergy nonjured, taking an unknown number of laity with them in England and Wales. In Scotland, the vast majority of the 607 Episcopal priests and all the bishops did likewise: with them went the sympathies of up to two-fifths of Scots. This was a serious secession, the more so that it lasted up to the early nineteenth century, and that the High Church party included many fellow travellers with the Nonjurors who remained in the juring Church, appeasing their consciences by 'distinguishing between a *de facto* and a *de jure* sovereign' (e.g. Sacheverell himself, Bishop Crewe of Durham and Francis Atterbury, later Bishop of Rochester). Those who adopted the High Church position arguably realized that 1688–9 represented a serious decoupling of the Church from legitimist caesarosacramentalism: the Church's necessarily more conditional alliance with a *de facto* monarchy (which in William's and the Hanoverian case was occupied by non-Anglicans) seriously weakened the traditional 'imperial' High Anglican position, born of the medieval struggles between Crown and Papacy. The assertion of the king's right over church government as the counterpart to papal claims to secular power lay at the heart of Anglican apology, and the legitimacy of the monarchy carried quasi-apostolic connotations in this context. Many of those who protested against James thus did not wish to see his line usurped, as only the true monarch could be the sacramental head of the Church. James's power to give the Royal Touch was a sign of his ability to bind and loose: so Louis XIV, in his own Gallican differences with the Papacy, intensified the practice of the Touch in France.[56]

The Nonjuring secession endured for more than a century, and many were brought up in its traditions or under its shadow. Nor was it a moribund, marginal movement: its members provided some of the most adventurous theology and ecumenism of the eighteenth century, and though later plagued by divisions, the inevitable accessory of secession, continued as a vital force through almost to the period of the Oxford Movement: 'tractarianism ... identified with the old Scottish non-juring tradition'.

Though there were many convinced Protestants in the ranks of the Nonjurors, one of their more interesting features is their renewed attempt (following Laud and some of the Aberdeen Doctors) to build a middle way between Rome and reform. Their habitual rejection of Lutheranism and Calvinism in favour of an aboriginal Catholicity was known and disliked by their opponents: for example, an anti-Jacobite tract aligns them with French Catholicism, claiming that Charles Edward's baggage contained

A Project left by Doctor *Leslie*, the famous Nonjuror, for incorporating and reconciling the *Gallican* Church with the High-Church of *England*.[57]

The language and concepts of the Nonjurors themselves were not calculated to allay suspicions of this kind, as evidenced in the intense sacramentalism of the reported letters and dying speech of the Reverend Robert Lyon, executed in 1746:

Our holy persecuted mother, the Church of Scotland, in which I have the honour to die a very unworthy priest ... this once glorious but now declining part of the Church Catholick ... her steadiness to principle and Catholick unity ... now, at last, alas ! devoted, in the intention of her adversaries, to utter destruction ... Her oratories have been profan'd and burnt, her holy altars desecrated, her priests outrageously plundered and driven from their flocks ...

Whatever 'errors' were declared by priests like Lyon as subsisting in the Church of Rome could seem little more than token to an audience for whom what the Nonjurors said and the way that they said it reeked of being 'soft' on Catholicism. The Nonjuring bishops described themselves (as at Jeremy Collier's consecration in 1713) as 'Catholic'; their clergy on occasion appear to have used the Roman liturgy, at least in private devotion; James II and III, through agents, maintained in Scotland in particular a grip on the nomination of their bishops, apparently with the tacit compliance of the Papacy. At an interview with James II in 1693 concerning new consecrations, 'his majesty expressed his esteem of the deprived bishops and clergy, and of the laity that suffered with them ... with tears in his eyes'. Such guilt by association with Catholic sovereigns was compounded by the influence French mysticism, such as that espoused by Mme Guyon and Archbishop Fénelon, had on the Nonjurors, as well as the drift among Episcopalian and Anglican Nonjurors abroad to the Christian universalism found in organizations such as the élite ranks of the early Masons; Jacobite propagandists such as George Flint also proposed schemes of 'Christian Union'. Moreover, Scottish Episcopalian theology already contained thinking that was highly suspect in a Protestant age. The seventeenth-century Aberdeen divine Dr William Forbes had claimed that 'Purgatory, Praying for the Dead, the Intercession and Invocation of Angels and Saints' could be derived from Scripture, while Professor John Forbes of Corse had displayed a belief in transubstantiation and Professor Henry Scougall was an admirer of SS. Thomas à Kempis and Teresa. Later, Scottish Episcopalian Jacobites founded a religious retreat at Rosehearty. Such thinking went on in the heartland of Scottish Episcopacy, whose mysticism 'flourished under foreign influences, and most of the authors whose works became popular belonged either to pre-Reformation or Roman Catholic Christianity'.[58]

This desire to return to pre-Reformation practices is perhaps borne witness to in the 'Usages' controversy which divided the Nonjurors in the 1720s, and which centred round whether to restore Catholicizing practices (including the prayer for the faithful departed) to the liturgy: it was accompanied by debate over related issues, such as a desire to use Roman Catholic clerical dress. More evidence of the special qualities of Nonjuring thought comes in the conversations held in 1717–21 with the Orthodox Church in an attempt to seek union: these are apparently still among the most important theological documents of Orthodoxy. Ecumenism of this type was only further evidence to its opponents of the divergence of the Nonjurors from mainstream Anglicanism, and Nonjuring apologists such as the Reverend Deacon can only have encouraged this view in making statements such as 'When I came to consult history, the less defensible I found the Church of England'. Though Deacon went on to disclaim the title 'Papist' as well as that of 'Protestant', the position he and other Nonjurors adopted moves close to Newman's attempt to reconcile the Thirty-Nine Articles to Catholicism in Tract 90, with consequences for Tractarianism and his own career which lend some credence to Protestant suspicions of the true ecclesiastical preferences of at least some in the Nonjuring Churches of England and Scotland (in 1836 Newman described the Anglican Church as having 'been in an unutterable stupor' since 1688). The Nonjurors endured and flourished longer than mere Jacobitism might have entitled them to do through their opposition to Latitudinarianism; here, too, Newman's opposition to liberalism in the Church forms an apposite parallel.[59]

Marginal Societies in Britain

The Episcopal Church in Scotland and the English Nonjuring community were in most respects the same church: their bishops were present at each other's consecrations, and in the 1770s most of the remaining English Nonjuring congregations were handed over by Bishop Gordon to the care of the Scottish Church, itself then on the point of becoming the mother church of the Episcopalian Church of America. Yet one of the paradoxes of Scottish Episcopalian culture, which has often proved difficult to grasp, was that, whereas Scottish Presbyterianism was largely politically unionist and ecclesiastically nationalist, the Episcopal Church was the reverse. Opposition to Union among Scottish Episcopalians was widespread, if not universal: for them Union was the latest in a series of judgements (the 1690s famine was another) against an ungrateful Scotland which had rejected both its hereditary monarchy and its independence. The government recognized this, burning Episcopalian meeting-houses and intimidating their clergy, as well as infiltrating them with licensed Anglican priests under the jurisdiction of juring bishops in England and Ireland. Partly as a result, where there had been over 600 Scottish Episcopal clergy in 1689, there were only 125–30 in the 1730s and 1740s and as few as 40 after 1745, when Scottish orders were outlawed. Although it maintained strongholds (several hundred were confirmed in ceremonies at Edinburgh and elsewhere as late as the 1770s), the fate of Scottish Episcopalianism shows that persecution does work: a church which had two-thirds of the support Presbyterianism had in 1690 declining to under one-twentieth today, and that tiny figure including the juring Anglicans of the eighteenth century, who united with the Episcopalian remnant after the threat of Jacobitism was extinguished. It was the demise of the Episcopalian Church under Anglican persecution which left Scotland a Presbyterian country.[60]

One of the features of Episcopal culture (which it shared with Roman Catholicism) was its sympathy towards Gaelic: the Scriptures were available in that tongue, and consecrations conducted in it. This was no doubt, at least in part, an example of the converging interests of groups and societies marginalized by the development of Britain after 1688. Just as relatively little attention has been paid to the Nonjurors by the central historical narrative, so not much has been said of other religious and linguistic minorities, particularly those of mainland Britain. It would perhaps be not too far off the mark to suggest that about a quarter of the Scottish population spoke Gaelic in 1700 (the vast bulk of the rest speaking Scots, a tongue (now attenuated almost to extinction) as separate from English as Dutch is from German). Wales and Ireland were very heavily Celtic-speaking at the same date. In England, 10 per cent or so of the population were Catholics, with a significant number of Dissenters in addition; in Scotland, 35 per cent were outwith the established Church; in Ireland, over 90 per cent. Given early eighteenth-century population statistics of 5 350 000 for England and Monmouthshire, 3 000 000 for Ireland, 1 100 000 for Scotland and 375 000 for Wales, it is clear that over two-fifths of the population of the British Isles did not belong to the established churches, and that a majority were not Anglicans; perhaps up to a quarter of the population did not speak English *or* Scots as their first language. Such fragmentation can be too readily subsumed under a dominant narrative in our picture of the eighteenth century.[61]

By the end of the seventeenth century Dublin had a population of 60 000, twice the size of Edinburgh and more than twice the size of any other British city outside London. The country as a whole was over 70 per cent Catholic, with under 20 per cent dissenting Presbyterians and fewer than 10 per cent in communion with the established Church of Ireland. Although Catholics had recovered some of the land they had lost under Cromwell (having 20 per cent in 1685 as opposed to 8–9 per cent under the Protectorate), their share was still far lower than the 60 per cent which had obtained at the outbreak of rebellion in 1641 (later it was to sink as low as 5 per cent, though this figure is not supported by strong evidence and has recently been challenged as an effective underestimate). As S. J. Connolly argues:

> much of the fall in Catholic landownership after 1704 was due to the conformity of proprietors or their heirs to the established Church ... Secondly, there was the substantial amount of land held on long leases by Catholic middlemen and tenant farmers: a less prestigious asset than outright ownership, but nevertheless one that brought with it economic advantage, social authority, and also – where there were Protestant under-tenants – political influence.

Whatever the truth of the matter, many Catholics did suffer. Some dispossessed landowners 'turned tory' and took to the hills, thus echoing the crossclass outlawry also found in Scotland. The new regime's alteration of property rights even outside Ireland (not least in the case of the monarchy) called into question the whole legal framework of society for some Jacobite ideologues. The Acts of William and Mary deprived Catholics of various rights of residence, worship and education in England and Wales; further acts of George deprived them of professional employment rights and facilitated the appropriation of Catholic estates (a process already virtually complete in Ireland), while a subsequent Act placed financial penalties on Catholic worship. Penalties such as the double land tax (1692), barring from legal practice (1696), the Irish Banishment Act of 1698 directed against the clergy and prohibition from land purchase and inheritance (1700) compounded the situation. In 1719, the Irish Commons suggested that 'unregistered priests caught in the country should be branded on the face with the letter P [Papist], a punishment amended by the Irish privy council to that of castration'. By 1709, only explicitly anti-Jacobite Catholics could vote in Ireland, and by 1727 'all catholics ... were deprived of the franchise'.[62]

It has been objected that such anti-Catholic legislation was seldom acted on with full vigour (for example, the 1710 report to Cardinal Paolucci stated that only the land tax and public office prohibitions were in force in England and Wales), but that is perhaps not altogether the point: any more than the fact that English juries failed to convict in the case of numerous petty capital crimes in the later eighteenth century can be used to demonstrate the liberality of the government which so multiplied them. The rise in such crimes in English law from 50 in 1688 to more than three times this number in the early years of George III (and yet more thereafter) was a sign of a regime on the defensive with regard to property rights. The idea that crime was the result of poverty (caused by Hanoverian corruption) was present in the Jacobite press, while Jacobite sympathizers offered support for criminality (particularly smuggling, in defiance of Hanoverian duties) as a destabilizing agency in the context of an illegitimate administration founded on an unnatural act against property rights. The boundaries of legality were also stretched by the French and Spanish use of privateers against British shipping up to 1714, in ventures frequently financed by expatriate Irish commissioned by Louis XIV or the Stuarts: 'the captains and crews of the vessels involved were also in many cases Irish'. Among highwaymen, often among the better-educated criminals, ideological attitudes towards post-1688 property rights are clearly, if only occasionally, visible. A sense of social banditry as the duty of restoration from an expropriating grasp dates back in English folklore at least to Robin Hood; and, as Frank McLynn has shown, some eighteenth-century highwaymen adopted such rhetoric, promising to steal only from 'stockjobbers', while the scholar can also find others characterized as social bandits in folksong. In a society which, in the long eighteenth century, came to view the acquisition and security of property as core metaphors in the stability and maintenance of civil society, controversy over the legitimacy of property rights was bound to be a fundamental issue which agitated greed and paranoia, as well as that deep political uncertainty which undermines financial markets, which I will examine in more detail in the next chapter. In this sense, the prospect of a Stuart restoration caused in the minds of many a terror and loathing reserved in our day for the thought of a confiscatory Socialist administration. As has been argued effectively in recent years, there was much in Stuart policy, both known and feared, that was radical rather than reactionary. Far from being the friend of the aristocrats against the legitimate demands of the bourgeoisie (admittedly a rather crude and outdated historical model), on subjects as diverse as enclosure, the restoration of Church lands and Catholic property rights, Charles I and his successors were unsound in the eyes of many supporters both of entrenched magnate power and commercial opportunity.[63]

One of the measures of our constitutional democracy today is the tacit agreement that Parliament will not in general pass retrospective legislation. But the Stuarts had a habit of threatening or implementing such legislation, indeed, they could not have posed as the radical threat some saw them as without taking this line. In 1660, the Act Recissory effectively annulled nearly a generation of Parliamentary decision, while the War in the Three Kingdoms itself was partly rooted in the fear that Charles and Laud sought to restore confiscated Church lands, a fear amplified when Juxon, the Bishop of London, became the first cleric to hold office in a royal administration since the days of Wolsey. Although Charles II did not reverse Cromwellian changes wholesale, nevertheless there was a drift towards the *status quo ante*, as witness the shift back to Catholic landownership in Ireland. Laud's opposition to enclosures and James II and VII's reputed sympathy with traditional land rights may also have formed part of an overall atmosphere of apprehension that a new Stuart regime might annul certain property rights built up since 1688, and become in effect confiscatory. The anxiety over property and the explosive question of legitimate title to it in the eighteenth century thus need to be seen as part of a broader zone of concern as to how far the dynasty in power could be trusted to guarantee matters. A Stuart restoration raised many other spectres beside dynastic, national and religious ones, not least after the development of extensive credit financing of the state under William and his successors. It was not for nothing that the Bank of England was in crisis and that taxes began not to be paid as Charles Edward advanced through England in 1745.[64]

If property rights were viewed as both fundamental and always in jeopardy, this was truer nowhere than in Ireland. After

Ormond's vice-royalty of 1661–9 and 1677–85, when Catholics were returned 'about a third of what they had held when the war in Ireland began in 1641' (a conditionally retrospective move designed to build up royalism), James in 1689 agreed 'to an act declaring that the English parliament had no right to pass laws for Ireland' (the Parliament of 1689 also permitted Catholics and Ulster Presbyterians to pay tithes to their own clergy). But this was the high watermark of the Catholic community, who had lost a third of the land then held by Anne's accession, while the 'popery act' of 1704 'severely curtailed rights and interests that had been lawfully enjoyed in the time of Charles II'. By it, a Catholic could not leave his estate to his eldest son, unless Protestant; an apostate son rendered a Catholic father a life tenant in his own property (shades here of the unnaturalness of James's Protestant nephew and son-in-law, William), and no Catholic could buy land or take leases for more than 31 years. Both this and the 1709 requirement for Catholic clergy to take the Oath of Abjuration were against the articles of the Treaty of Limerick of 1692, under the conditions of which the Jacobite forces in Ireland had surrendered. Central British interests intruded on the terms of a negotiated treaty just as the Scottish Privy Council was abolished and English treason law extended to Scotland following the Treaty of Union in 1707. Limerick was no union treaty, but it was similar in that it bought Irish compliance to English interests on what appeared to be favourable terms, until those terms were breached. The first article in particular, whereby Catholics were to have the same privileges as under Charles II or as were consistent with the laws of Ireland, was roundly abused, both in the letter and the spirit. It was indeed, as J. G. Simms concludes, 'to be many years before Catholics regained the status and opportunities they had briefly enjoyed under a Jacobite administration'.[65]

The 12 000 soldiers who left Ireland for James II and VII',s and subsequently the French service, kept alive in their longstanding exile (where over the following century they were joined by tens, if not hundreds of thousands of their fellow countrymen) a culture of resentment at the betrayal of Limerick, as expressed at Fontenoy in 1745, when six Irish battalions

> advanced with bayonets ... the bagpipes, fifes and drums of the
> Irish played the Stuart hymn 'The White Cockade', and the

officers yelled 'Cumhnigidh ar Liumreck agus feall na Sassanach' ('Remember Limerick and Saxon perfidy').

In the ensuing victorious charge, the Irish were (according to Voltaire) motivated by a desire to 'avenge "their kings betrayed, their country, and their altars"'. A coherent group in exile, who for many years tended not to marry outside their own community, the Irish abroad arguably played a more significant part in the history of other countries than that of Britain in the century before the French Revolution.[66]

Recruiting for the Irish Brigades in the French service continued for decades not only in Ireland (with 10–20 000 recruited in 1713–14, and 'somewhere under 1000 men per year' in the 1720s and 1730s, of whom scores if not hundreds were hanged, drawn and quartered for enlisting), but also in Scotland, where the Gaelic-speaking community in particular provided a source of men. After 1745, Highlanders were sent to their own glens to bring out soldiers for the French service. The Gaelic speakers of both nations seem to have shared a common cultural vision, one later confirmed in Scotland by the Clearances, and exemplified in Aodh Buidhe Mac Cruitin's lament for the passing of the open-handed chiefs and their replacement by 'foreigners and the cunning avaricious merchants'. Such merchants, as later in W. B. Yeats' quasi-nationalist play *The Countess Cathleen* (1892), symbolized the corrupt new order and its emphasis on non-traditional property relations: a critique in fact close to that offered in England of the new 'moneyed interest'. From such a situation, Irish bardic Jacobitism (sometimes still under the traditional forms of patronage) expresses the hope of deliverance in forms such as the *aisling* poem, where a female and abandoned Hibernia foretells her forthcoming messianic deliverance by an heroic Stuart prince, a figure who by the early nineteenth century has been transmuted into that of Daniel O'Connell, who created 'a mass national public' in Leinster and Munster through use of the older traditions. O'Connell, who stated that 'the restoration of our [Irish] rights ... would have been the certain consequence of the success of the Stuart family', himself had an uncle in the Irish Brigades, the last surviving officer of which died in 1859. Like the culture of the Nonjurors (the last of whom died in 1875), that of the Irish Brigades survived well into the nineteenth century, remaining pro-Stuart until a late date.[67]

Notwithstanding the lack of a Jacobite rising in eighteenth-century Ireland, the country itself was unstable and resentful, with thousands of its inhabitants serving in foreign wars or fomenting banditry and agricultural disturbance at home. When in fact a rising belatedly came in 1798, it found elements among the Irish Defenders and even the French (to Wolfe Tone's irritation) still looking for a Stuart solution to the Irish problem, for throughout the eighteenth century much unrest had taken a Jacobite form. As Daniel Szechi informs us:

> This underground culture was naturally resistant to the forces of change, disillusionment and despair that destroyed Jacobitism elsewhere in the British Isles, and consequently may have lingered into the 1790s. Hence the oaths and rhetoric of the Defenders ... who were recruited to fight for Ireland's freedom by republican, Protestant, United Irishmen between 1796 and 1798 still contained references to the Stuarts.

Perhaps between a quarter and half a million people left Ireland between 1700 and 1776, many for France. The New World was at this stage less welcoming: for example, 'the zealous Protestants of New England were so hostile to "St. Patrick's Vermin" that few Irish Catholics ventured to settle there'. In this context, it was small wonder that a deeply resentful inferiorism developed among exiled Irish Catholics in non-Catholic countries, with damaging long-term consequences. Even in 1959,

> the autobiography of an Irish labourer in post war Britain, reported that many of his fellow navvies still blamed Cromwell and the Penal Laws for Ireland's contemporary problems and for their own involuntary expatriation.

This rooted culture of complaint was to exact a high price for earlier intransigence in the Troubles of the twentieth century.[68]

In outlining the minoritization of Irish Catholics, and the corresponding harshness required when such minoritization was imposed on a majority position, it is important not to forget the complexity of Irish society, which was one where Protestants themselves 'can no longer be seen as a monolithic group with a single set of views'. Many Protestants were of course alienated by the bill of 10 May 1689 to repeal the Restoration land settlement, but this did not lead the Presbyterians (twice as numerous as the Anglicans) towards any enthusiasm for British rule. Themselves disadvantaged under the Anglican ascendancy, the exclusion of Dissenters from power in the eighteenth century eventually led them towards Irish nationalism (not until 1719 were they free to practise their religion, and they were excluded from municipal corporations until 1780). Like the Catholics, they too felt colonized; and indeed there is some evidence of fellow feeling between the two groups before the United Irishmen period, on occasion ethnic as much as religious. In the rebellion of 1641, for example, 'it was the declared policy of the rebels ... that the Scottish Presbyterians should be left alone because of their "Gaelic" origins'. Though this was not fully adhered to, it is interesting to note that in the Troubles of the later twentieth century, it is IRA policy not to attack Scottish targets: something apparently not realized by the major insurance companies who put up premiums in Glasgow following bomb attacks in the City.[69]

In Ireland as elsewhere in the British Isles in the eighteenth century, the demarcation between Catholic and Protestant was not so clear-cut as might be supposed. Not only were many Irish Anglicans, whether or not under Ormond's influence, sympathetic to the Jacobites (four Anglican bishops had attended James's 1689 Dublin Parliament, 'though they explained subsequently that they were merely protecting the interests of their flocks'), but there were also significant crossover conversions from different ethnic groups. Ian Adamson suggests that 20 per cent of Anglicans in Co. Down were native converts, whose political sympathies might not be expected to be 'Anglican' in all respects. Moreover, there were significant numbers of what might have been called in England and Scotland 'Church Papists', persons of Catholic sentiment who accepted Anglicanism for ambition's sake. Such may well have been Edmund Burke's father, and indeed his famous son, whom political cartoonists shrewdly enough portrayed as a Jesuit, and whose political sentiments towards his native land were those of the minor Catholic gentry whence he sprang. In Scotland, closet Catholicism of this type was well known in the later sixteenth and early seventeenth centuries: the Covenanting owner of Provost Skene's house in Aberdeen decorated the ceiling of his private chapel with various suggestive medieval iconography, including the coronation of the Blessed Virgin as Queen of Heaven. James I and VI's Scottish Chancellor, the Earl of Dunfermline, was among the most prominent of such crypto-Catholics. It is more difficult to trace the development of this group into the eighteenth century, but by that time a new alliance of sorts was emerging on the east coast of Scotland between Roman Catholicism and Episcopalianism. Describing the port of Montrose (later a major Jacobite centre) in the late seventeenth century, Duncan Fraser writes that 'Scotland was ... hovering on the brink of turning Roman Catholic again and Montrose Town Council had quite a few members who would not have resisted the change'. In the north-east generally, 'the Popish lords naturally threw their weight in with the prelatic party within the Church of Scotland who were far more likely to tolerate their presence than the Presbyterians'. In the Rising of 1745, the close cooperation between Episcopalian and Catholic in north-eastern Scotland was remarked on. Catholicism proper may also have been gaining: despite an act of the Scottish Parliament of 1700 which offered a reward for the apprehension 'of each priest and Jesuit', who were to be banished, with death the penalty for return in the same capacity, Catholic seminaries were opened in northern Scotland, first in Loch Morar, then in Scalan in Glenlivet. In 1706, the Presbytery of Kincardine O'Neil recorded that 'they [the Catholics] give out that upward of 200 persons were in one day confirmed by him [Bishop Maxwell] at Stretin': the Presbytery suggested the provision of Gaelic (called 'Irish') bibles to combat this threat. On the margins, in particular, there were shifting boundaries of identity.[70]

If Scotland had its Glenlivet, Wales had its Monmouthshire, with the Jesuits having founded a college there in 1622 (it was sacked during the Exclusion Crisis 'and four of its priests were executed'). Elsewhere in the principality, Catholicism was weak, though religious belief gave strongly positive linguistic connections to Welsh publishing, something that was not the case in the Gaelic-speaking countries. Nonetheless, only the poorer clergy tended to be Welsh, and Welsh-speaking was a bar to promotion in the Church. The gentrifying of Wales led to a decline in native culture: as early as 1686, William Richards feared for the end of the language, which

'The Society of Ancient Britons' (1715) and later 'The Honourable Society of Cymmrodorion' (1751) were to a degree established to defend. Sympathetic gentry 'could be quite well disposed towards Welsh activities ... But they expended only a minute part of their time and their resources on such matters' . This process speeded the decline of Welsh bardic culture, itself well on the way to extinction by the late seventeenth century. Even Sir Watkin Williams Wynn, who maintained it after a fashion, could hardly be said to think of himself as a Welshman in any terms more serious than those of a cultural hobby: for example, in 1748 he entered a horse called 'Old England' for the race-meeting at Lichfield. Although the gentry might subscribe to the revival in Welsh patriotic publishing, they were simultaneously (as were those that aped them) moving away from Welsh speech and Welsh names for their children (though it is fair to say that some commentators interpret their actions more sympathetically).[71]

As Britain became more centralized, the role of marginal groups and societies appears to shift in the English consciousness. Catholicism had been a bugbear since the reign of Mary Tudor and the era of the Armada; the 1641 Rising had brought anti-Irish feeling to a pitch. But as the British state developed, such tendencies appear more accentuated: they are perhaps, to import a word applicable to British foreign policy, 'colonial'. Scottish, Irish, Welsh, Catholic and Episcopalian difference were all to a greater or lesser degree in opposition to a post-1688 British identity which sought out incorporation rather than the multiple kingdom monarchy of the later Stuarts. There had been earlier gestures towards centralism, by Charles I and (particularly) Cromwell, but these paled into insignificance beside the post-Revolution push towards the final exaltation of the sovereignty of the London Parliament in opposition both to local rivals and royal quangos. The end of the Council of Wales, the Treaty of Limerick, the restrictions on Irish Parliamentary sovereignty (in fact 'there had been suggestions at the time of the Revolution ... to abolish the Irish parliament ... transferring full control of Irish affairs to England', a move which may only have foundered owing to the apprehended backlash), the perpetual adjournment of the Edinburgh Parliament following Union, the end of the Scots Privy Council, the end of the Stannaries parliament in Cornwall, the end of separate Scottish currency, the undermining of Irish money, the taxation of all Britain in pursuit of Anglo-Hanoverian goals – all these and more were great alterations in the state, and heralded the massive concentration of power in the London House of Commons which we currently enjoy.[72]

As this process progressed, a greater degree of stigma became attached to displays of any separate identity. Chapbooks appear carrying the kind of Irish jokes recognizable today (indeed, by the end of the eighteenth century one can witness 'the lumping of Irish Protestants along with Catholics into a single Hibernian stereotype'); the Welsh are sneered at as stupid, irritable and poverty-stricken (in 1701, Ned Ward described Wales as 'the fag-end of Creation; the very rubbish of Noah's flood'); the Scots are sex-mad, infested with vermin, eat children, and put their feet in the lavatory while excreting on the floor (this print, *Sawney on the Boghouse*, appears to have been a mid-century favourite); even people from the West Country are cannibals. It is certainly arguable that in the eighteenth-century print and chapbook the British often show more xenophobic hatred towards their fellow countrymen than to the French enemy. On the other hand, as the century progressed, Scots and to a lesser extent Irish who did away with the more obvious differences of language, accent and manners (in other words, eradicated difference) became more acceptable. Burke, whose 'accent never quitted the banks of the Shannon', remained suspect on this count, while in Wales, 'scholarly Welsh clerics could not find livings … whilst monoglot Englishmen were appointed to Welsh-speaking parishes'. Nor was this altogether a general move towards an early form of Anglophone Received Pronunciation: English regional accents remained acceptable at the highest levels of government and society, as Lord Curzon's flat 'a''s bore witness to more than a century later.[73]

In the process of marginalization and alienization, the Jacobite leadership was characterized in terms of the disgraced and disliked Celtic fringe. James Francis's status as Prince of Wales was deliberately confused with Welsh nationality, rendering him and by implication the whole Jacobite project marginal: 'Perkin ap Dada, Prince of Wales' is a base-born Welsh pretender, bastard of a Papist priest. 'My Welsh blood's up', exclaims Perkin in another poem. Fiery Welshmen, touchy Scots and the ever-violent Irish are eighteenth-century as much as modern models, and are depicted as Jacobite backwoodsmen in government propaganda. Transmuting himself from Welshman to Gaelic Highlander in another pro-government poem, James whines 'Take care on your Sell, Sir, now', like an ingratiating stage Gael. When such margins are felt to be a threat, they can always be characterized in terms of a dominant foreign enemy in order to suggest their alien quality: so Jacobites are presented in prints as strongly associated with Franco-Italian Catholicism, and a Welshman from 'Goatlandshire' is, in at least one chapbook, conflated with the French 'other' to reinforce his unacceptability to the incorporating narrative of 'Britishness'.[74]

The Rhetoric of Britain

The Rose and the Thistle together are gane ...
An' wae to the loons wha their growin' wad mar

Long before the consummation of Anglo-Scottish Union, 'Britain' as a concept had a long history. But it is important to realize that the 'Britain' so conceptualized was significantly different from the development of the 'imagined nation' following 1707. English enthusiasm for Britain had been (and up to perhaps 1770 entirely remained) of a firmly imperialist cast, being linked to foundation-myth-derived claims of sovereignty and hegemony. Modern Welsh ideas of Britain had begun to emerge following the accession of Henry VII. Henry called his eldest son 'Arthur' and later Welsh origins were claimed for the Anglican Church, for 'David was the most famous saint of the early British church, who could be taken as a permanent reminder that the Church in England and Wales could claim an ancestry independent of papal Rome'. Attempts were even made to claim the Stuarts as a Welsh dynasty, through both the Tudor and Fleance connections, with Humphrey Llwyd, for example, emphasizing 'the Celtic origin' of the Stuarts.[75]

In Scotland, the Scoto-Britanes, writers and courtiers at the court of King James VI, had long welcomed in anticipation the accession of their king to the English throne. Their idea of a new British imperial monarchy was of one not merely ruled by a Scottish monarch, but with major Scottish input and influence. Such a projection of a British partnership with strong Scottish elements was unwelcome in England, which was one of the reasons

why James's attempts to promote closer cooperation foundered
(just as did the Covenanters' later attempts to unite Britain under
a Scottish agenda). Various suggestions were put forward for the
Anglo-Scottish flag: one, which portrayed the crosses of St George
and St Andrew conjoined, each occupying half the flag, indicates
the magnitude of the role sought for Scotland. (Most of the proposals indeed, contained a more marked presence for the Scottish
flag than did the later Union Jack). However, as Henry VII had
once prophesied on the marriage of his daughter to James IV, the
greater drew the lesser into its orbit.[76]

Part of the frustration felt at the fairly rapid failure of the
Scoto-Britannic ideal may have played its part in the ignition of
national resentment against the ecclesiastical and (as it was perceived) Anglicizing reform in 1638. Certainly after 1603 the
virtual cessation of separate Scottish diplomatic representation
abroad further helped to weaken the links with France already
slackened by the Reformation. Scotland was strongly anti-
English, but for all that was becoming more British, a process
which was to a degree curtailed by the multi-kingdom monarchy
of the later Stuarts, and accelerated thereafter (though Scots
retained the right to French citizenship up to the time of the
Entente Cordiale in the early twentieth century). The very nature
of the absentee monarchy and the success of Scots in London
naturally caused problems: there had been only fifty-odd Scots in
the English capital in the 1560s, but after 1603 their numbers
burgeoned. Dr Arthur Johnston, Medicus Regius to both James
and Charles, and an eminent Latin poet, wrote ironically of the
careers of such London-based Scots as Sir William Alexander,
Earl of Stirling:

Sad was the day when Alexander of Menstrie entered the Court
circle, deserting Phoebus and the Muses. A chieftain of Poets
then said to the poetic art: 'Farewell, and for ever!' and hung
up his lyre no longer strung. As soon as he of Menstrie saw the
Thames, he became a confidant of the throne, but I wish he
had withdrawn thence to other, though far ruder, climes. Even
in this bleak land of Scotia the Muses can live. So Naso lived in
Scythia, and Orpheus in cold Thrace. The Court is a clime
unfavourable to pensive Elegiac song. 'Tis like the abode of
Circe, imposing spells of silence.

The spell of silence, of eradication of voiced difference, affected Scottish prose and poetry from the Reformation in a trend completed after 1603, driving native Scottish forms and vocabulary out into the vernacular localities.[77]

From the English point of view, Scottish claims to a shaping role in the new monarchy were resented (indeed, continued to be resented up to the age of Wilkes). For this reason, there was much English scepticism of Union with Scotland: the Cromwellian union was driven more by military necessity than ideology, and was of course dissolved after the Restoration. English attitudes towards Scotland continued to be hegemonic and to speak in terms of restoring rightful overlordship; Ireland did not even reach that position, although certain Irish people (of the right religion) were accepted as English on terms more favourable than Scots then experienced. Yet if Ireland was to be a possession, Scotland was to be little better: 'in this Union are Lands and People added to the *English* Empire', as Daniel Defoe put it, 'an entire Coallition ... as has been formerly Settled between the Kingdom of *England* and the Principalities of *Wales*'. Hardly any Scottish unionist, then or now, could have accepted this description: just as Scottish unionists tend and tended to regard the Union as an unalterable treaty in international law (and there is legal opinion for this stretching at least into the 1950s), while the British political system has abrogated the force of certain of its clauses as convenient. Not that the English advocates of Union were impressed by its constitutional safeguards at the time: for example, Defoe saw the preservation of Scots law as similar to the specifics of local administration in Lancashire and Durham.[78]

After 1707, the idea of Britain still hovers between a synonym for a greater England (indeed, this is perhaps even the case in Jacobite poetry like Pope's *Windsor Forest*) and the limited common purpose sought by the Jacobite Britain of multiple kingdoms. The Union itself did not become embedded in a rhetoric of partnership to any convincing extent (*pace* early Scottish imperial efforts such as James Thomson's *Rule Britannia* (1740)), until the Stuart threat had been beaten off, and large numbers of Scottish troops had fought alongside their English counterparts in the Seven Years' War. Parliamentary attempts by Scottish Jacobite MPs (who won 16 of Scotland's 45 Commons seats in 1710, showing 'all the characteristics of a contemporary political party') to end the

Union went on until the death of Anne (who, as Edward Gregg tells us, was upset by such attempts), coming in 1713 very close to success. George Lockhart of Carnwath, later James's agent in Scotland, was among the leading lights in such moves.[79]

It should perhaps be noted that Lockhart and other passionate anti-Unionists of his stamp were not necessarily 'separatists' in the way twentieth-century anti-nationalist rhetoric uses the term. They tended rather to recognize the Union as the means whereby the Act of Settlement had been forced on Scotland: an insult both to the nation and its ancient dynasty, thus excluded. Hardly any Jacobites (except perhaps in 1708) thought of a Stuart restoration in Scotland alone: it was not feasible without continuous French aid, for one thing. But what they did want was a multi-kingdom monarchy with separate parliaments, not a unitary Britain. The Jacobite case was that the Union was an act of slavery, which cut their country adrift from its past, and bound it to English ends: 'the handcuff of Scotland'. Even those who were its supporters were conscious of its dual interpretation: in Scotland, a partnership; in England, possession. Consciousness of this endured, as did the resulting alertness of Scots of every stamp to quickly resent even symbolic encroachments on the idea of 'partnership'. Parallels can be seen in the attacks on EIIR pillarboxes in the 1950s, or criticism of the monarch in Scotland for not flying the Scottish quarterings, a grumble which dates back to George IV's visit of 1822. The gap between Scottish and English perceptions of 'Britain' reaches from the optimistic Scoto-Britanes of the 1580s to our own day.[80]

NOTES

1. Cf. J. H. Plumb, *The Growth of Stability in England 1675–1725* (London, 1967); Paul Langford, *A Polite and Commercial People* (Oxford, 1989); Thomas Babington Macaulay, *History of England to the Death of William III*, Volume I (London, 1967), pp. 220, 223, 224.
2. G. M. Trevelyan, *England Under the Stuarts*, 19th ed. (London, 1947 (1904)), pp. 402, 431.
3. *The Poems of Alexander Pope*, ed. John Butt, one-volume Twickenham Pope (London, 1963), p. 570 ff.; Macaulay, I, p. 274.
4. Cf. David B. Kramer, 'Onely victory in him: the imperial Dryden', in Earl Miner and Jennifer Brady (eds.), *Literary Transmission and Authority* (Cambridge, 1993), pp. 55–78.

5. See Geoffrey Holmes, *The Trial of Doctor Sacheverell* (London, 1973).

6. Cf. Linda Colley, *Britons: Forging the Nation 1707–1837* (New Haven, 1992) for the idea of Protestant solidarity; Holmes (see above) for Sacheverell's sales figures.

7. S. Bruce and S. Yearley, 'The Social Construction of Tradition', in David McCrone, Stephen Kendrick and Pat Shaw (eds.), *The Making of Scotland* (Edinburgh, 1989), pp. 175–88 (182, 184).

8. Keith Brown, 'The vanishing emperor: British kingship and its decline, 1603–1707', in Roger Mason (ed.), *Scots and Britons: Scottish Political Thought and the Union of 1603* (Cambridge, 1994), pp. 58–87 (86–7); James Kinsley, 'A Dryden Play at Edinburgh', *Scottish Historical Review* 33 (1954), pp. 129–32.

9. Murray G. H. Pittock, *The Invention of Scotland: the Stuart Myth and the Scottish Identity, 1638 to the Present* (London and New York, 1991), p. 17; Bruce and Yearley (1989), p. 181; Kinsley (1954), p. 130; Hugh Ouston, 'York in Edinburgh', in John Dwyer, Roger Mason and Alexander Murdoch (eds.), *New Perspectives on the Politics and Culture of Early Modern Scotland* (Edinburgh, n.d. (c. 1983)), pp. 133–55 (133).

10. Cf. Ouston, pp. 133–55 (134).

11. William Thoirs' commonplace-book has been recently catalogued by the National Library of Scotland; Julia Buckroyd, *William Sharp* (Edinburgh, 1987), p. 115; G. M. Trevelyan, *English Social History* (London, 1945 (1942)), p. 256; the 1708 Synod lists are discussed in Jean McCann, ' The Organization of the Jacobite Army, 1745–46' (unpublished Ph.D. thesis, Edinburgh, 1963), and in Murray G. H. Pittock, *The Myth of the Jacobite Clans* (Edinburgh, 1995), p. 47.

12. Peter Berresford Ellis, *The Celtic Revolution* (Talybont, 1985), p. 167; Ronald Hutton, *Charles II* (Oxford, 1991), pp. 207, 362, 423, 437; S. J. Connolly, *Religion, Law and Power: The Making of Protestant Ireland 1650–1760* (Oxford, 1992), pp. 13–15, 19, 21–3.

13. Lawrence Smith's 1994 Edinburgh Ph.D. on the 4th Earl of Orrery; Connolly (1992), pp. 3, 105, 118, 120.

14. Hutton (1991), p. 407; Connolly (1992), 32.

15. Geraint H. Jenkins, *The Foundations of Modern Wales 1642–1780* (Oxford, 1987), pp. 43, 87, 98, 143; Connolly (1992), p. 44; John Davies, *A History of Wales* (London, 1993 (1990)), pp. 235, 272, 275, 292; A. H. Dodd, *Studies in Stuart Wales*, 2nd ed. (Cardiff, 1971 (1952)), pp. 1, 19, 33–4.

16. Dodd (1971), pp. 49, 50, 51–52, 59–61, 66, 67, 68, 71, 74, 218, 220, 226; John Rhys and David Brynmor-Jones, *The Welsh People* (London, 1923 (1900)), p. 66 ff.; Prys T. J. Morgan, 'The clouds of witnesses: The Welsh Historical Tradition' in R. Bruley Jones (ed.), *Anatomy of Wales* (Glamorgan, 1972), pp. 17–42 (27, 29); G. Jenkins (1987), p. 145.

17. Cf. Murray G. H. Pittock, *Poetry and Jacobite Politics in Eighteenth-Century Britain and Ireland* (Cambridge, 1994), pp. 25, 27 ff.; Marc Bloch, *The Royal Touch*, tr. J. E. Anderson, (London, 1973), p. 41.

18. Hutton (1991), pp. 358–66, 391; Macaulay, I, (1967) p. 370.

19. F. C. Turner, *James II* (London, 1948), pp. 237, 240; Gordon Donaldson, *Scotland James V to James VII* (Edinburgh and London, 1965), p. 380.

20. J. R. Jones, *The Revolution of 1688 in England* (London, 1972), p. 112; Turner (1948), pp. 306–7, 309, 314, 323, 327.

21. Macaulay (1967), I, p. 589; II, p. 126; Murray G. H. Pittock (1991), p. 19; Tim Harris, 'London Crowds and the Revolution of 1688' in Eveline Cruickshanks (ed.), *By Force or By Default? The Revolution of 1688–1689* (Edinburgh, 1989), pp. 44–64 (48); Philip Jenkins, *The Making of a Ruling Class: the Glamorgan Gentry 1640–1790* (Cambridge, 1983), p. 125; Leo Gooch, *The Desperate Faction?* (Hull, 1995) for the position of Catholics in northern English society.

22. Macaulay (1967), I, p. 599; Turner (1948), p. 375; Gordon Donaldson, 'Scotland's Conservative North in the Sixteenth and Seventeenth Centuries' in *Scottish Church History* (Edinburgh, 1985), pp. 191–203; Bruce Lenman, *The Jacobite Risings in Britain 1689–1746* (London, 1980).

23. G. W. Keeton, *Lord Chancellor Jeffreys* (London, 1965) for a revisionist view.

24. Sir George Mackenzie, *A Defence of the Antiquity of the Royal Line of Scotland* (London, 1685), pp. 3, 5, 6, 21, 186–9.

25. Sir George Mackenzie, *The Antiquity of the Royal Line of Scotland Farther Cleared and Defended* (London, 1686), pp. 80, 82.

26. William Dauney, *Ancient Scottish Melodies From a Manuscript of the Reign of King James VI* (Edinburgh and London, 1838), p. 23.

27. E. P. Thompson, 'Patrician Society, Plebeian Culture', *Past and Present* (1974), pp. 391, 393, 400; Frank McLynn, *Crime and Punishment in Eighteenth-Century England* (London, 1989) for Fielding's attitude; Ronald Hutton, *The Rise and Fall of Merry England* (Oxford, 1994), pp. 233, 235; Nicholas Rogers, *Whigs and Cities* (Oxford, 1989), p. 363.

28. *The Oxford Authors: John Dryden*, Keith Walker (ed.) (Oxford, 1987), p. 321.

29. Peter Burke, 'Popular Culture in Seventeenth-Century London' in Barry Reay (ed.), *Popular Culture in Early Eighteenth-Century England* (London, 1988 (1985)), pp. 31–58 (45); David B. Kramer in Miner and Brady (1993), p. 58; Keeton (1965), p. 337; Lois Potter, 'Politics and popular culture: the theatrical response to the Revolution' in Lois G. Schwoerer (ed.), *The Revolutions of 1688–1689: Changing Perspectives* (Cambridge, 1992), pp. 184–97 (196).

30. Dauney (1838), p. 19.

31. *A Copy of a Trayterous Libel which was Printed and Cent about the Streets* (1689); Tim Harris in Cruickshanks (ed.), *By Force or By Default?* (1989), p. 58, also Eveline Cruickshanks, 'The Revolution and the Localities', ibid., pp. 28–43 (29); John Miller, 'Catholic officers in the later Stuart army', *English Historical Review* 88 (1973), 35–53 (40, 49, 53); Pittock (1995), p. 23 ff.

62   *Inventing and Resisting Britain*

32. See Gooch (1995), p. 43 ff. for government distrust of the keelmen; James Hogg, *The Jacobite Relics*, 1st series (Edinburgh, 1819), preface for Fletcher of Saltoun, p. xi ff.; Macaulay (1967), I, p. 326.
33. P. W. J. Riley, *The Union of England and Scotland* (Manchester, 1978), pp. 204–5; *An Account of the Proceedings of the Meeting of the Estates in Scotland* (London, 1689), p. 8; Pittock (1991), p. 25; Philip Lawson, *The East India Company: A History* (London, 1993), pp. 33, 54.
34. Cf. Pittock (1995), p. 58; Keith Brown, *Kingdom or Province? Scotland and the Regal Union 1603–1715* (Basingstoke, 1992), p. 181.
35. Michael Lynch, *Scotland: A New History* (London, 1991), p. 200 ff.
36. Cf. above, n15–n17; Philip Jenkins, *A History of Modern Wales 1536–1990* (London, 1992), p. 83; Jenkins (1983), p. 79.
37. Roger Mason, 'Scotching the Brut: Politics, History and National Myth in Sixteenth-Century Britain' in idem (ed.), *Scotland and England 1286–1815* (Edinburgh, 1983), pp. 60–84 (60, 61, 63); Colin Kidd, *Subverting Scotland's Past* (Cambridge, 1993), p. 47.
38. Brown (1992), pp. 81, 83; Dauvit Broun of the Scottish History department at the University of Glasgow is one scholar working on the continuing use of Irish foundation myth in Scottish royal genealogies.
39. Pittock (1991), p. 37 ff.; Pittock (1994), p. 52.
40. Pittock (1994), p. 49, Brown, *Kingdom or Province?* (1994), p. 185; Edward Gregg, *Queen Anne* (London, 1980), pp. 130, 147–8.
41. Daniel Szechi, *The Jacobites* (Manchester, 1994), p. 22; Pittock (1994), pp. 52, 54; Lawson (1993), p. 51.
42. Pittock (1994), p. 51; Riley (1978), pp. 282, 304; Lockhart's sentiments are to be found in his *Memoirs*, the most available edition of which is Daniel Szechi's, *'Scotland's Ruine': the Memoirs of George Lockhart of Carnwath* (Aberdeen, 1995); *A Discourse on the Necessity and Seasonableness of an unanimous Address for Dissolving the Union* (n.p., 1715), p. 5; Daniel Szechi and David Hayton, 'John Bull's Other Kingdoms: The English Government of Scotland and Ireland', in Clyve Jones (ed.), *Britain in the First Age of Party 1680–1750: Essays Presented to Geoffrey Holmes* (London and Ronceverte, 1987), p. 241 ff.
43. Elizabeth Carmichael, 'Jacobitism in the Scottish Commission of the Peace, 1707–1760', *Scottish Historical Review* 58 (1979), 58–69 (58).
44. *The Muses Farewel to Popery & Slavery*, 2nd and revised ed. (1690); *Virgil's Aeneid*, trans. John Dryden (New York, 1968), p. 35.
45. *Popery and Slavery* (1690), p. 105; Paul Korshin, *Typologies in England 1650–1720* (Princeton, 1982), p. 119.
46. Frances Yates, *Astraea* (London, 1985 (1975)), pp. 33, 59; Madge Dresser, 'Britannia' in Raphael Samuel (ed.), *Patriotism: The Making and Unmaking of British National Identity*, 3 vols. (London and New York, 1989), III, pp. 26–49 (32).
47. James Winn, *Dryden and his World* (New Haven, 1987), p. 485; cf. Murray G. H. Pittock, 'The *Aeneid* in the Age of Burlington: a Jacobite Text?', in Toby Barnard and Jane Clark (eds.), *Lord Burlington: Architecture, Art and Life* (London, 1995), pp. 231–49.

48. Annabel Patterson, *Pastoral and Ideology: Virgil to Valéry* (Oxford, 1988), pp. 169, 170, 180, 225; Pittock (1994), p. 31; Korshin (1982), pp. 5, 119; Eirwen Nicholson, unpublished Ph.D. thesis (Edinburgh, 1994), plates 6, 9, 11, 14, 25; F. Marian McNeill, *The Silver Bough*, 4 vols. (Glasgow, 1957), I, p. 77 for Druidic oak; David Greenwood, *William King* (Oxford, 1969), pp. 77–9, 170–1, 226.

49. Brian J. R. Blench, 'Symbols and Sentiment: Jacobite Glass', in R. Woosnam-Savage (ed.), *1745: Charles Edward Stuart and the Jacobites* (Edinburgh, 1995), pp. 87–102 (97); Howard Erskine-Hill, *The Augustan Idea in English Literature* (London, 1983), pp. 236–37; *Mr Addison Turn'd Tory*, by a Gentleman of Oxford (London, 1713).

50. Roberta Florence Brinkley, *Arthurian Legend in the Seventeenth Century* (Baltimore, 1932), p. 8.

51. Patterson (1988), p. 171.

52. Cf. Pittock (1994), pp. 36–7; Paul Monod, 'Pierre's White Hat', in Cruickshanks (1989), pp. 159–89 (164–7, 170–1); Macaulay (1967), I, p. 250 ff.

53. Monod in Cruickshanks (1989), pp. 160, 164, 166.

54. Holmes (1973); Jenkins (1987), p. 141.

55. Cf. Holmes (1973), p. 263; Nicholas Phillipson, 'Politics and Politeness in the Reigns of Anne and the Early Hanoverians', in J. G. A. Pocock with Gordon Schochet and Lois Schwoerer (eds.), *The Varieties of British Political Thought 1500–1800* (Cambridge, 1993), pp. 211–45 (213).

56. Clyve Jones (1987), p. 25; Gooch (1995) discusses Bishop Crewe's case in detail; cf. Pittock (1994) for extended discussion of sacramental monarchy.

57. *Scottish Notes and Queries V* (1890–91), pp. 40–1.

58. Bishop Robert Forbes, *The Lyon in Mourning*, ed. Henry Paton, 3 vols., (Edinburgh, 1895), I, pp. 10, 15; J. H. Overton, *The Nonjurors* (London, 1902), pp. 87, 119; D. Macmillan, *The Aberdeen Doctors* (London, 1909), pp. 173–4; G. D. Henderson, *Mystics of the North-East* (Aberdeen, 1934), p. 14.

59. Henry Broxap, *The Later Nonjurors* (Cambridge, 1924), pp. 66, 323; Rev. Canon George Farquhar, *The Episcopal History of Perth* (Perth, 1894), pp. 111–12; Newman, cited in Peter Nockles, *The Oxford Movement in Context* (Cambridge, 1994), p. 157; Timothy Ware's (Bishop Kallistos') *The Orthodox Church* (Harmondsworth, 1982 (1963)) confirms importance of Nonjuring contacts with the Orthodox; the Usages controversy also has good coverage in Daniel Szechi (ed.), *Letters of George Lockhart of Carnwath* (Edinburgh, 1989).

60. Overton (1902), p. 375; Gavin White, 'The Consecration of Bishop Seabury', *Scottish Historical Review* 63 (1984), 37–49; Bruce Lenman, 'The Scottish Episcopal Clergy and the Ideology of Jacobitism', in Eveline Cruickshanks (ed.), *Ideology and Conspiracy: Aspects of Jacobitism* (Edinburgh, 1982), pp. 36–48 (46); Forbes, *Lyon*, Volume III, pp. 305–8; Farquhar (1894), pp. 171, 190.

64   *Inventing and Resisting Britain*

61. William Donaldson, *The Jacobite Song* (Aberdeen, 1988) discusses Episcopal sympathies towards Gaelic.

62. Cf. Pittock (1994), p. 108; John Cannon, *Samuel Johnson and the Politics of Hanoverian England* (Oxford, 1994), p. 11; Connolly (1992), p. 147; Oliver Rafferty,*Catholicism in Ulster 1603–1983* (London, 1994), pp. 64–5.

63. McLynn (1989), p. 57 ff.; Cannon (1994), p. 12; Connolly (1992), p. 236.

64. Pittock (1991), p. 12; Eveline Cruickshanks, *Political Untouchables* (London, 1979), pp. 80–1; Audrey Cunningham, *The Loyal Clans* (Cambridge, 1932) gives a sympathetic reading of James's sympathy with traditional forms of landholding.

65. J. G. Simms, *Jacobite Ireland* (London, 1969), pp. 3, 80, 260, 267; Connolly (1992),p. 157.

66. J. G. Simms in T. W. Moody and W. E. Vaughan (eds.), *A New History of Ireland* (Oxford, 1986), p. 636.

67. Pittock (1995), p. 86; Brian Ó Cuin in Moody and Vaughan (1986), 397, 407; Kerby A. Miller, *Emigrants and Exiles: Ireland and the Irish Exodus to North America* (New York and Oxford, 1985), p. 241; Connolly (1992), p. 237; John Cornelius O'Callaghan, *History of the Irish Brigades in the Service of France* (Glasgow, 1870), pp. 193, 634, 638. See the ongoing work of Breandan Ó Buachalla for the fate of Irish recruits.

68. Szechi (1994), p. 133; Kerby Miller (1985), pp. 114, 137, 145.

69. Raymond Gillespie, 'The Irish Protestants and James II', *Irish Historical Studies* XXVIII, 10 (1992), 124–33 (131); Ian Adamson, *The Identity of Ulster* (Ulster, 1982), p. 20; Cannon (1994), p. 13.

70. Adamson (1982), p.15; Alexandra Walsham, *Church Papists: Catholicism, Conformity and Confessional Polemic in Early Modern England* (New York, 1993), p. 116; Conor Cruise O'Brien, *The Great Melody* (London, 1992), p. 174; Duncan Fraser, *Montrose (before 1700)* (Montrose, 1970), p. 109; Alexander Keith, *A Thousand Years of Aberdeen* (Aberdeen, 1972), p. 134; *Aberdeen Notes and Queries IV* (1911), pp. 145–6; Pittock (1995), p. 48; Cannon (1994), p. 13.

71. Davies (1993), pp. 287, 289, 301, 302–4; G. Jenkins (1987), pp. 220, 226, 300.

72. Connolly (1992), p. 75.

73. E. D. Evans, *A History of Wales 1600–1815* (Cardiff, 1976), p. 72; George Fasel, *Edmund Burke* (Boston, 1983), p. 5; cf. Pittock (1995), ch. 1.; G. Jenkins (1987), p. 87.

74. Pittock (1994), p. 33; National Library of Scotland Rosebery Collection Ry. iii.a.10, 124; Pittock,(1995), pp. 23–4.

75. William Allan, *Rose and Thistle* (London, 1878), p. 3; Pittock (1994), pp. 202, 205.

76. Examples of the early designs for the Anglo-Scottish flag are on display at the National Trust for Scotland Bannockburn Heritage Centre.

77. *Musa Latina Aberdoniensis*, ed. Sir William Duguid Geddes (vols. 1 and 2) and William Keith Leasle (vol. 3) (Aberdeen, 1892–1910), I, pp. 180n, 219.

78. Daniel Defoe, *An Essay At Removing National Prejudice Against a Union with Scotland* (London, 1706), pp. 5, 7, 8.
79. Daniel Szechi, *Jacobitism and Tory Politics 1710–14* (Edinburgh, 1984), pp. 63, 67.
80. Pittock (1991), chs. 4 and 5 for discussion of later Scottish protests.

2 Blest Paper Credit: Financing the Revolution

The Financial Revolution

> Blest paper credit: last and best supply!
> That lends corruption lighter wings to fly ...
> Pregnant with thousands slips the scrap unseen,
> And silent buys a king – or sells a queen.

Pope, *Epistle to Bathurst* [1]

Daniel Defoe's famous apophthegm, 'That an Estate is a Pond; but that a Trade was a Spring', which animates both his manual *The Complete English Tradesman* and his novel *Roxana*, contrasted the spendthrift ways of the traditional aristocracy with the efficient husbanding of new money under a new regime. One of the key differences between the two financial worlds Defoe was describing is that between borrowing money to spend, which burdened the gentry with debt, and borrowing money to invest, which geared the tradesman's higher returns. Like Defoe's virtuous tradesman (and most unlike Charles II, kept afloat by French subsidy), the post-1688 regime borrowed to expand its resources in order to oust its competitors from the marketplace and become the major player: the British Empire.[2]

Charles II had introduced centralized control of customs and excise in the early 1670s, but progress in the efficient use of state resources had nonetheless been slow. When William II and III came to the throne, there was a gradual shift in favour of policies which would in the end underpin the British state and empire as they developed into a greatness resting on an ever-expanding national debt (which in 1995 stands in the region of £300 000 million). William came from a country with an already

mature and flourishing stock market, which in the tulip craze
had suffered the first modern speculative crash. By 1688, Dutch
dealing had developed many of the features of a modern
financial market, such as commodities futures: 'there was
forward buying of herring before it had been caught and wheat
and other goods before they had been grown or received', as
Fernand Braudel tells us. Commodities prices had been published in Holland since 1585, though regular share prices were
still some distance away. In England, the introduction of
financial practices 'in the Dutch style' helped William 'to tie to
his still-fragile cause a large number of government stockholders': and the ability to do this derived from the emplaced role
credit had gained in the Dutch financial system. England itself
had market conditions which enabled it to take advantage of
such opportunities: 'as early as 1689, George White was accusing
... "stockjobbers"' of setting out 'to devour men'. By 1695,
'Change Alley', the stock exchange, was full of 'the howling of a
wolf, the grunting of a hog, the braying of the ass, the nocturnal
wooing of the cat' as trading reached frenzied levels, and two
years later, an Act restricting the number of 'brokers and stockjobbers' was brought in 'following a wave of market-rigging and
insider-trading'. Although progress was gradual, the government moved steadily towards financing its long-term needs and
ambitions through what was effectively futures trading on its
fiscal revenue, turning on a supply of private capital to purchase
an interest in the returns of future taxation:

> The country's rulers gradually realized that there was a possible
> market for long-term loans at low interest rates; that there was a
> fixed ratio as it were between the real volume of taxation and
> the potential volume of loans (the latter could rise to a third of
> the total without danger), between the size of the short-term
> debt and that of the long-term debt. The only real danger lay in
> attaching interest payments to sources of revenue which were
> uncertain or difficult to estimate in advance.[3]

After 1692, the subscriber to such a loan could transfer his title
to a third party, and thus the bond market was born: 'this was the
miracle: the state never recovered the loan, but the lender could
recover his money whenever he wanted it'. At first, 'tontines, life

annuities' and 'lotteries' were used to raise funds, but gradually the English government moved towards a policy of steadily funding long-term or even 'perpetual' loans (a twentieth-century example of the latter is the undated War Loan: this was of course the purpose for which much of William's monies were raised). In our own century, inflation has ravaged sterling bonds (especially undated stock), and rendered them a marginal and inefficient holding in the private market from which they once drew their strength. The far higher proportion of bonds held in private portfolios in the US and Germany reflects these countries' closer adherence to the policies which, ironically as it turns out, sustained the English bond market in its infancy, and helped to build the British Empire. The Bank of England, established in 1694, 'promptly lent all its capital to the state', but this did not prevent a financial crisis from developing in the same year, when the pound sterling collapsed on the Amsterdam market, the golden guinea rose from 22 to 30 shillings in value, and a premium of up to 40 per cent in paper money had to be found in order to obtain specie. Bad harvests and the amount of cash being exported to fund the war of the League of Augsburg were to blame: government borrowing was sending the value of money into decline. There was strong pressure to accept the effective devaluation, but then as now a result would have been a risk premium on the interest payable on government stock in a weak currency, and possibly a lack of confidence which would sap the government's ability to raise capital.[4]

At this critical juncture, John Locke argued successfully for the retention of the pound sterling as 'an invariable fundamental unit', and what followed was a reduction in the value of the guinea and the beginnings of a movement towards a gold standard, one which in fact overvalued gold relative to silver in terms of the European norm. But this move had its advantages in the long-term securing of overseas markets by the arbitrage which it enabled to be practised through silver export:

> When England attracted gold, by the same token she exported silver, whether to the Netherlands, Russia, the Mediterranean, the Indian Ocean and China, where silver was essential for trade. Venice had done precisely the same thing, in order to make it easier to transfer to the Levant the silver which was

indispensable for her purchases there. What was more, England had been further propelled in this direction since her trade victory over Portugal, sealed by Lord Methuen's treaty (1703), whereby she gained access to the gold of Brazil ... so could it be said that the English chose gold rather than silver, without consciously realizing it – and in doing so became a world power?

Naturally the increasing volume of trade and London's commensurately boom status as a mercantilist capital swelled the flow of credit which in turn financed the military operations by which Britain gained control of a huge empire. There were difficulties along the way, notably the South Sea Bubble of 1720, but possibly because of the greater maturity of English markets, this was in the end far more easily absorbed than the disastrous experiment with a paper currency secured on national assets which the Scottish financier John Law introduced in France. Law's system, which collapsed under a general demand for specie, appears to have caused a lasting aversion to paper, and with it modern systems of credit and supply, in France, with the result that France was less competitive economically with Britain than she should have been in the eighteenth century.[5]

The English development of a massive long-term debt depended, however, not only on a state which was creditworthy, but also one where the regime was secure (hence the run on the Bank of England in 1745, although the Jacobites did not disown the National Debt). The necessity for politico-military as well as financial security was one of the reasons why England showed such hostility to Scottish commercial ventures at the turn of the eighteenth century. Successful Scottish colonial enterprise raised on Scottish credit and in the context of a militant Scottish Parliament among which were many Jacobites, was a nightmare the supporters of the National Debt did not want to see manifested. For England and later for Britain, the National Debt was the key to empire: 'a technically effective masterpiece', or as Pitt put it in 1786, 'upon this matter of the national debt repose the vigour and even the independence of the Nation'.[6]

Naturally, there was a downside in the use of this enormously successful financial instrument. The gigantic amounts of credit were raised on the back of earmarked taxes, for 'every new loan made it necessary to create a new tax, a fresh source of income, so that the interest could be paid'. During the eighteenth century this led to Britain becoming heavily taxed. One estimate suggests that taxation was 22 per cent of Gross National Product, compared to only 10 per cent in France. On the other hand, although this burden was to an extent noted and resented (even if humorously so, as in the well-known print *French Liberty and British Slavery* from the end of the century), the use of indirect taxation served to disguise the extent to which taxes were rising:

> *Direct taxation*, which made up the greater part of the burden in France, was always both politically and administratively unpopular and difficult to increase. In England *indirect taxation* ... made up the largest share of the tax burden (70 per cent between 1750 and 1780).

Nevertheless, it was possibly only increasing prosperity that made this acceptable: Britain was probably 20 per cent ahead of France in GNP per capita during the eighteenth century.[7]

This was the century in which the English became confirmed as a nation of shopkeepers. Just as in government policy, the domestic economy thrived on credit, praised by Defoe to the extent that it has been said of him that 'credit was at all times to be placed above honesty, decency and fear of God'. Defoe took Thomas Hobbes's commercial metaphor from *Leviathan* (1651) about the worth of a man being the value of his power to the extent where creditworthy appearance could outweigh all other considerations, in 'the necessary and justifiable immorality of commerce'. The toning down of some of Defoe's sentiments in the 1745 edition of *The Complete English Tradesman* may indicate, in Bram Dijkstra's words, a 'moral retrenchment', which was the result of a move towards respectability and the 'idea of the gentleman' in a commercial world blunting its pioneer edge in the process of social integration.[8]

If this was the case, credit was the whetstone of the process. It was gained either by a usually interest-free loan within the trade, or an external loan at 5 per cent interest. Some large concerns such as the East India Company sold directly for cash, thus obviating the need to borrow, and buying themselves time. It may also have helped them operate in emerging markets with less well-developed trading in bills of exchange (the East India Company had four times the revenue of its French equivalent in the eighteenth century). In Britain, however, credit was the rule, and on the back of it shops spread at a rate. In both the markets and in trade generally, news was important (indeed a rapid news service is one of the principal lubricants of urban capitalism). Merchants such as Medina (who paid Marlborough £6000 to have a man accompanying him on all his campaigns) cornered an information market which repaid him many times, as he could buy on the news of what others were still selling as rumour.[9]

The social impact of these changes was considerable, the more so since the long-term benefits of England's great experiment with the public finances remained to a degree unrecognized for many years. London's already remarkably dominant position in England (only Bristol really offered an alternative economic centre of any weight) was further confirmed by its accentuated role as a focus of credit and mercantilism. By the middle of the eighteenth century, the Great Wen had a population of around 675 000, more than ten times that of Edinburgh. Scotland, unlike Wales, where the population of Cardiff was only 2000 in 1801, though other centres were bigger, did not suffer from urban underdevelopment: around 1750, there were five or six Scottish towns among the largest 25 settlements in mainland Britain, Edinburgh being second, Glasgow fifth and Aberdeen eleventh. In England (where only Westmorland and Huntingdonshire were as thinly populated as the five least populous Welsh shires), the need to link suppliers with markets led to solidly improving communications throughout the eighteenth century (in Scotland, such improvement was primarily due to fears of Jacobite unrest). The development of the turnpike road network, which had its beginnings in the seventeenth century, and later the canal system (a horse could pull up to 16 wagons' load on a towpath), served to increase the rapidity of travel, threatened as this continued to be by highwaymen and footpads.

Supplies came from overseas too, and the rapid growth in the availability of commodities had a considerable impact on social stratification, with the early development of what might be called 'lifestyle' products, such as bohea. Susannah Centlivre's *A Bold Stroke for a Wife* (1718) mixes the provision of such commodities in Jonathan's coffee house with the discussion of stocktrading: the two worlds were related. Moreover, 'the consumption of imports' was not merely a benefit of the rich, for it 'led directly to new opportunities for home manufacturers', 'from Black Country kettles to Sheffield plate'. During the eighteenth century, exports more than doubled as a percentage of output: between 1709 and 1748, exports to Asia rose by 100 per cent, but this was more than matched in the rise of tea imports from 200 000 lb annually in 1711–17 to 3 000 000 lb by 1757.

The development of the national and provincial press in the period was doubtless important in such developments: a large proportion of newspapers were taken up by advertisements, which in turn served to highlight the fashionability of high-ticket products over a wide area and prepare the ground for a homogenization of the requisite standards for social display.[10]

Nevertheless, the commodification of society, symbolically important as it was (as will be discussed in the next section), was as yet on a limited scale, for while 'in a modern consumer society, things are cheap, people are expensive', the opposite was the case in the eighteenth century. In 1700, a living-in servant could be had at £2 to £3 a year, two maidservants at £14 10s, which

> was less than one-quarter of the family's clothes bill, half the charge for keeping a horse in stable and straw, one-tenth of the expense of maintaining a four-wheeled carriage with two horses.

The cheapness of labour and the relatively high cost of possessions may have reflected themselves in the cultural stress on 'show', criticized as nouveau by Tory writers from Pope to Austen and beyond. Such 'show' was particularly important in the marriage market, and as an expression of right to hold social and political opinions, for as Sydney Smith later remarked, 'it is always considered a piece of impertinence in England if a man of less than two or three thousand a year has any opinions at all on important subjects'.[11]

The increase in English law's severity towards property crime (a tendency traced back by Linda Colley to the 1671 Game Act) was a natural consequence of holding property to be the chief determinant of social importance, and thus the very warp and woof of social stability. Landed property was the foundation of social posi-

tion, but exemplary penalties fell even more heavily on the appropriation of personal property, the property of the new moneyed
class, as many landowners had reservations about the post-1688
regime. The landowning classes (though they tended to pay less
in land tax than was the case before 1714) could identify themselves as victims of the national debt, while those in society whose
business in general was 'show' might be said to join them in the
unfortunate position of being used as a source of assigned
revenue to cover fresh loan debt:

> certain categories of the population – landowners who paid
> one-fifth of their income to the state in land-tax, usurers and
> retailers of certain highly-taxed products – considered that
> they were paying for the whole operation, as opposed to a
> class of parasites and profiteers – rentiers, money lenders,
> businessmen whose income was not taxed, the 'moneyed
> men' who strutted about and thumbed their noses at the
> hard-working nation. Did not these profiteers have every
> inducement to be warmongers, since they stood to gain from
> any conflict which meant the further raising of state loans
> and a rise in interest rates?

Given that English stocks were tax-free, and that 'between 1702
and 1713 31.4 per cent of English war expenditure was financed
by public loans', these complaints were not without foundation.
Indeed, the avarice of war grew ever greater. Military expenditure
was between 60 and 75 per cent of total expenditure during the
War of the Austrian Succession, and 10–15 per cent of national
income in the Seven Years' War and War of American
Independence, by the end of which 66 per cent of revenue was
used up in servicing debt. The early bias towards Whigs in the
Bank of England directorate (23 out of 25 under William) and
elsewhere in the political and financial world underlined the
problem, since many landowners leant towards Toryism. The proportion of Tory MPs and peers holding Bank of England stock
trailed that of their Whig counterparts all the way to 1760, but the
gap was closing steadily, no doubt in response to a greater and
greater acquiescence in the new order. The large-scale purchase
of Bank of England stock by Tories in 1744–6 was an interesting
phase in this development.[12]

Politics and the Price of Things

Even though landownership's dependence on credit arrange-
ments (for example, mortgages and other bills of security) grew as
the century progressed, its paramountcy remained unchallenged.
This was not unique to Britain, as the continental proverb 'land
never lies' makes clear: the trend which saw 'ruined noblemen'
give place to 'rich bourgeois' was found in mainland Europe also.
Nevertheless, English society iconized land as the measure of
social power in an intense fashion. When 'people bought land',
they were 'buying up the perquisites of a social class, the undis-
turbed control of the life of a neighbourhood'. The power of this
status and its possible consequences is made plain in novels such
as Samuel Richardson's *Pamela* (1740) and William Godwin's
Caleb Williams (1794), where the squirearch's place at the corrupt
heart of a web of power and patronage is essentially unchallenged: on his own land, squire is king. The squirearchy of
England in particular was anomalous in European terms. Far
fewer Englishmen had or were connected to titles than was the
case elsewhere. In France, the aristocracy was some 1 per cent of
the population at the time of the Revolution; in Scotland 2 per
cent at the time of Union. Yet for all this, plain Mr So-and-so in
England might command (as Mr Bingley does in Jane Austen's
Pride and Prejudice) an estate of several thousand a year, a huge
sum when a curate such as Parson Adams in Henry Fielding's
Joseph Andrews has only £23 (though the living standards of the
clergy improved as a result of a rising yield from land during the
long eighteenth century; in Scotland, with its established
Presbyterian system, their status was generally more consistent).[13]
   Titled or not, the English aristocracy and gentry were a close-
knit society: 400 families owned one-fifth of cultivated land in
England, and the gentry as a whole 'held about half the total cultivated land'. Small as the group at the top was, its holdings were
mobile: of 31 great estates in 1700, only one was held by a direct
male descendant in 1750. To join the gentry group at some level
was a widespread ambition which unsurprisingly tended to
increase the price of land, a finite resource (land prices in France
had also been high in the seventeenth century). By the late eighteenth century, £100 000 was needed to buy 10 000 acres and a
suitable house. This was prohibitive, and most families sought a

crabwise route into the gentry over a number of generations through marriage. This naturally led to 'an undue apprehension of the risks of an injudicious Union' among the propertied, and the close measuring of wealth and status in the case of prospective spouses.[14]

If land was in demand because of its status, there were other features which reinforced that status. One of these was improvement, which raised the rental value of land, the other was urban growth: for example, it was discovered in 1743 that 'the rents of the Conduit Mead estate' in Westminster, 'had risen in the space of less than half a century from £8 to £14 240 15s'. These processes were mutually reinforcing: as land rose in price, so did the pressure to improve its yield, which in turn provided the fundamentals to maintain and further increase the price. 'The expansion of trade and manufactures' also created a new set of buyers, and prices continued high until suffering a collapse in the later stages of the American War of Independence, a critical juncture for many political and economic certainties. The general value of land and the rents arising from it were placed in bolder relief by the continuing 'impoverishment' of wage-earners compared to 'the enrichment of those who sold farm produce or leased farms at rents they could raise':

> The cost of labour ... and the costs of some leading industrial products were halved in terms of foodstuffs. This pervasive and deepgoing change must have transformed the real incomes of those who were able to share in the higher real earnings of farming as a business.

By 1685, it has been argued (though this may turn out to be an exaggeration), real wage rates had dropped to less than half of what they had been in 1510; and though the eighteenth century witnessed a partial recovery of lost ground (in 1745 reaching three-quarters of the early sixteenth-century level), wages generally remained low in real terms, though improving more rapidly for unskilled than skilled workers. As 'the enclosure movement and the more intensive techniques of farming developed in the eighteenth century' pushed land into fewer and fewer hands, wage-earners suffered in comparison unless, like country rectors, they benefited from the increasing value of tithes, and hired a curate to do their work for them at a low stipend. Between 1690 and 1790, rents doubled while wages barely increased. High wages were rare, and they did not tend to be used as a measure of social qualification for service as a Justice of the Peace or similar, for 'almost all statutory qualifications were expressed by a formula permitting either land or personal property to qualify, the former as an annual rental value, the latter as a capital sum'. In other words, capital was more important than income as a measure of social worth, for the income which was chiefly acceptable was only that which arose from capital. Similarly, a qualification act of 1711 'insisted that' MPs should be landed.[15]

Those without capital were, like those suffering under religious disabilities, effectively excluded from most offices. But those whose only capital was a small landholding suffered too: for the enclosure movement not only abrogated common land rights, but sent to the wall many yeomen and tenant farmers 'whose want of capital made it difficult for them either to fight enclosure before the event or benefit from it afterwards'. Attempts made to ameliorate their position were generally unsuccessful, and they became the circumstantial victims of social change. The enclosure movement itself could in a sense be seen as the ascendancy of the aggrandizing moneyed interest at the heart of land price push, evidence that '*Power*, which according to the old maxim, was used to follow land, is now gone over to money', as Swift put it. The rural topos long popular in pro-Stuart writing was expressed afresh in the contrast between a true ruralism, protective of folkways and uninterested in accumulating capital, and its moneyed rival. Alexander Pope was among those who expressed such sentiments, exactly opposite to the criticism of landed expenditure made by Defoe. The 'Man of Ross', John Kyrle, is a hero *because* he spends money:

> Behold the Market-place with poor o'erspread!
> The MAN of ROSS divides the weekly bread;
> He feeds yon Alms-house, neat, but void of state,
> Where Age and Want sit smiling at the gate;
> Him portioned maids, apprenticed orphans blest,
> The young who labour, and the old who rest.
> Is any sick? the MAN of ROSS relieves,
> Prescribes, attends, the med'cine makes and gives.
> Is there a variance? enter but his door,
> Balked are the courts, and contest is no more.

Despairing Quacks with curses fled the place,
And vile Attorneys, now an useless race ...
Of Debts and Taxes, Wife and Children clear,
This man possest – five hundred pounds a year.

In 'the Market-place' Kyrle spends money charitably; he does not trade. In the first half of this apostrophe he spends money on others; in the second, he saves them money by spending time with them. The emphasis is that Kyrle's life and money are both spent on human beings, in contrast to the inhuman world of Sir Balaam, where 'stocks and subscriptions pour on every side/ 'Til all the Demon makes his full descent/ In one abundant shower of Cent per Cent'. Moreover, those that Kyrle benefits – the poor, the orphan and the labourer – are all likely victims of changes through clearance, improvement and enclosure, while the parasitical doctors and lawyers journey to gentility through the exploitation of the poor who cannot afford to pay them. Pope's rural idealism, like that of seventeenth-century Royalist poetry, is one where the whole community is succoured and pro-tected by a responsible landowner, whose fertility (like that of the Stuarts as magical monarchs) is linked to his care of the land. Archbishop Laud himself had been criticized for opposition to enclosures, and similar sentiments are at the heart of at least some Stuart rural ideology. Jacobite protests at Henley (1743), in the south-west (1753) and Sussex (1766) may have been linked to reactions to changing land use, which Jacobite and radical alike agreed were chiefly motivated by the profiteering of a ruthless landowning class: for 'the loss of common land rights was a serious blow to very many of the poor'. John Clare's attack on the threat to open land in 'The Lamentations of Round-Oak Waters' is more explicit than Pope's, but in essential agreement with him:

Ah cruel foes with plenty blest
    So [h]ankering after more
To lay the greens and pasture waste
    Which profitted before.

In fact, both rents and in all probability output rose following enclosure: but this 'profit' was for the landlord's benefit.[16]

The situation in Scotland was not dissimilar. The relation between the laird and his tenants/tacksmen, favoured lessees who might well be his blood relations, was beginning to break down in the seventeenth and eighteenth centuries, in the Lowlands earlier than in the Highlands. The traditional system of 'runrig', where strips of land were interspersed, so that in case of attack, a man would have to defend his neighbour's property as well as his own (for a strip of his neighbour's land might be sandwiched by two fields of his) was in retreat as fields began to be enclosed (the first major case of this was in Galloway in 1700, when cattle dealers sought to pen their merchandise before driving it over the border). Despite the fact that 'mob riots followed these early enclosures', the move towards changing patterns of land use intensified. In this process, 'the small farmers lost, without recompense, their age-old right of free grazing on the moors and hillsides', and the 'new small farmer, usually the strongest member of the original communal group of possessors, ousted the cottager with his toft and cow'. The consequence of this was a 'slow, agonising exodus' from the old 'ferm touns' to the colonies, and 'the mills and slums of Glasgow and Dundee'. These were, 'in fact, the first of the Clearances', and were largely complete when their better-known Highland counterpart began in the 1790s.[17]

Neither Edinburgh nor Glasgow, however, raised a corresponding ruralist indignation to that found in English high culture towards London (though Fergusson's lament for Edinburgh's decline leans towards it). Although Pope's vision of the corrupt city (one shared with John Gay and Samuel Johnson) progresses from satirical gaiety to despair between *The Rape of the Lock* (1713) and the 1744 *Dunciad*, a deep unease is nonetheless evident in the earlier poem. Mock-heroicism is used to underline the corruption of the post-1688 regime, where 'The hungry Judges soon the sentence sign,/And wretches hang that jury-men may dine', while Queen Anne herself 'Dost sometimes counsel take – and sometimes Tea', the zeugma (as throughout the poem) indicative of a moral equivalence between government and the recreational value of luxury commodities. This reification of spiritual and moral worth is a sophisticated restatement of the key Tory critique of the moneyed interest, and the manner in which it has colonized the state whose colonies are exploited to provide these corrupting commodities. Pope (as later Johnson) is drawing also on a much older tradition which goes back at least to Juvenal (the model on which Johnson drew in 'The Vanity of Human Wishes'), which berates the imperial state for being corrupted by what it has conquered:

Iam pridem Syrus in Tiberim defluxit Orontes
Et linguam et mores. (*Satire* III)
('The Syrian Orontes has now long been discharging in Tiber
Its language and morals').

Fear of the Orient is a lot older than the recent age of Western colonialism, and Pope, in his characterization of a London obsessed with commodity, corruption and above all 'show', emphasizes the newfound gains of Eastern trade as incipient indicators of the decline of the state. Belinda herself is artificially composed of tortoiseshell, ivory, Indian gems and Arabian perfumes, while Anne's monarchy is levelled with commodity in the gossip of Hampton Court society:

One speaks the glory of the British Queen,
And one describes a charming Indian screen ...

This view in *Rape of the Lock* extends to the analysis that not only have moral values become commodified, but that these new commodities and the habits they generate act as corrupting social drugs. In Canto III

Coffee, (which makes the politician wise,
And see through all things with his half-shut eyes)
Sent up in vapours to the Baron's brain
New strategems, the radiant Lock to gain.

In Canto IV Belinda, mourning her fall, claims she wishes she had remained 'Where none learn Ombre, none e'er taste Bohea!', far from the court and the corruption of London, where new luxuries inflate and feed desire which prevents people seeking out the nature of true value, as known to the Man of Ross.[18]

Nationality, Religion and Money

Where London's column, pointing to the skies,
Like a tall bully, lifts the head and lies;

There dwelt a Citizen of sober fame,
A plain good man, and Balaam was his name.

Pope, *Epistle to Bathurst*

Pope's evil man of money, Sir Balaam, is a faithful Anglican and a
frequent attender at the Stock Exchange ('Constant at Church,
and Change'). He is also depicted living in the shadow of the
column on Fish Street Hill, which attributed the Great Fire of
London to Catholics. This sleazy beneficiary of the financial revolution is thus closely associated with the ferocious anti-Catholicism
of elements not only of the London mob, but also of London
society, which broke out in open violence as late as 1780. As in the
Popish Plot crisis, it is the 'modern' figure of Whig money who is
the superstitious sectarian, not the 'outdated' jacobitical Catholic
poet who depicts him.[19]

An association of this nature between moneymaking and religion is unsurprising. Notwithstanding the fact that the full rigour
of English, Scottish or Irish penal legislation was seldom inflicted,
Catholic tenure of property was extremely insecure, especially in
an age where the possession of capital and the ability to transmit
it were central to the perpetuation of social consequence.
Restrictions on Catholic ownership of land were not significantly
eased in England until 1778, and not until 1791 could Catholics
worship in public or practise at the Bar. Though there had been a
creeping gradualism, not always reflected in legislation, throughout the eighteenth century, it was still possible as late as the 1820s
for pro-Catholic agitation to depict its subjects as a 'negro in
fetters', thus capitalizing on the anti-slavery movement. Generally
speaking, Catholics did not have the same networks as benefited
Nonconformists in their pursuit of trade and the relaxation of
civil penalties (for example, in 1727 the Dissenters organized to
evade the effects of the Test and Corporation Acts). The Quakers
in particular were outstandingly organized in easing the restrictions of religious penalties, winning several victories beginning
with the 1696 Affirmation Act (which excused them from oaths –
it was blocked in Ireland by the bishops), though they and the
Baptists did not benefit to the same extent as other Dissenters
from the lax enforcement of the conformity laws, which transformed their general position during the eighteenth century:

together indemnity [the extension of the period of qualification] and occasional conformity ensured that generations of ... Dissenters were untouched by the law.

In addition to this, conformity could be a 'token gesture', and as such might secure to a Dissenter an office from which he might have been supposed debarred. In 1779, an act ensured the abandonment of 'the requirement that Dissenting ministers subscribe to the Thirty-Nine Articles', in further relaxation of restrictions which had not been consistently imposed: yet their presence had spurred Dissenters to network in their own interests in both society and trade, and already there were signs of spectacular success on the latter front.[20]

In Scotland, the position of the Episcopalians was considerably worse, especially after 1747, but those who could accept the Hanoverian succession and attended the licensed Anglican meeting-houses fared much better: it could be argued that only political disaffection ensured anti-Episcopalian discrimination north of the border by the latter part of the eighteenth century, and even in such cases there seems often to have been little strict pursuit.[21]

Ireland presented a more difficult case. As the established church represented only a small fraction of the population, it sought a correspondingly strong grip of events, especially in view of the fear of disaffection, both within the Church of Ireland itself, and more intensely throughout the Catholic population. Despite the fact that the Catholic hierarchy were in general nominated by James III and VIII (as were Episcopalian bishops in Scotland), the Catholic leadership in Ireland increasingly played down Jacobitism in return for a tacit go-slow on the implementation of the penal laws.[22]

Ireland's position in the financial revolution was nevertheless unstable. Although Dublin was the second-largest city in the British Isles, and in 1760 'Ireland still ranked second ... in population, in revenue and expenditure, and in volume of trade' among the colonies of the British Empire, it was a country with a history of unstable money and widespread poverty. Many in the English governing classes were in any event jealous of Irish trade: Edmund Burke lost his seat at Bristol at the end of the 1770s because of his opposition to tariffs on it.[23]

The exploited and irregular quality of Irish money was highly significant, and contrasted strongly with the English government's perceived need for a strong pound sterling (against which the exchange rate of the pound Scots was fixed after 1707). The problem dated back to 1689, and the issue by James II and VII of a large-scale minting of base metal tokens made of 'brass ... from old cannon, bells and other scrap metal'. Called first 'Brass Money' then 'Gunmoney', these tokens had a notional redemption value against sterling silver which could only be realized in the event of a Jacobite victory: they were in fact a means of debasing the currency to get campaign funds. The situation worsened in 1690, when, running low on metal, the Jacobite administration reduced the sizes of halfcrowns and shillings, while the 1689 halfcrowns were reminted as crowns. Later that year there were pewter strikes with 'a plug of brass through them to distinguish the genuine pieces from counterfeits which might be cast in lead'. After the Williamites took Dublin, the coins were reduced in value: in 1691 they were demonetized, the larger shillings being subsequently received as halfpence and the smaller ones as farthings.[24]

Even though it was a relatively brief episode, the Gunmoney debacle was an important one. The Tudor devaluation had seriously shaken confidence in the English currency of the day, despite being a debasement of far less hazardous proportions: within two or three years, the value of Gunmoney specie had dropped by over 90 per cent. Insecurity over the stability of Irish money was compounded not only by the failure to produce a copper coinage after 1696, but also through the methods by which it was proposed to bring the resulting shortage to an end: the patent granted to William Wood in 1722, which allowed him to strike underweight Irish copper and pocket the difference. Since the coin was in any case to be minted at Wood's Bristol foundry, the whole process brought nothing to Ireland and smacked of straightforward colonial exploitation. In a country where the scars left by James's bad money still smarted, it was little wonder that the furore whipped up by Dean Swift in his *Drapier's Letters* (and backed by the Irish Parliament and its officials) brought an end to Wood's project. Swift's Drapier even threatens that the Irish might have to turn to Jacobitism: indeed, it has been said that in the *Letters*, Swift 'struck the first blow in the cause of home rule, and so powerful was the stroke that the impulse of the blow was never lost'. Swift's attitude to Irish liberty, in fact, almost looks like a transposition of his possibly Jacobite sympathies into a fresh channel (his letters were still being opened as late as 1738):

> Upon Queen ANNE's Death the Whig Faction was restored to Power, which they exercised with the utmost Rage and revenge ... *Ireland* utterly ruined and enslaved, only great Ministers heaping up Millions, and so Affairs continue until this present third Day of May, 1732, and are likely to go on in the same Manner.

Swift's opposition to the financial revolution operated in a context of colonial exploitation. The Drapier's victory, did, no doubt, help to ensure that when 'a new coinage of halfpence was put in hand at the London mint' in 1736, 'to allay further public outcry it was directed that any profit accruing from the coinage should be credited to the public revenue of Ireland'.[25]

In Scotland, the Bank of Scotland (1695), set up only a year after its English counterpart, testified to the rapidity of financial development in Scotland on the eve of Union, even though the grandiose scheme of Darien was to come to nothing. The Bank, set up by expatriate Scottish merchants, was 'the first instance in Europe, and perhaps the world, of a joint-stock bank formed by private persons ... solely dependent upon private capital'. It was also 'the only bank ever to be incorporated by Act of the Scottish Parliament'. After Union, the Bank of Scotland fell out of favour because it was tainted with Jacobitism (David Drummond, its Treasurer from 1700–46, was 'a staunch supporter of the Stuart cause'). The foundation of the Royal Bank of Scotland (1727) provided a Whig alternative: 'the founding of the Royal Bank may be seen, not unfairly, as part of Walpole's system of political control in Scotland' (despite this, thousands in specie was paid out by the Royal to Charles Edward Stuart during the occupation of Edinburgh). Subsequently, the Scottish banks were at the forefront of banking development: the limited liability principle, note issue, overdrafts, interest-paying deposit accounts, joint-stock banking and exchange stabilization being among their areas of innovation. The most important long-term shift brought about in Scottish economic development through Union was the transfer of the country's economic nexus from the European-oriented east to the colonial-oriented west coast. This led to a massive expansion in the population of Glasgow on the back of a rapidly developing mercantilism, particularly in the area of the tobacco trade with North America. Such a change no doubt served further to entrench the Presbyterian character of Scottish culture, historically strongest in the south-west and west central belt and weakest in the north-east: economic and demographic shifts thus reinforced the outcome of the political battles of the first half of the eighteenth century.[26]

In such battles, fiscal issues had loomed large: it was an important campaigning plank of Jacobite nationalists that taxes would be restored on 'the old Scots footing' in the event of a Stuart victory and the end of Union. The Earl of Mar consented to collect taxes only on this basis in 1715, while in 1745 the hated malt tax (which had almost ended the Union when it was first mooted in 1713) brought many into Charles Edward's camp. The heavy load of British indirect taxation (of which the excise was an example) necessary to pay the interest on stock seemed to bear particularly hard on Scotland, an argument still heard today in the context of the disproportionately severe taxation of whisky.[27]

Just as the eighteenth century saw the imposition of taxation regimes geared to specifically English needs throughout the British Isles, so it also witnessed the extension of English currency: the triumph of sterling was not significantly challenged until the flotation of the Irish punt in 1979 (which is currently (1995) exchanged at 0.97 to the £ sterling). Although the Irish pound was not formally amalgamated with sterling until 1821 (following the merger of the Irish exchequer in 1817), it was the Scottish currency of pound and merk which had centuries of significant divergence behind it. In 1603, it had stood at £12 to the pound sterling, the rate around which it exchanged thereafter. No longer tradeable after 1707, the pound Scots remained as a unit of domestic currency and account until the end of the eighteenth century (the Bank of Scotland continued to issue Scots £ denominated notes for some years after Union), and badly worn coins of the independent currency survived in circulation until at least the 1730s, and quite possibly very much longer (James III and VIII's pattern coinage of 1716 was, however, denominated in sterling). By 1800, the merger of Scottish currency (and indeed weights and measures) with its English counterpart was more or less complete, though terms such as 'bawbee' to describe a half-penny (originally 6d Scots) survived for many more years, if not to the date of decimalization itself. As late as 1803, the British Parliament, in revising the 1696 Scots Education Act which required 'the establishment of a school in every parish', allowed the schoolmaster's salary to be expressed in Scots merks (13s 4d Scots).[28]

Economic Woman

Just as the Revolution of 1688 did not betoken improved standards of liberty and civil and religious freedom for marginal groups in general, so also it did not serve the position of women in society. Indeed, the long eighteenth century's somewhat defensive obsession with property rights (no doubt partly derived from an anxiety over their legitimacy) tended to a reification of women as just one more commodity for 'show'. As Paul Langford explains:

> In his diatribe against the Marriage Act of 1753 John Shebbeare had his Earl of Womeaton describe marriage as 'taking Money with the Mortgage of a Wife to pay off a Mortgage on an Estate'.

The 'instructive tendency of the age was to express any relationship of unequals in terms which equated power over people with possession of things'. Marriage, like landowning, benefited from 'enclosure': it was a place of fenced-off territory. The jovial Lockean mutuality of the marriage contract in William Congreve's *The Way of the World* (1700) gives way in later writing to the legal and illegal entrapment of women in novels such as Samuel Richardson's *Pamela* and *Clarissa* and William Godwin's *Caleb Williams*. In *Pamela*, even when the heroine has gained the hand of Squire B— by refusing all the contracts offered her under duress to be his mistress, an exclusive and admonitory marriage agreement is made, which emphasizes a continuing disparity of status: Pamela is nonetheless grateful for it, having suffered, in a Christian paradigm, 40 days in the wilderness of being kidnapped and abused. The extent to which human oppression can go beyond the vows of obedience in Christian marriage is made clear in *Clarissa*, where the heroine suffers at the patriarchal hands of her father, brother and lover, and their string of female accomplices, in an unendingly brutal manner, repeatedly characterized in the language of invasive sexual assault. Clarissa dies at last, raped and unmarried, in the arms of her ultimate spouse, calling 'COME – Blessed LORD JESUS!' Richardson's great novel epitomizes the suffering of contemporary women martyred to their family's inclinations, and (in Clarissa's case) envied for their money: it is made clear that she is hated by her family for owning property, rather than merely being it.[29]

In the context of such social mores as these, it is perhaps unsurprising that some of the earliest feminists leant towards a Jacobite perspective, with its distrustful and rebellious attitude to the new property rights and laws. Though it might have appeared to the careless observer that the Stuart monarchy was the ultimate in patriarchy, women were among its strongest supporters, as contemporary reports testify: a fact used to feminize and romanticize Jacobitism into the margins (Charles Edward, who of course crossdressed as Betty Burke, was depicted as a woman in government propaganda). Scottish and Irish society had historically provided at least marginally more diverse and interesting roles for women, a fact which it has been argued continues into this century, when women have been among the most prominent figures in the nationalistic cause in both countries. In Scotland, women's ability to divorce on the grounds of adultery or desertion in the eighteenth century (347 cases came before the Edinburgh Commissary Court between 1708 and 1780, initiated roughly equally by men and women and across a range of social classes) was an important feature in indicating slightly greater equality. Education for girls, sometimes including Latin, was not uncommon in Scotland in the 1700s, while women such as Mrs Ruddiman carried on their husband's businesses (she produced a seventeenth edition of Ruddiman's *Rudiments of the Latin Tongue* in 1768). In England, too, women were found continuing their husband's enterprises. The attitude concerning wife-battering in Scotland was similarly not entirely unenlightened: in 1631, David Bowman was sent to prison for assaulting his wife. During the Jacobite period, many women found themselves managing the family estates. In 1745, Whig propagandists were outraged by the 'unnatural' behaviour of Colonel Anne Mackintosh, who raised a regiment for Charles Edward, and subsequently took her own husband (a Hanoverian captain) into custody:

> Of all the Rebel Beauties here,
>   There's one I will not name, Man,
> Who there did head five hundred men,
>   For which she's much to blame, man ...
>
> No *Bathsheba*, nor *Venus* fair,
>   Could e'er so well appear, man,
> As she did in her Feelabeg
>   Before the *Chevalier*, Man.

Madam Mackintosh is here accused of three kinds of 'unnatural' behaviour: her Jacobitism, as a woman raising soldiers and her implied promiscuity. Yet she was only one of a veritable gallery of Jacobite women, ranging from the Duchess of Buckingham through Mrs Charles Caesar to the Oglethorpes. As Patricia Hill writes:

> To such a woman there was an intense appeal in Jacobitism. This subversive movement ... would accept all volunteers, regardless of sex. In work for the Pretender, ladies could correspond personally with their 'King over the Water', giving him encouragement and advice; they could smuggle messages back and forth across the Channel; they could use their charms to help corrupt important politicians into supporters of 'King James III'. Often they organized secret meetings in which they took leading roles and helped plan the great 'risings' for overthrowing the government and establishing their monarch's reign.[30]

One stage removed from this network of conspiratorial and quasi-conspiratorial Jacobites were women like Delariviere Manley, who 'assisted Jonathan Swift in writing Tory pamphlets', and Elizabeth Powell, the editor of *The Orphan Reviv'd or Powell's Weekly Journal*, founded in 1718 as a 'High Church and Jacobite newspaper'. More central than either of these, however, was Mary Astell, one of the first ideological feminists. Her teaching tended towards the separatist feminism of flourishing without men, rather than the redefinition of marital relationships sought by

later writers such as Mary Wollstonecraft (there are some small
indications that Wollstonecraftian feminism tended to be more
Whig/contractual, while separatist feminism, which could be associated with nunneries, as in Astell's own monastic recommenda-
tions in *A Serious Proposal to the Ladies* (1694, 97), leant more
towards the Jacobites). Astell, who 'idealized Charles I as a religious and political martyr', was kept afloat in her early years as an
independent woman in London through the patronage of
Archbishop Sancroft, remaining 'a divine-right monarchist to the
end', though she had seemed sympathetic at the time towards the
Revolution. Her praise of retreat can be aligned with the use of
this topos in the pro-Stuart poetry of Denham and Pope, while
her tract *Moderation Truly Stated* quotes Dryden's *Aeneid* as a com-
mentary on the Civil War: a Jacobite way of reading the text.
Astell, who has been suggested as a model for Clarissa, was also
associated with Jacobitism through the work she carried out in
charity schools, regarded as a hotbed of disaffection in the eighteenth century. In 1715, she counted Atterbury and Ormond
among her friends. For at least one of her recent historians, she
exemplifies

> the paradox that feminism in its earliest phase, owed as much,
> if not more, to conservative and Anglican values than it did to
> the anti-authoritarian and secular impulses in Restoration
> culture.[31]

Anne Finch, the Countess of Winchilsea, who had been
appointed maid of honour to Mary of Modena in 1682, was a
more traditional figure: yet her writing implicitly aligns women
with the other minorities suffering discrimination in the aftermath of 1688:

> How are we fallen! fallen by mistaken rules,
> And Education's, more than Nature's fools,
> Debarred from all improvements of the mind,
> And to be dull, expected and designed ...

Only too aware that 'a woman that attempts the pen' is 'an
intruder on the rights of men', the Countess is nevertheless in
agreement with her disaffected male contemporaries in praising

the merits of 'A sweet, yet absolute retreat'. In 'The Petition for an Absolute Retreat', Winchilsea describes the 'lonely stubborn oak ... sapless leaves all bent and shrunk', perhaps a symbol of Stuart monarchy, the fall of which threatens the retreat and is metaphorically linked to the 'fall' of 'Ardelia' herself:

> So the sad Ardelia lay
> Blasted by a storm of fate
> Felt through all the British state;
> Fallen, neglected, lost, forgot
> Dark oblivion all her lot ...

Winchilsea's ruralist retreat poetry combines Jacobitism with 'a feminocentric protest' against displacement, and such apparent descriptions of politics in quasi-erotic terms are found elsewhere in the Countess's work, as in 'A Song on the South Sea, 1720', which complains that 'brokers all the hours divide/Which lovers used to share', an image of movement away from idyllic mutuality to division and exploitation. Likewise, her comments on the Postmaster-General's censorship of Jacobite correspondence aligns the display of female and Jacobite passion as alike suppressed:

> Cornwallis breaks up every seal
>   To guard the state from harms
> How can we then our hearts reveal
>   Or Arrabella's charms?

A leading Nonjuror (she contributed to the Usages controversy, and her poetry deals with her attempts to provide support for the Nonjuring clergy) and friend of Swift (who encouraged her to publish), Winchilsea in her writing is one of the best exponents of the common purpose of the dispossessed found in the language of radical Jacobitism. Even core imagery like that of 'Augustus' succumbs to a striking feminist playfulness: 'Livia so influenced Augustus that his accomplishments in world dominion were brought about "thro' a woman's wit"'.[32]

In contrasting mode, there were of course Whig ladies, such as Susannah Centlivre the playwright, who incorporated the pace of financial and social change into their own work, while the question of women's economic independence was addressed by Defoe in two novels, *Moll Flanders* and *Roxana*. For the heroines of these books, sexuality is the route to wealth and power, but the economic independence derived from it is clearly a two-edged sword, given the sociopathic nature of an independence earned through prostitution and dishonesty. Roxana and Moll succeed through wit, calculation, device and fraud: they also commodify their own bodies to the same extent as does male-dominated marriage, the difference being that they earn through selling themselves rather than being merely property. Unlike Defoe's Complete English Tradesman, these women do not benefit from networking and its associated fruits (free credit internal to the trade, for example). The isolation of Moll and Roxana is repeatedly stressed: without a network, they fall back on self, and self's most obvious presence in the world, becoming entrepreneurs of the body. And when their own bodies will not do, another can be used: one of the most disturbing scenes in *Roxana* occurs when the heroine prostitutes her own maid, Amy, and watches the transaction. Defoe's heroines do not redefine the eighteenth-century status of women as possessions: they simply sell themselves slowly rather than entering an irreversible bargain. As authors of their own careers, they trade their narrative for royalties rather than making an outright sale of the rights: yet in either case they remain a marketable resource, to be used up.[33]

The approach taken by women to the accumulation of property in Defoe's writing lay at the margins of legitimacy. Women at these margins were not usually portrayed as successful entrepreneurs, but bandits' molls and brassy balladeers: the 'lower-class Female Warrior heroine'. Such figures 'multiplied noticeably' in popular literature after 1660 'and the loosening of restrictions on ballad publishing' (which tended to be Royalist, just as arguably after 1688 it tended to be Jacobite). John Gay's jacobitical reading of English society in *The Beggar's Opera* (1728) has as one of its themes the 'lowness' of women who sing of love and despise, or affect to despise, property; while in the same author's *Polly*, banned as subversive, the heroine herself belongs to the class identified by Dianne Dugaw in her study of *Warrior Women and Popular Balladry*. To disassociate oneself from the dominant politico-economic system was to step outside it, so that even disaffected noblewomen could be portrayed as sharing the pursuits and situation of the humblest peasant:

O gin I live to see the day,
 That I ha'e begg'd, and begg'd frae Heaven,
I'll fling my rock and reel away,
 And dance and sing frae morn till even.
For there is ane I winna name,
 That comes the beingin bike to scatter;
And I'll put on my bridal gown,
 That day our king comes o'er the water.

The Countess Marischal may never have begged, lived in a 'wee croo house' or used a 'rock and reel', like the women of the folk tradition: but the presence of such images in 'Lady Keith's Lament' symbolizes the honesty of common purpose with the poor and excluded which Jacobite propaganda often alluded to, and which gave it a moral (and given the domestic sphere of poverty, sometimes a gendered) separatism from the great property concerns of the Whig state.[34]

Property is Theft?

Since the post-1688 regime was illegitimate, it followed that in a sense all its property relations were bogus, and that the highwayman was merely claiming back what had been stolen. Anticipating Proudhon, the Jacobite insinuated the idea 'that all Hanoverian property was theft'.

Frank McLynn [35]

The Black Act of 1723 marked a new phase in the intensity of the conflict between the state and challenges to property rights. As E. P. Thompson put it when describing the vast increase in capital crimes in the eighteenth century, there is 'some complicity between the ascendancy of the Hanoverian Whigs and the ascendancy of the gallows'. The anti-landlord activities of the Blacks were simply part of a whole range of agricultural unrest taking place in a century of changing land use, stretching from the south of England to the Irish Whiteboys: but since the Blacks' activities had the misfortune to occur in England in the shadow of the Atterbury plot, the group was stigmatized by Walpole's regime as

Jacobite malcontents. As a result, they suffered from what has been called (by Sir Leon Radzinowicz) 'the most severe legislation of the eighteenth century'. It was in particular the Blacks' activities in the royal forests which warranted hostile attention: in violating the game laws they seemed to strike at the heart of royal authority in a manner easily read to be Jacobite.[36]

More worrying for government perhaps than the immediate aims of the Blacks was the evidence for what Eveline Cruickshanks and Howard Erskine-Hill have identified as 'a social continuum' between the Blacks and fellow travellers of Jacobitism such as 'Pope, Goring and Atterbury'. This evidence of the crossclass nature of Jacobite sympathies can also be found in the protection granted to smugglers and bandits by Jacobite-leaning landowners and lairds, and their returning the compliment by acting as agents for high cultural propaganda, as in the 'distribution of Jacobite medals, prints and portraits' by smugglers in Kent.[37]

This 'social continuum' had a number of focal points, one of which was to be found in the character and activity of the highwayman, or Irish gentry bandit. Highwaymen were, as Frank McLynn has pointed out, usually of higher social standing than other criminals, and on occasion politicized their own thefts (interestingly, the Blacks compared themselves to Robin Hood). Tim Buckley, for example, held up 'pawnbrokers and stockjobbers', while other highwaymen were ex-officers in James II and VII's army, many of whom had refused to serve William. With other criminals, particularly smugglers, they could fulfil the role of what E. J. Hobsbawm has identified as a 'social bandit', banditry with a political programme. Just as highwaymen challenged property rights, so smugglers challenged taxation laws. It may be in this context no coincidence that the 1736 Porteous riots in Edinburgh, with their anti-Union undertones, ultimately had their roots in the prosecution of a smuggler.[38]

Smugglers, like highwaymen and the Blacks, were directly associated with Jacobitism through legislation: 'the Smuggling Acts of 1698, 1717, 1721, and 1745 were passed amid great anxiety over Jacobite activity in England', and subsequently an international network of Jacobite business related to smuggling developed, for

English smugglers who professed to be (or actually were) Jacobites had an easy entree into the merchant community of the French Atlantic seaboard ... and were thus able to ply their trade more freely.

Landlord support for smugglers was useful for their continued success: it also helped to provide 'one of the most difficult public-order problems British governments have ever had to deal with'. In Scotland, smuggling could be a protest against the post-Union imposition of the English customs system: this was especially true in east coast ports like Montrose, called by the Jacobite captain John Daniel 'a fine loyal seaport town', and a source of considerable Jacobite support in 1745.[39]

Gay chose a highwayman for the lead role in his *Beggar's Opera*, with its extensive critique of the financial and criminal justice systems of Walpole's Britain. Macheath's very name, his title of 'Captain', and assertion that 'gentlemen of the road [that is, highwaymen] may be fine gentlemen', all serve to reinforce the idea of Gay's hero as a politicized figure: possibly a Scot (hence a Jacobite), possibly an ex-officer and possibly better-bred than his pursuers like Peachum. The notorious case of Jonathan Wild, reflected in the characterization of Peachum, could be seen to emblematize the roots of corruption in the financial revolution, for the great thief-taker was a frontier capitalist, trading in stolen goods and the lives of criminals, and profiting through arbitrage in legitimate and illegitimate markets (for Fielding, Wild, like Walpole, was ironized as a 'Great Man'). The 1692 Highwaymen Act in England had ensured a £40 reward for the betrayal of a highwayman. Thus, when Peachum states that 'like great statesmen, we encourage those who betray their friends', he is alluding to the acceptance at the highest levels of the state of the use of money to legitimately bribe for the purposes of legitimate betrayal. Macheath may sing 'Lilliburlero', but the set expressed to the air is one which deprecates the money-based society of Whig England.[40]

Gay may have based Macheath on Captain James Hind, 'the great Robber of England', whose exploits circulated in eighteenth-century chapbooks and who had been the subject of a 1651 play, *An excellent Comedy called the Prince of Priggs Revels or The Practises of that grand Theif Captain James Hind*. Hind was a displaced Royalist, like so many of James's soldiers after 1688, and his loyalty (he fought for Charles II at Worcester) and fate mirrored that of the Jacobite heroes of a later age. Such traditions concerning the social background and political outlook of highwaymen long persisted: they are found, for example, in R. D. Blackmore's *Lorna Doone*, two centuries after Hind, where the Doones are a colony of Royalist gentlemen turned bandits.[41]

If the instability of a property-based regime with its roots in perceived usurpation was one side of the coin, the other was the destitution and poverty which followed from enclosure and agricultural un- or under-employment. There are signs that the Jacobites could take advantage of both these aspects: on the one hand, as reflected in Chevalier Ramsay's assertion that 'if you deny hereditary right in kingship, you cannot have it in property'; on the other, through the recognition that poverty can cause criminality, found in Mist's *Journal.* There was also a 1728 report to James on the same theme. In 1751, 'General James Oglethorpe told a Jacobite visitor that he had not finished walling in his park at Haslemere in Surrey because it was doing'

> a bad thing to the Poor ... he rather thought as the Civill Law does that in Case of Necessity every Man had a right to take what was absolutely necessary for his support.

The same argument was used in Ireland in the 1890s. Then, as in the eighteenth century, it evidenced distrust of the socio-political developments of its day, and was a boost to criminality. In such areas of debate, Jacobite agents sought to take advantage of disaffection, while the fact that crime against property rights was so central to the Whig criminal justice system helped to politicize the question of criminality itself, a trend intensified by Jonathan Wild's entrepreneurial career. The criminalization of Jacobitism and the severe penalties threatened for even very low-key Jacobite activity, compounded with religious penal legislation, pushed certain sections of otherwise respectable society in the direction of connivance at more commonplace criminality. If the Jacobites did not go as far as Proudhon, they still understood the arbitrariness of the legal system under a Whig ascendancy. Political and religious exclusion which was itself in part exclusion from property rights became interlinked with more general attacks on property. This was the ideological root of the 'social continuum' which posed the threat of the politicization of crime itself.[42]

NOTES

1. *The Poems of Alexander Pope* ed. John Butt, one-volume Twickenham Pope, (London, 1963), p. 574.
2. Bram Dijkstra, *Defoe and Economics* (Basingstoke, 1987), p. 15; cf. Daniel Defoe, *The Complete English Tradesman* (Gloucester, 1987 (1726)).
3. Fernand Braudel, *Civilization and Capitalism 15th–18th Century: II The Wheels of Commerce*, tr. Siân Reynolds, (London, 1985 (1982)), pp. 101, 103, 525, 526; Colin Chapman, *How the Stock Markets Work* (London, 1994), pp. 9–10.
4. Braudel (1982), pp. 175, 376.
5   Ibid., pp. 360–1.
6. Ibid., p. 375.
7. Braudel (1982), pp. 376, 384; *French Liberty and British Slavery* is most appropriately reproduced on the cover of H. T. Dickinson's *Liberty and Property* (London, 1977).
8. Dijkstra (1987), pp. 8–9.
9. Braudel (1982), pp. 107, 451; Philip Lawson, *The East India Company: A History* (London, 1993), p. 83.
10. Braudel (1982), pp. 109, 583; Daniel Szechi and Geoffrey Holmes, *The Age of Oligarchy* (London, 1993), appendix and *Scottish Population Statistics*, ed. James Gray Kyd, (Edinburgh, 1952) for Webster's population census; John Rule, *The Vital Century: England's Developing Economy 1714–1815* (London, 1992), pp. 230, 258; Lawson (1993), pp. 73, 97.
11. Paul Langford, *Public Life and the Propertied Englishman* (Oxford, 1991), pp. 10–12.
12. Linda Colley, *In Defiance of Oligarchy: The Tory Party 1714–60* (Cambridge, 1982), pp. 9, 11, 15; Braudel (1982), p. 527; Rule (1992), pp. 277–9.
13. Braudel (1982), pp. 249, 261; John Burnett, *A History of the Cost of Living* (Harmondsworth, 1969), p. 140; Eric Evans, 'The Anglican Clergy of Northern England', in Clyve Jones (ed.), *Britain in the First Age of Party* (London, 1987), pp. 221–40 (221).
14. Burnett (1969), pp. 140, 141, 150; Langford (1991), pp. 3, 39.
15. Langford (1991), pp. 40, 42, 46, 234; Burnett (1969), pp. 140, 141, 172; Henry Phelps Brown and Sheila V. Hopkins, *A Perspective of Wages and Prices* (London, 1981), pp. 70, 100; A. J. S. Gibson and T. C. Smout, *Prices, Food and Wages in Scotland 1550–1780* (Cambridge, 1995), p. 343 shows reservations concerning the Phelps Brown findings; John Cannon, *Samuel Johnson and the Politics of Hanoverian England* (Oxford, 1994), p. 15.

16.   Langford (1991), p. 370; William Speck, *Society and Literature in England 1700-60* (Dublin, 1983), p. 22; Pope (1963), pp. 574–82; Murray G. H. Pittock, *The Invention of Scotland: the Stuart Myth and the Scottish Identity, 1638 to the Present* (London and New York, 1991), p. 12; E. P. Thompson, *Customs in Common* (London, 1991), pp. 179–81, 246–9.

17.   R. J. Brien, *The Shaping of Scotland* (Aberdeen, 1989), pp. 4–5, 8, 9, 11, 22.

18.   Murray G. H. Pittock, *Poetry and Jacobite Politics in Eighteenth-Century Britain and Ireland* (Cambridge, 1994), pp. 160–1; Pope (1963), pp. 197–227.

19.   Pope (1963), p. 574 ff.

20.   Langford (1991), pp. 8, 72–3, 82, 86, 98; cf. H. T. Dickinson, *The Politics of the People in Eighteenth-Century Britain* (Basingstoke, 1995), p. 83 ff; S. J. Connolly, *Religion, Law and Power: The Making of Protestant Ireland 1650–1760* (Oxford, 1992), p. 174.

21.   The ideological position of Episcopalianism is outlined in Murray G. H. Pittock, *The Myth of the Jacobite Clans* (Edinburgh, 1995), p. 88 ff.

22.   Pittock (1994), p. 200; cf. Connolly (1992), p. 158.

23.   Francis Godwin James, *Ireland in the Empire 1688–1770* (Cambridge, MA, 1983), p. 1; *Cassell's History of the British People*, V (London, 1923), p. 1732.

24.   Cf. Seaby's *Coins of Scotland, Ireland and the Islands* (London, 1984), pp. 154–5.

25.   Cassell (1923), V, pp. 1611–12; Seaby (1984), pp. 162–3; Ian Higgins, *Swift's Politics: A Study in Disaffection* (Cambridge, 1994), pp. 87, 97, 133.

26.   S. G. Checkland, *Scottish Banking: A History 1695–1973* (Glasgow and London, 1975), pp. xvi, 18, 23, 58, 59, 73.

27.   Pittock (1995), p. 97.

28.   Brien (1989), p. 89; Checkland (1975), pp. 14, 32; Seaby (1984), pp. 5, 83, 91, 169.

29.   Langford (1991) pp. 3, 6.

30.   Rosalind Marshall, *Virgins and Viragos* (London, 1983), pp. 100, 196–7 and *Women in Scotland 1660–1780* (Edinburgh, 1979), pp. 7, 25, 52; William Donaldson, *The Jacobite Song* (Aberdeen, 1988), p. 60; Murray G. H. Pittock, 'Jacobite Culture', in R. Woosnam-Savage (ed.), *1745: Charles Edward Stuart and the Jacobites* (Edinburgh, 1995), pp. 72–86 (82–4); Howard Erskine-Hill, 'Under Which Caesar? Pope and the Journal of Mrs Charles Caesar 1724–1741', *Review of English Studies* (1982), 436–44; Valerie Rumbold, *Women in Pope's World* (Cambridge, 1989), p. 231; Patricia Kneas Hill, *The Oglethorpe Ladies* (Atlanta, 1977), p. ix.

31.   Mary Mahl and Helenne Kean (eds.), *The Female Spectator: English Women Writers Before 1800* (Bloomington and London, 1977), p. 179; Paul Monod, 'Pierre's White Hat' in Eveline Cruickshanks (ed.), *By Force or By Default? The Revolution of 1688–89* (Edinburgh, 1989), pp. 159–89 (164–7, 170–1); Katharine Rogers, *Feminism in Eighteenth-Century England* (Brighton, 1982), pp. 71, 250; Ruth Perry, *The Celebrated Mary Astell*

Blest Paper Credit: Financing the Revolution   97

(Chicago and London, 1986), pp. 41, 68, 71, 100, 172, 193, 238 ff.; Joan Kinnaird, 'Mary Astell and the Conservative Contribution to English Feminism', *Journal of British Studies* 19 (1979), 53–75 (54–5, 70).

32. Anne Finch, Countess of Winchilsea, *Selected Poems*, ed. Denys Thompson (Manchester, 1987), pp. 7, 14, 26, 53, 57, 80; Barbara McGovern, *Anne Finch and her Poetry* (Athens, GA, and London, 1992), pp. 1, 2, 24, 87, 95, 182, 185.

33. Mahl and Kean (1977), p. 209.

34. Dianne Dugaw, *Warrior Women and Popular Balladry 1650–1850* (Cambridge, 1989), pp. 47, 91; James Hogg, *The Jacobite Relics*, Series I (Edinburgh, 1819).

35. Frank McLynn, *Crime and Punishment in Eighteenth-Century England* (London, 1989), p. 57.

36. E. P. Thompson, *Whigs and Hunters* (Harmondsworth, 1985), p. 23; Pat Rogers, 'The Waltham Blacks and the Black Act', *Historical Journal* 67 (1974), 465–86; John Broad, 'Whigs and Deer-Stealers in Other Guises: A Return to the Origins of the Black Act', *Past and Present* 119 (1989), 56–72.

37. Eveline Cruickshanks and Howard Erskine-Hill, 'The Waltham Black Act and Jacobitism', *Journal of British Studies* 24 (1984), 358–65 (365); Paul Monod, 'Dangerous Merchandise', *Journal of British Studies* 30 (1991), 150–82 (161).

38. E. J. Hobsbawm, *Bandits* (London, 1969) for the idea of social banditry.

39. Monod (1991), p. 153; Szechi (1994), p. 26; Duncan Fraser, *The Smugglers* (Montrose, 1971), pp. 10, 85, 164.

40. John Gay, *The Beggar's Opera*, ed. Edgar V. Roberts (London, 1969), pp. 7, 48, 63, 82.

41. John Ashton, *Chap-Books of the Eighteenth Century* (London, 1882), pp. 433 ff.

42. McLynn (1989), pp. 57–58; Monod (1991), p. 158.

3 Crown Culture and Counter-Culture

Religion and Politics: Change and Continuity

Although the increase in capital crimes in pursuit of the protection of property arguably had a bark worse than its bite (for example, in the 1590s as many had been executed in one year in Essex as in the whole of the Home Counties in the mid-eighteenth century), there was still a marked shift of legal focus in tandem with the ideological centrality of property in political and, given the effect on the living standards of the clergy, religious, culture. Although the property rights proclaimed and defended by the British Government after 1714 were vulnerable and of doubtful legitimacy, the defensiveness of the Whig ascendancy over the next 46 years was almost certainly a political mistake. Sir Robert Walpole in particular, throughout more than 20 years in power, played up the Jacobite theme to encourage Whig solidarity and paranoia. As a result, it has been argued that the Tories were driven, through exclusion, to be a Jacobite party. If this was the case, it would mean that the representatives of a very significant body of political opinion were devoted to overthrowing the state: but if it is getting to be uncommon to hear the view that the Tories did not exist as a coherent political force after 1714, the case that a majority of them, rather than a rump of irreconcilables, were Jacobites, has yet to be widely accepted. It does, however, seem likely that Whig solidarity benefited from the Jacobite odour surrounding the 1710–14 Tory administration, especially following Bolingbroke's and Ormond's explicit defections to James. When the Whigs came to power with George I, there was certainly widespread dissent:

With the advent of Hanover, the political calendar became a calendar of riot. Disturbances were reported in 26 English and Welsh towns on Coronation Day; and the next five years saw ... seditious demonstrations in a further 31, if we include London and Westminster. Virtually every town with a population of 10 000 inhabitants or more was implicated in the rash of disorder, Colchester and Great Yarmouth excepted; and very few towns with over 5000 remained unscathed ... popular hostility to the new reign was a good deal more widespread than most historians have allowed.

If this was disturbing, the 1715 Rising, which mobilized a Scottish army almost equal in size to those of the victorious Covenanters of three-quarters of a century before, put the very state at risk. Just as Hanoverian indifference to the political ambitions of the Earl of Mar and the concerns over Union in Scotland had served to inflame the Rising, so the suspicion the regime attached to the Duke of Argyll and others for their lack of brutality in suppressing it alike indicated an increasingly centralized government.[1]

Although the majority of the 1100 or so Englishmen who rose in arms in 1715 were Catholics, anti-Catholicism appears to have had little impact in anti-Jacobite sentiment and activity (this was not to be the case in 1745). The fact that Bolingbroke and Ormond were Anglicans, and that the latter was very much identified by the High Church party as their own, no doubt had something to do with this. The Nonjurors were still strong in England (Norwich had a 'great congregation ... presided over by notable preachers', and the Bishop was arrested in October 1716: it also had a Jacobite press), while the High Church party generally leant towards the Jacobites. People toasted 'JOB' (James/Ormond/Bolingbroke) as a compound (and two-thirds Anglican) entity, and the parish clergy campaigned 'like madmen' for Jacobite candidates in the election of January 1715:

> marshalled by Atterbury, the clergy ... threw themselves into the 1714–15 Election campaign with almost as much fervour as they had displayed in 1710. Along with such slogans as 'No Hanover' and 'Down with the Roundheads' the cry of 'High Church and Sacheverell' was heard for the last time at the hustings.

When the Rising itself came, 'hundreds of country clergy were known to have sympathized with, if not actively supported, the action of the rebels', and 'three Tory bishops refused to subscribe to the declaration of loyalty to the throne'. As in the political sphere, government reaction was swift, and from the time that Benjamin Hoadley was elevated to the see of Bangor in December 1715, 'unrepentant High Churchmanship would convey any aspiring young divine to second-class citizenship'. The damage inflicted by the Revolution on sacramental High Anglicanism was intensifying: by 1727, five years after the Atterbury Plot, the whole bench of bishops was Whig.[2]

Yet the Whig regime's tendency to appropriate the power bases of those whose loyalty it doubted, combined with the lengthy tenure of power achieved by its first prime minister, served to undermine confidence in a government already weakened by the accession of a German dynasty whose prime loyalty was widely suspected of being directed towards their electorate rather than their kingdom. The military vulnerability of Hanover in European power politics, combined with the evident concern shown for it by George I and II, helped create an atmosphere of distrust in foreign as well as domestic policy. In their turn, George I and II were uneasy with British pluralism. As the latter said in 1755,

> There are kings enough in England. I am nothing there. I am old and want rest and should only go to be plagued and teased there about that D——d House of Commons.[3]

In the world of political debate, doubts amounting to disaffection with the government were often aired through an unusually oblique kind of political comment, centred on 'codes, cryptograms and symbols', as well as classical or biblical typologies and beast fables. Interest in such codes, and 'the hidden significance of an apparently innocuous vocabulary' peaked at the time of the Atterbury trial, and furnished Swift (himself no mean practitioner of the art) with material for satire in his description of Lagado in *Gulliver's Travels*. As Paul Langford puts it:

> A sieve signified a court lady, a lame dog an invader (an obvious reference to the evidence given in the Atterbury Plot),

a chamber-pot a committee of grandees. No parody of Swift's could have exceeded the absurdities of reality.

Codified political discourse survived throughout the period of the Jacobite threat. Apart from its humorous side, it was also symptomatic of a distortion of open communication and debate resulting from the presence of serious political divisions in the state. Whig distrust of folk culture (which paralleled that of the earlier Cromwellian regime) was perhaps in part an attempt to control the spread of such sedition, drawing, as the codes did, on many folk topoi. Fielding's *Inquiry into the late Increase in Robbers*, for example, 'advocated an all-out effort to destroy popular culture and the folkways of the "lower orders"'. In particular, the recommendation that 'wandering' itself could be a crime could be seen as striking against travelling chapmen, balladeers and those who simply brought the news from place to place.[4]

Such attempts were to some extent the outcome of the restriction of the fruits of the regime (particularly property rights) to a narrow elite, 'a radical doctrine, more radical than many of those who subscribed to it liked to admit'. The sectional interests of such views were those attacked in moderate oppositional political propaganda, whether that of Bolingbroke's 'One Nation' Patriot King rhetoric, or the associated politics of the Patriot Whigs of the 1730s. Bolingbroke's (perhaps codedly Jacobite) hope that '*patriotism*' should fill 'the *throne*, and *faction* be banished from the *administration*' was a nostalgic return in spirit to the party-free politics of an idealized Stuart era. The 'hierarchical but benevolent society' invoked by Tory apologists was rather vague in its definition.[5]

Even in explicit Jacobite writing there may be little definition in the way of identifiable political change. Lord Forbes of Pitsligo, one of the most dedicated of all Jacobites, even praises the British Constitution in his *Essays Moral and Philosophical* (1734). Nor is this mere window-dressing: in his unpublished writing of the 1720s, Forbes had aligned himself to the Whig doctrine of popular consent, and in his apologia for joining the '45, he identifies the corruption of good government and the withdrawal of such consent as his justification for appearing in arms. The Episcopalian community to which Lord Forbes belonged strongly supported the restoration of the Scottish Parliament (Lord Forbes himself had opposed Union), but they nevertheless saw themselves as linked, in a broad and loose way, to the conduct of affairs at a British level. Lord Forbes was no Sinn Fein Scottish nationalist: like many of those with whom he identified, he doubtless saw the British Constitution as having room for a rightful king and a Scottish Parliament, but being apparently otherwise satisfactory, the *status quo ante* having been restored. Such views were a feature of a kind of Whiggish Jacobitism. Eveline Cruickshanks describes the situation under Walpole thus:

> Tory speeches in Parliament ... show not regard for the prerogative but frequent use of revolution principles (not surprisingly since these were of more use to the Tories than the Whigs after 1714) and strident anti-Hanoverianism. They also reveal dislike of the Lutheranism of the first two Georges, whom the Tories regarded as Occasional Conformists.

Such anti-Lutheran views were strongly shared by some among the Scottish Episcopalians, the most militantly Jacobite group in mainland Britain.[6]

Whigs, Tories and Jacobites

The political and cultural effects of the development of governmental and church practice in 1714–60 were diverse, not only in ideological and religious, but also in national terms, and deserve separate consideration. As a number of commentators have noted, the iconography of the pro-Hanoverian establishment in the years after George I's accession lacks conviction: given the contested nature of many of the native, classical and sacred discourses of kingship, George I's apologists lacked fully coherent media of cultural expression. Meantime Arthurianism, which had carved out a place in Williamite iconography, largely through the efforts of Sir Richard Blackmore, began a century of decline before its Victorian renaissance. The deracination of the heroic under the first generation of Hanoverian administration is borne witness to in the strength of mock-heroic, satire and burlesque in literary production at all cultural levels, a process intensified by the rise of the 'Great Man', Walpole. The development of Grub Street and the massive expansion of a factionalized press were further factors in this destabilization of the heroic and sacramental.[7]

If Arthur and Arthurianism were beginning to fade, the same was not true of Merlin. Throughout the early part of the eighteenth century, but particularly in the 1730s, as opposition to Walpole developed, a number of supposedly antique prophecies of the legendary mage were 'discovered', along with those of other prophets. This whole cultus of coded political (though of course not always Jacobite) oppositionalism was linked to a growing interest in the antiquarian, itself no doubt connected to a nostalgia for the past under a monarchy which had to an extent been forced to disown its implications. Antiquarianism also provided a useful shelter for political oppositionalism, not only for English Nonjurors, but for Scottish patriotic publishing. Allan Ramsay's 'The Vision' (1726), a supposedly medieval poem which Ramsay claimed to date from the Scottish Wars of Independence in the fourteenth century, makes a strongly nationalist case he could not have hoped to have published more overtly. Later in the century, James Macpherson and Thomas Chatterton would, in their different ways, further develop this cult of antiquarianism, while in Ireland 'already in the 1720s and 1730s antiquarian and historical writers were showing a greater interest in pre-Norman Ireland and a new willingness to acknowledge its cultural achievements'. By the 1780s, Charlotte Brooke's *Reliques of Irish Poetry* 'offered a literary backing ... to the patriotic fervour surrounding the constitution of 1782'. In Wales, printers and publishers, beginning with Thomas Jones in Shrewsbury in 1695 (the first official printing press in England outside London and the university towns) developed

> activity, from collections of poetry to dictionaries to raise the status and improve the public knowledge of the language ... The culture revival was that of the princely part of ancient Wales: but it was revived for a literate middle class of yeomen and merchants.

Where such a target market obtained (as, with the exception of Ireland, it usually did), antiquarianism was depoliticized into a heritage zone for the aspiring middle class, enveloping them as it did in the glamour of a fake aristocratic past.[8]

In the 1730s, the Patriot Whigs helped to rehabilitate the oak tree as a national, rather than simply a Stuart symbol, thus casting

into oblivion the anti-oak inheritance of Williamite iconography.
One of the central themes through which this rehabilitation was
achieved was in the adoption of the Druids (for whom the oak
had reputedly been the chief of magical trees) as companions for
Merlin in the image of primitive British antiquity which directly
challenged the images of Stuart classicism and sacramentalism (as
did the 'Patriot Gothic' of Saxon liberty, which some by implication saw as freed from centuries of Norman yoke by the accession
of a Lutheran Prince of Germanic race). In plays such as
Hildebrand Jacob's *Brutus the Trojan* (1735), Druid and Trojan
Britons are conjoined in a patriot vision which after the fall of
Walpole in 1742 becomes generally integrated into the language
of Hanoverian patriotism. The intense defence of a native British
nationality in the writing of the Patriot Whigs can be seen in ret-
rospect as having helped to wrench control of political iconography from the Jacobites. Whether or not Bolingbroke intended his
Patriot King to hover ambivalently between the Stuart and
Hanoverian dynasties, by the end of the 1730s a more plausible
set of images was sustaining the rule of the latter than had been
the case twenty years before.[9]

A similar trend can to some extent be traced in sacramental
symbolism. The systematic marginalization of the jacobitical High
Church party during the 1720s and 1730s diminished the presence of internal Anglican conflict over sacramentality and authority. Partly as a result of the decline in establishment Anglican
Jacobitism, the tone of anti-Jacobite propaganda became more
decidedly anti-Catholic, and 'in England, the very areas which saw
a massive purge of Dissenting meeting-houses in 1715, witnessed
threats upon Catholic chapels in 1745 and 1746'. The aftermath
of the Atterbury Plot, which witnessed a last push against the
High-Flyers, did indeed mark a turning-point. In what was at least
a partly parallel movement, established Presbyterianism in
Scotland moved further away from Jacobitism. In 1715, quite a
number of nationalist-inclined Presbyterians seem to have leant
towards Jacobitism; in 1745, this trend was much less noticeable,
as a good number of disconsolate Jacobite recruiting agents
averred.[10]

The established Churches in both Scotland and England could
thus be said to have become gradually more fully reconciled to
the post-1707 and post-1714 British state, and the dissident

minorities within them steadily shrank. This was not so true of Episcopalians, Catholics or Irish Nonconformists. In England, repeated protests by and deep hostility towards Dissenters should not be underestimated, even though the vast bulk of them accepted the *status quo* on terms. The fact, however, that the last disabilities imposed on Dissenters (for example, the right to attend the universities of Oxford and Cambridge) were not lifted until the 1870s, should give us pause to acknowledge that the notion of a pan-Protestant common cause is a trifle illusory in the early and mid-eighteenth century. As late as 1788 the Dissenter Gilbert Wakefield found the marks of Antichrist in the Church of England; in 1787, Pitt, arguing against the repeal of the Test and Corporation Acts, had stated that 'there is a natural desire in sectaries to extend the influence of their religion; the dissenters were never backward in this, and it is necessary for the Establishment to have an eye to them'. As late as 1831, Samuel Taylor Coleridge opined that he 'had known very few dissenters indeed, whose hatred to the Church of England was not a much more active principle of action with them than their love for Christianity'. Thirty years later, Matthew Arnold was still castigating 'the Dissidence of Dissent' in *Culture and Anarchy*. British Protestant identity only very slowly replaced Anglican hegemony.[11]

Nonetheless, there was evidence of a growing desire for Britishness in the contributions of Scots such as James Thomson and the Gothic strain in Patriot Whiggery, which began to separate off (ideologically, if not factually) a naturally 'Saxon' Lowland Scotland from the Celts of the Highlands and Ireland. In the aftermath of Culloden, Lowland areas of Scotland which raised thousands of Jacobite troops were less badly treated than the clan heartlands of the Gaeltachd, and within a few years the cult of Ossian was allowing Lowland Scots to divide themselves into emotionally Celtic and in practice Saxon, a constructed consciousness which endures to our own day. The Patriot Whig account of 'Saxon liberty' offered a vision of a new nation, as well as giving rise to an artistic impulse which, as Christine Gerrard argues, provides a link between the political poetry of the 1730s and the more canonical art of 'Collins, Gray, and the Warton brothers'. Meanwhile, the role of Hanover in British foreign policy was diminished by the patriot cult of Elizabethanism, and its associations of unfettered patriotic struggle against a hostile

Catholic Europe. The rehabilitation of the rhetoric of antiquity and the agenda of large-scale resort to a heroic Anglo-British past was further reinforced by the Stuartism of the Hanoverian heir, Frederick Prince of Wales. Thus by the early 1740s, the cultural positioning of Frederick and the Patriot Whigs had usurped a significant portion of Jacobite rhetoric, and in so doing had blunted its force.[12]

If Jacobitism was losing control of the high cultural discourses of classicism, patriotism and antiquity in England, the same was not true north of the border. The Union represented a deep break with the Scottish past, and any benefits it brought appeared outweighed in the early and mid-eighteenth century by taxation and English contempt. The Stuarts remained consistently opposed to Union up until 1750 at least, and not simply out of a sentimental attachment to their 'ancient kingdom'. The Union had not only ended the multi-kingdom polity of the later Stuarts; it also encapsulated a direct insult to their dynasty, being the means whereby the Act of Settlement, rejected by the Scottish Parliament, was forced on the Scottish people. The Union thus was an instrument which excluded the Stuarts, and as such they were likely to oppose it, aside from the strong political benefits which might accrue from taking up a Scottish nationalist position. There was clearly a major positive shift in support for the Stuarts after Union: in the 1640s and 1680s, Montrose and Dundee had failed to raise more than 3000 Scots for the King's cause, but when that cause became the nation's, up to 20 000 followed Mar, and 12–14 000 appeared in arms for Charles Edward's risky and uncoordinated venture. As Frank McLynn points out when describing an incident at Holyrood in 1745, the dynasty became the means for national self-expression, not merely its end:

> On the steps of Holyrood palace, Hepburn of Keith … acted out a piece of theatre. He ostentatiously went ahead of the prince in a gallery touch meant to convey to the crowd that Scotland took precedence over the House of Stuart and that to oppose Union with England was logically to be a Jacobite.[13]

In Wales, there was very much less evidence of a nationalist dimension to Jacobitism. Welsh Jacobites were usually Anglo-Welsh magnates (though there were some popular celebrations, as in Wrexham on 10 June 1716, when 'the bells ... rang incessantly from eight until dusk and devout Jacobites wore feathers in their hats and carried oaken boughs'). The gentry, though they might show some interest in local folk customs, generally echoed the songs, sentiments and organization of their English counterparts, making little or no use of Welsh versions of the 'heroic legendary history' of the Scots: they were 'more concerned with assimilation into the English social and political scene than otherwise'. Only occasionally did faint nationalist sentiments surface, as in Sir Watkin Williams Wynn's belief that 'corruption in electioneering was an English characteristic'. The military occupation of large areas of Scotland after 1745 had no counterpart in Wales; nor does there appear to have been recruitment to the Irish Brigades there. The Stuarts were

> allied to Welsh sentiment neither through nationality nor religion ... Wales was already joined to England by the Tudor annexation, and there was no nationalist dimension to the events of 1688–1707 ... Wales was less geographically remote than either Scotland or Ireland.

For a combination of these reasons, Welsh Jacobitism appeared to lack an effective national dimension. Although it is true to say that declining folk traditions and the decline of the Welsh language itself could be linked to a past of which the Stuarts were a key part, on the Hanoverian side patriotism and its use of Merlin also made their obeisance to Welsh Druidism. Geraint Jenkins sums up the situation by saying that 'Welsh Jacobitism survived not as an effective political force, but as a waning romantic ideology ... the dog that barked but never bit.' Two hundred and forty years earlier, Charles Edward put it even more succinctly: 'I will do for the Welsh Jacobites what they did for me. I will drink their health.' Even the central Welsh Jacobite song, 'Robin John Clark', betrays a deep passivity:

> Let each bung his eye till the vessel's quite dry,
>   And drink to the lowering extravagant taxes;
> The spirit of Britain, by foreigners spit on,
>   Quite low by oppression and tyranny waxes.
> Then take off the toast, though the battle be lost,

> And he that refuses, a traitor we'll mark;
> Success to our prince, our rightful true prince;
>   For this is the chorus of Robin John Clark.
>
> To the brave duke, his brother, we'll fill up another,
>   Not meaning that blood-thirsty cruel assassin;
> May the Scotch partizans recollect their foul stains,
>   Their force twenty thousand in number surpassing.
> May they enter Whitehall, St. James's and all,
>   While for safety the troops are encamped in Hyde Park;
> And Heaven inspire each volley of fire.
>   Success to the chorus of Robin John Clark!

The Welsh Jacobites, acknowledging 'the battle ... lost', drink to tax cuts while they expect a Scottish army to take London for them singlehanded: such was their mettle both in rhyme and reality.[14]

In Ireland a vicarious patriotism operated through the achievements of the Irish Brigades abroad: soldiers were often recruited by explicitly Jacobite propaganda, as in Dublin in 1714 when men were promised 'that they should immediately march to Lorraine and see the young king'; 'others, signed up in County Wexford, were assured that "they were to serve King James the Third, and that they should not fight a battle till they landed in England or Ireland"'. At home, the breakdown in bardic culture in the late seventeenth and early eighteenth centuries, compounded as it was by the loss of power of the 'old Catholic' gentry, no doubt helped to reinforce the generally strongly nationalist and pro-Stuart stance of Irish bardic writers such as Aoghan Ó Rathaille and Eoghan Rua Ó Suilleabhain. As in Scotland, folk cultural expression became strengthened by a dispossessed high culture, and this was especially true given the scale of dispossession in Ireland: on 26 December 1702, the Jacobite Colonel Maurice Hussey wrote that 'the Tories in the province are lately grown highwaymen'. Bardic writing linked the Stuart deliverer to ancient heroes: he was 'Caesar', 'Charles Rex', 'The Lion', 'Angus Og' or 'Conall Cearnach': 'Charles, Son of Seamus, it was that name or no name, his standard or none, if the past were to live in the future, if the Gael were to endure'. In such a context of uncompromising nationalism, it is interesting to note Swift's possible links with Irish bardic culture (Protestant Jacobitism was also well-known, particularly in Kilkenny (Ormond's city), Derry, Waterford and Galway, where there were 'strong parties' of disaffected Protestants in 1716). Swift's own condemnation of 'the right claimed by the British parliament of binding Ireland by legislation' placed him on the side of Jacobite nationalism (his sympathies with Ormond and Viscount Dundee were also suspect in this context), as well as of those Protestant Irish patriots who rioted in Dublin in 1759 on the mere suggestion of an impending union with England. Ireland had two kinds of strong nationalism in the eighteenth century, Scotland one (plus a Cameronian patriot fringe). For all of them, religious difference was important, and social change strengthened the hold of declared opposition to the development of the British state in the form it took after 1707.[15]

Jacobite Culture

The breadth and significance of Jacobite culture remains of key importance in any attempt to account for the variety and strength of Jacobitism. Once it is accepted (as surely it should be) that armed uprising was an extreme manifestation of Jacobitism rather than a normative one, it becomes clear that the phenomenon of Jacobite interest and support, and particularly of culture, the tissue of its communication, is widespread. In any apportioning of political commitments, there are only ever a few willing activists to be found: and in a context where activity carried such risks, this is truer than ever. Jacobite culture is the manifestation of the breadth and depth of other, lesser but not insignificant, expressions of Jacobite identity.[16]

Although it may be argued that Jacobite cultural statement was a way of avoiding the realities of Jacobite political activity (as in the Welsh situation, discussed above), there are many reasons for rejecting this view, apart from its questionable assumption that 'real' Jacobitism is only to be found in major conspiracies (which few had the chance to participate in) or armed rising (very much a last throw of the dice). Jacobite culture was strongest in militant Jacobite areas; it played a significant role in communicating sympathies and sentiments, and the high, folk and crossclass elements of Jacobite culture indicate both its richness and permeation of society. The essential conservatism of high cultural Jacobites should not mask their strong traditional contacts with folkways and the poorer members of their often highly localized landed society. Such connections were strengthened by discrimination against the elements in the old ruling elite who clung to pre-1688 religious or political values. Most prevalent in Ireland and Scotland, this kind of high cultural Jacobitism is found throughout the British Isles; its idioms, based on a shared European high culture of classical and biblical reference, do not differ greatly in (for example) English and Gaelic.[17]

The strength of Jacobite symbolism in folk and popular culture is of at least as much interest. Whereas high cultural Jacobitism can be found in artifacts almost as readily as in poetry or sermons, its folk and popular counterpart is (for obvious reasons of wealth) far more rooted in music, oral and broadside verse, the coded or explicit cries of the mob and popular symbolism such as the use of flowers, rural pursuits, or the burning of Hanoverian 'guys' in public demonstrations of Jacobite support. High cultural supporters of the Stuarts supported and even helped to circulate such ballads, lamenting their decline in folk culture's 'ancient order'. Popular Jacobitism could be unexpectedly radical, as in the 'self-consciously heretical Jacobitism ... of the forest yeomen and cottagers in defence of their customary rights'. Many of the areas which witnessed Jacobite unrest in the earlier eighteenth century were centres of radical activity in the French Revolutionary period: it has been suggested by Paul Monod that political protest in early nineteenth-century England could have based itself on Jacobite models.[18]

The area of convergence between high and folk/popular Jacobitism thus derived not only from common dynastic, religious or national aims, but also from high cultural opposition to the financial revolution, enclosure and other social developments which increased mobility and threatened rural communities. Pro-Stuart writers already had a long tradition by 1700 of idealizing ruralism and folkways, and the common label of criminality attaching to both groups served drastically to reduce the social distance between them: 'gentlemen of the road may be fine gentlemen'. There were also strong traditional links in ballad culture, dating back to the early part of the seventeenth century and beyond:

Ballads were hawked in the alehouses and markets, but at the
same period they were sung by minstrels in the houses of the
nobility and gentry ... Chapbooks which sold for twopence, and
appealed to 'honest folks that have no lands', were also bought
by a Staffordshire lady and carefully left to her clergyman son.

The ballad was a major political weapon: up to 3–4 million of
them were circulating by the late sixteenth century, and the
attempts by the authorities in the Cromwellian and post-1688
periods to suppress them are signs of their potency, and the
difficulty of any attempt to control a mixed medium, where
'ballads passed down from years of tradition could co-exist in the
minstrel's repertory with songs originating from manuscripts or
printed texts'. As Raphael Samuel reminds us, 'John Aubrey ...
claimed that he could construct a consecutive history of England
from the Norman Conquest onwards, on the strength of the
ballads which he had learned from his nursemaid'.[19]

The ballad was part of a network of coded communication,
partly oral and partly written, and different groups in Jacobite
society suffered to different degrees in connection with various
kinds of treasonable display. Street balladeers seem to have got
off quite lightly, printers of broadsides and propagandists less so
(one at least was hanged). Gentlemen and members of the professional middle classes were apparently proportionately likely to
suffer seditious words prosecutions, while in the aftermath of the
1745 Rising, two-thirds of those executed were officers. Jacobites
from differing social groups thus shared a vulnerability to prosecution greater than the differences of wealth or outlook which
might have divided them: and this was underlined by the instability of property ideology after 1688, discussed earlier. On the
margins, Jacobitism forced divergent social and political groups
together in a cultural exchange: hence in the 1740s and 50s,
English Tory gentlemen sported the badge of the impoverished
and despised Gaeltachd in wearing tartan at fashionable meets
and resorts such as Bath, while Sir John Hynde Cotton's own
bespoke set proclaimed his Stuart patriotism.[20]

Such actions amplified and publicized high cultural Jacobitism
in a popular mode, while not detracting from educated and
gentry Jacobitism's three central themes: the sacramental authority of the Stuart monarchy in the context of the caesaropapist

English Reformation; the hereditary right of the Stuarts enshrined in the classically derived Brut myth; and the identification of the king as a magical monarch (on a symbolic level, at least) capable of restoring his realms and the lives of his subjects from poverty to plenty. This third theme drew on that element in Scoto-Irish foundation myth which identified the monarch as male and the land as female: and all three themes drew on the deep-seated connotations of the King's Two Bodies.[21]

The sacred messianic approach was linked to the classical elements of Jacobite high culture, particularly the Brut myth and its connections to Aeneas and the Augustus of Vergil's Fourth Eclogue, themselves messianic deliverers. In addition the magical monarch/fertility king topos could correlate identical symbols in varied contexts: thus the Aenean oak of Book VI, the royal oak of the Stuart badge and Boscobel, and the Druidic oak of ancient British lineage could suggestively interact in Stuart representation across cultural boundaries. The Jacobite leader was the fresh springing oak of the 1750 '*Revirescit*' medal of the Royal Oak Society; he was also the green man of the Highland Laddie song-cycle. The restorative fertility of the just king was a particularly strong belief in both Scottish and Irish Gaelic culture.[22]

While sacred and classical aspects of high cultural Jacobitism found echoes in folk and popular culture, it was perhaps the fertility imagery of the magical monarch which appealed most to customary beliefs. There were two major points of contact between popular celebration and the ideology of Jacobite high culture: traditional 'big house' modes of patronage, and the revelry of carnival, street, theatre and the inn. Here the 'improvised oral communication' of folk culture met the printed ballads of a popular culture, whose written texts, often displaying high cultural symbolism, interacted with folk models. Street culture under Charles II displayed a convergence between the interests of different classes, and this may have intensified after 1688. Allusive codes revealed Jacobite sympathy publicly while rendering prosecution less likely, and to achieve this end, well-known folk songs and motifs were adapted for Jacobite use. Such motifs were probably recognized by the Jacobite leadership: Charles Edward appeared as the prophesied 'Highland Laddie' in 1745, and so did his troops, as he uniformed Lowlanders (and even Englishmen and Franco-Irish troops) in Highland dress. The potency of the image of Charles as Highlander was recognized both by the Jacobites and the Hanoverians, who portrayed him as a Pied Piper-like seducer. On occasion (especially after dressing as a woman in the Betty Burke episode), Charles was identified not just as the land's lover but as the female personification of the land itself: hence *perhaps* he is shown as a woman on Jacobite drinking-glasses (six of which survive). Hanoverian propagandists took the episode as an excuse to deride Charles's masculinity.[23]

Music was also a central part of popular Jacobite celebration. Setting pro-Stuart verses to a familiar air was a common device: thus in mixed company, or when danger threatened, the Jacobite piper could play an air that was recognizable to sympathizers, but which it would be difficult for the authorities to take action against. As Nicholas Rogers explains:

Those who disapproved of its ['The King Shall Enjoy his Own Again'] seditious sentiments, or who feared prosecution, could simply have whistled it, for the Whigs revamped its verses with Hanoverian doggerel in 1714 and inadvertently gave it a plausible legality. Several ballad singers argued this out with a London constable in 1723.

The use of such airs for recruiting purposes may be borne witness to in 'The Piper o' Dundee':

He play'd 'The Welcome Owre the Main',
And 'Ye'se be fou and I'se be fain',
And 'Auld Stuarts back again',
  Wi' muckle mirth and glee ...

And wisnae he a roguie,
A roguie, a roguie,
And wisnae he a roguie,
  The Piper o' Dundee?

Cultural expressions of sympathy for the Stuart cause were widespread, and not only in Scotland. Pedlars and chapmen carried chapbooks to villages and individual homes, while women, both in that sphere and elsewhere, were important in transmitting Jacobite traditions. The song-culture of Jacobitism, one of its main means of popular expression, was integrated into the Risings themselves. It may have served to display a national and international commonalty of purpose, as in its use by the Irish Brigades and the playing of Jacobite verse in Scots by Highland pipers in England in the 'Fifteen (e.g. 'Little ken ye wha's coming'). Such similarities of expression among diverse communities are signs of the complexity of a movement which embraced questions of monarchy, property and national identity. Its legacies are with us yet, and some of the questions it asked have never been answered. Jacobite culture represented far more than the dynasty whose cause it supported, and the variety of ways in which its opponents categorized it as 'other' indicated the diversity of its threats.[24]

Folk Culture and Rebellion

The term 'folk culture', normally referring to those kinds of story or poem which are orally transmitted, is one vexed with complication in the print age, particularly in a period of growing literacy such as the eighteenth century. As Tessa Watt has recently demonstrated, even in the sixteenth century there had been significant interplay between material which circulated orally, and that which was written down: sometimes even the illiterate, alert to the growing power of print, would paste broadsides of poems they could not read up in their houses.[25]

In the eighteenth century, this process was naturally becoming more advanced, though in a context of increasing withdrawal from folkways by a high culture more bent on self-definition. In Scotland, this process was to an extent slowed by the development of a patriotic Scoto-Latin and vernacular culture in the aftermath of 1603, and still more 1707. Already a culture with strong forms rooted in an overlapping set of registers such as the flyting, a court entertainment with folk parallels enduring into the twentieth century, after the Union Scottish writing to some extent adopted the vernacular as a defence mechanism.[26]

There were also points of cultural interchange in England, such as Tyburn, with its broadside trade. In Wales, gentry such as Sir Watkins Williams Wynn supported the traditional harper, John Parry, who from the 1740s to the 1780s, in *Antient British Music* and the collections which followed, made harp airs available in printed editions. The Jacobite Irish aristocracy likewise supported the remnants of a bardic tradition. In Scotland and Ireland, the surviving topos of the sleeping ruler is found in both folk cultural anecdote and high cultural poetry (and continues to be found in both into the twentieth century: the last sleeping hero was Kitchener!). Such figures were well adapted to classical or biblical notions of the returning hero or messiah. As Paul Monod argues:

> In retrospect, the upsurge in popular Jacobitism after 1714 can be seen as the last great effort to preserve a traditional political culture which united the elite and the common people.

The attempt to return this increasingly detached elite to the common voice, made as a Romantic gesture through Primitivism and the *Lyrical Ballads* of Wordsworth and Coleridge, was thus in part a project which had extensive links with Jacobitism, and was in the end to revivify it, albeit in a Romantic version shorn of political content.[27]

Just as Protestant songs appear to have outnumbered Catholic ones in the Scotland of the 1550s, Royalist Cromwellian ones a century later and Jacobin songs government ones in the 1790s, so Jacobite songs outgunned their opposition. As the Scottish patriot Andrew Fletcher of Saltoun opined, 'if a man were permitted to make all the ballads, he need not care who should make the laws of a nation'. If this was indicative of a general oppositionalism in ballad culture (Saltoun, who had fought with Monmouth, was on the whole no Jacobite), such was confirmed at the end of the century when Joseph Ritson identifed Jacobinism and Jacobitism alike as having opposition to tyranny as a common denominator, and wrote of Robin Hood as a social bandit in this mould.[28]

By 1745 popular Jacobitism was in its last decline in London, where white roses were last reported on the 10th of June in 1723, though it survived in provincial England for rather longer. In Scotland, however, the high cultural patriotism which rejected the new metropolitan norms emplaced the folk tradition as central in a distinctively Scottish literary culture: and this can be seen as a key to the Scottish literary tradition from that day to this, through the work of people such as Ramsay, Fergusson, Burns, Scott, Hogg, Oliphant, Stevenson and Muir, to name but a few examples. Without undue romanticizing, the strong links across cultural boundaries in Scotland may have had something to do with the more egalitarian cast of Scottish society, a feature long noticed, and remarked on by Robert Southey:

> More offences are committed in England than in other Countries because there is more wealth and more want; greater temptations to provoke the poor, greater poverty to render them liable to temptation, and less religious instruction to arm them against it. In Scotland, where the puritan clergy retain something of their primitive zeal, the people are more moral, poverty is almost general there and therefore the less felt, because there is little wealth to invite the contrast.

However true this was, it was clearly the case that 'in Scotland there [was] ... a long-running interaction of high and folk literature'. This manifested itself increasingly as literacy expanded:

> the chapbooks and the broadsides derived material from tradition and they also sent material into traditional circulation.

Such 'traditional' circulation was strongest in the north-east, the heart of Scottish folk culture and, perhaps incidentally, of Scottish Jacobitism: for example, 'Buchan ... has probably produced at least fifty per cent of all traditional song lore collected in Scotland', while one-third of Child's Scottish texts and 'almost one-third of his A-texts come from Aberdeenshire'. This may well be as true of the Jacobite song, for 'there is a considerable number of Jacobite songs belonging to Aberdeenshire, which are never heard except in the bothies and farm-kitchens of the north-east'. Even after the end of Jacobitism as a serious threat and the dilution of the folk tradition, Scottish society continued to display its crossclass links, evidenced both in the actual social background of many of those from whom ballads were collected (e.g. Mrs Brown of Falkland) and the enthusiasm for traditional music in general:

> The old Scots folk songs of love and courtship enjoyed great popularity with middle and upper-class ladies who sang them at their tea-parties in the 1770s and 80s ... Scotland was still a small country where the rich and poor mingled together in daily life.[29]

The link between patriotic high culture and the vernacular revival was evident from Ramsay's early connections with the world of Jacobite Latinity inhabited by such as Dr Archibald Pitcairne and Thomas Ruddiman. Likewise, the classicizing of 'Edina' or 'Scotia' by the 'Scottish nationalist Tory' Robert Fergusson marched hand in hand with a fervent defence of vernacular values, as in 'Elegy on the Death of Scots Music':

> *Fidlers*, your pins in temper fix,
> And roset weel your fiddle-sticks,
> And banish vile Italian tricks
>   From out your quorum,
> Nor *fortes* wi' *pianos* mix,
>   Gie's *Tulloch Gorum.*

Just as Ramsay had demonstrated 'that he possessed the Horatian elegance of the English gentleman by rendering an ode of Horace in vivid and handy Scots verse', so a succeeding generation of cultural patriots defended both the folk and classical traditions. Ruddiman published Ramsay, but he also glossed Bishop Douglas's Scots translation of the *Aeneid*, a late medieval defence of Scottish culture which combined vernacular elements and classical ambition, in Douglas's aim to 'Kepand na Sudroun, bot our awin langage'. Freebairn, who published the Douglas translation, was a patriot who contacted Jacobite sympathizers in June 1745 with an offer of subscription to Fordun's *Scotichronicon*, of which its author had written 'he is no Scot whom this book does not please'. This appeal to nationalist sentiment was well timed. Even later in the century, 'upper-class Scots ... in folk music ... found an expression of conservatism, of national identity, and of community with all social classes of fellow Scots'. The blending of classical and folk traditions was, it has been argued, one of the major developments in eighteenth-century Scottish music.[30]

One of the noteworthy features of Scottish Jacobite poetry was the fact that the imagery and ideas of the Gaelic tradition (still 'mostly composed for oral circulation') are very close to those found in writing in Scots, mixing allusive language with 'something very different, much nearer to the elusive *vox populi*':

we must therefore be prepared to recognise 'higher' and 'lower' styles, 'court' (*i.e.* 'bardic') and 'folk' strains ... we must allow for conscious manipulation of these categories by some of the more sophisticated of our poets ...

The invocation of folk topoi in Gaelic verse matches that found in Lowland Scotland: both alike could be divided into 'gentry' songs and songs for 'below stairs', for *ceilidh* or carnival. The much written-of 'Lowland/Highland division was not ... quite as straightforward as it might appear'.[31]

In Ireland the situation was not dissimilar, though there was on the whole much less incorporation of classical typology into the bardic culture, particularly strong in Munster, where secret societies such as the Whiteboys flourished. The rhetoric of a feminized and suffering land, found also in the English and Scottish traditions, was an enduring one in Ireland, passing into Mangan's 'Roisin Dubh' (a black rather than a white rose) and the revived symbolism of Cathleen Ni Houlihan, so histrionically used in Maud Gonne MacBride's twentieth-century nationalist rhetoric.[32]

Folk culture's role in eighteenth-century politics, and its subsequent adoption by Primitivism and Romanticism, reflected to a marked degree the priorities of disaffected high cultural groups who fostered, mediated and adopted it. As society shifted away from folk practice and belief, so those discontented with that society (either politically, or later spiritually and emotionally) had recourse to the folk and popular 'little' traditions. Such culture thus played an important role as a badge of dissent or difference: the profile it thus gained and the political frisson attached to it no doubt serving to enhance its status in the era of ballad-collecting and romanticization which followed so hard on the heels of the last major Jacobite Rising.[33]

Regional Societies

As late as 1861, 'when the Royal Commission on Mines sat in Westminster, interpreters had to be employed to translate the answers of the Northumberland witnesses'. The gap between life and society in London, Edinburgh or Dublin and their regional hinterlands could be significant even into the twentieth century;

150 years earlier, it was marked indeed. In the eighteenth century, however, there was little of the slightly patronizing idealism which was to infect urban attitudes to rural England from the late nineteenth century on. John Bull, born early in the 1700s, was in the process of being codified into 'Farmer John', the voice of old England, but otherwise, metropolitan attitudes to the hinterland were often contemptuous. To an extent this was understandable in terms of economic and political motivation: Ireland and Scotland were largely disaffected for much of the century, and most of their inhabitants spoke a different language (certainly if one includes Scots). This was also the case in Wales, which was 90 per cent Welsh-speaking in the eighteenth century: as late as 1866, *The Times* called Welsh 'the curse of Wales'. In addition, even in the late eighteenth century, there were huge disparities in living standards: the skilled workman earned half as much again in Exeter or Manchester as in Edinburgh (though Northumberland and Lancashire might pay no more than Scottish wages), and twice as much in London. In addition, unskilled labour was very badly paid in comparison with skilled work in both Scotland and Ireland owing to their historically lower growth rates: for every £1 an unskilled Irish labourer earned, a Scot might get 30s to £2 and an Englishman £3 or more, whereas Irish skilled craftsmen might earn up to two-thirds of the English rate. Deep poverty was widespread on unskilled wages on the periphery, especially in the context of widely fluctuating food prices.[34]

Poverty is not, of course, enough to explain central English characterizations of the Irish, whom Charles Kingsley viewed as 'human chimpanzees', or the Scots and Welsh who suffered markedly also. The former were viewed as filthy, verminous, grasping, dissembling and poor, while Wales, full of 'peasant farmers' and characterized as 'Goatlandshire', could be regarded as the habitation of irritable and indigent illiterates with hilarious accents – when they could speak English. The idea that the Scots Highlanders were cannibals was a real fear in the 1745 Rising, and of course the association of moral and geographical marginality of this kind surfaced again in the imperial era with reference to 'darkest' Africa: the eating of human flesh being a sure mark of the inhuman savage 'other' which could be thus justly colonized or destroyed by its more civilized superiors. It would be pleasant to imagine that such outlooks can be anatomized dispassionately in our own day, but the evidence does not altogether bear this out. A casual glance at the *Punch Book of Scotland*'s twentieth-century cartoons bears out some of the old canards, while the current London-based series of Xenophobes' Guides includes one on the Welsh. This eighteenth-century Irish joke has a familiar flavour to it:

> A gentleman who had been shooting brought home a small bird with him, and having an Irish servant, he asked him if he had shot that little bird? Yes, he told him. Arrah, by my shoul, honey, replied the Irishman, it was not worth the powder and shot, for this little thing would have died in the fall.[35]

In the north of England, rapid economic growth in Northumberland and Yorkshire (among the poorest counties in 1700) increased the population significantly, while previously leading regional capitals such as Norwich, for long the second city in England, stagnated. The north was releasing itself from the political disaffection which had had a disabling effect. Up to two-fifths of the gentry were ill-disposed to the regime in Lancashire in the early part of the century, and the 'unsympathetic gentle-man' who was 'the standard type of the Jacobite landowner' underlined a bumpkin image of stagnation and ignorance, which may have continued in the west, but was subject to attrition by economic growth north of the Humber (which by the 1760s clearly included Scotland). There was certainly a political need for Fieldingesque caricatures of the country landowner, if up to 40 per cent were alienated from the regime (over England as a whole the proportion has been estimated as a quarter, with a low of one-ninth in Sussex).[36]

If the rural squirearchy could be comfortably characterized in this way, it was less easy to deal with provincial urban societies which showed signs of disaffection. In Bath, Oxford or Norwich, where opposition to the regime was generally confined to the better sort, there might be little cause for concern; but the authorities feared the mob, particularly the mob made up of a single group of workers, like the keelmen or colliers of Newcastle. Because the dominant rhetoric of a fifth column 'other' within was Jacobitism, such groups, often no more Jacobite than average, were alienized as mainly such: similarly the Whig Ascendancy

cloaked criminality, sometimes unjustly, under a jacobitical cover-
ing. Sometimes these fears were not unreasonable: six troops of
horse were sent as late as 1750 to quell Jacobite rioting in the
Black Country, while Jacobite candidates were elected in Preston
in 1768, and there was a White Rose Day riot in Nottingham as
late as 1779. But it is hard to resist the feeling that sometimes, particularly after the early part of the century, a state of paranoic
alarm was created through a discourse of Jacobitism applied to
sporadic provincial rioting, a discourse fed by such rioting, but
not finally exemplified in the careers of many of the rioters. In
this context, there is a distinction between sporadic Jacobite
'show' and the longer-term presence of frameworks of jacobitical
cultural communication, richer and more varied in their texture
through both space and time. In 1715, the northern English
gentry who rose for King James were as disappointed in the inac-
tion of the urban workers who had been characterized as Jacobites
by both sides, as King George's infant administration was relieved.
On the other hand, it has been persuasively argued that both in
England and Wales, some of the chief centres of Jacobite popular
display (most of which had in any case been zones of Royalist
support in the 1640s), were subsequently at the heart of radicalism in the 1790s and even beyond.[37]

Particularly in the era of Sacheverell, there were strong 'Church
in Danger' overtones to urban dissent, as on 16 July 1715, when
the Wrexham mob 'gutted the Presbyterian Meeting House and
pulled down the Anabaptist chapel'. In Birmingham

> there was a continuity of Anglican-inspired mobbing from the
> Sacheverell outbreak of 1710, through the anti-Methodist and
> anti-Quaker riots of 1751 and 1759, to the Church and King
> demonstrations of the 1790s.

Anti-Methodist riots in Norwich in 1751 were in this sense possibly
an accurate expression of a strongly Anglican and indeed
Nonjuring tradition, rather than of a determination to alter the
dynasty. Whereas in Scotland significant and subsequently realized
Jacobite dissension underlay the Porteous Riots of 1736, in
England military interest and popular demonstration at a time of
real Jacobite threat was after 1715 largely limited to the west north
of Bristol. In this context, it may be noteworthy that although

there were 2000 seditious words prosecutions in England between 1689 and 1760, almost 3000 (mainly Scots) Jacobites faced legal proceedings in 1746 alone. The secret and semi-secret clubs and societies which flourished among local worthies in small towns in England and Wales kept a low profile. Freemasonry may have experienced a fourfold expansion in the immediate aftermath of the Atterbury Plot, but political practice (as opposed to belief) was well rooted in wise and comfortable equivocation.[38]

Language and religion were also both powerful forces for the crystallization of communities, though this was less true of economics. Unlike France, England was moving away from commercially important regional centres towards the model of an ever more powerful metropolis. One area where economics did contribute to community identity was in the strong and often regionally based networking among Dissenters in general and Quakers in particular, where marriage 'from Friends' (i.e. outside the Quaker community) remained frowned on into this century.

The process of industrialization and the rise of industrial magnates has long been linked with Dissenting economic activity, in a tradition dating back at least to Mrs Gaskell's *North and South* in the 1850s. Throughout the eighteenth century, the cooperative nature of such networking was securing the possibility of economic transformation for many humble tradesmen. The granting of favourable purchasing and leasing contracts between family members and (in the environment of intra-community marriage) an ever-expanding body of cousins, fed a mutual drive towards commercial success. Despite the fact that Dissenters appear in some areas to have successfully bypassed religious disabilities (though this route was not so open to Quakers), in general it remained true that Parliament, the law, the universities and other areas of the establishment remained closed to them until the nineteenth century: in one or two cases the later nineteenth century. Perhaps partly as a result, it might be speculated that instead of the Anglican marriage-pattern, which prioritized moving up the social scale through the professions to the gentry over a number of generations, the excluded Dissenters, and especially Quakers, emphasized the building of trade networks within their own group in their version of the marriage market.[39]

The eighteenth century also saw the development of what was to become a new church, with particular strengths in Wales and provincial England: Methodism. The Wesleys for a long time saw the movement they had done so much to build as a vehicle for Anglican revival rather than a separate confession in its own right. John Wesley's mother was a Jacobite, and it was perhaps not altogether a coincidence that Methodism in its early stages was influenced by the spiritual intensity developing in the writing of Nonjuring rather than mainstream Anglicanism: William Law's *Serious Call to a Devout and Holy Life* (1728) in particular 'greatly impressed John Wesley', and had a marked influence on him. Despite such youthful influences, by the 1740s, when Wesley's ministry was well under way (and by which time the Jacobite-leaning Duke of Beaufort had begun (1740) to organize anti-Methodist riots), it was Cumberland who welcomed Methodism into the British Army when it was still widely suspected elsewhere. Indeed, Anglican fears that Methodism was to prove a church within a church were substantially correct: Wesley himself began in his later ministry to ordain without (apparently) seeming to realize the irrevocable break with Anglicanism which such a practice invited. Particularly strong in the north-east, north midlands, West Riding, the potteries, Cornwall and mining and seaport areas generally, Methodism made little headway in Scotland, where the established Church had inherited much of the Covenanting spiritual tradition, where the issue of lay patronage of clerical livings was still so alive that it was to split the Church in 1843 and where Methodist-style field preaching was still a living memory. However, the effects of the new confession were in general powerful: 'the revivalist preaching of the Wesleys and Whitefield ... deeply moved a vast mass of human beings hitherto neglected by Church and State'. In Wales, Methodism followed a Calvinist pattern as opposed to Wesley's Arminianism: here it derived largely from the preaching of others such as Howell Harris, whose influence was opposed in Wales by Jacobite magnates such as the Duke of Beaufort. Its popularity was doubtless helped by Anglican neglect of Welsh: for 154 years from 1716 there was no Welsh-speaking bishop and 'scholarly Welsh clerics could not find livings in Wales whilst monoglot Englishmen were appointed to Welsh-speaking parishes'.[40]

In the famous case of Dr Thomas Bowles, appointed Rector of Trefdraith and Llangwytan in Ynys Môn (Anglesey) in 1766, 'only five of his 500 parishioners spoke or understood English'. The

Cymmorodorion Society and local dignitaries fought for his removal in a case at the Court of Arches, where Bowles's attorney argued that 'Wales is a conquered country; it is proper to introduce the English language, and it is the duty of the bishops to promote the English, in order to introduce the language'. The judge declared the Welsh plaintiffs right in principle, but Bowles kept his living. Such events could only help to drive the laity 'into the arms of Methodism', especially since many of the bishops were themselves enemies of Welsh. The anti-Methodist argument that the Anglican Church was the true 'Celtic' (i.e. aboriginally British) one was an inadequate defence by comparison. Moreover, in Wales there was not 'the close affinity between squire and parson' found in England, and consequently no united front between Justice of the Peace and rector, a powerful axis of local Anglican authority.[41]

Methodism appealed to the folk in its re-metaphoricizing of folk culture. Although, for example, Cornish Methodists attacked popular pastimes and folk superstitions, they 'replaced them with revivals, Love Feasts, watch-nights, hymn singing, providential interventions and colourful local versions of ... cosmic drama'. In Wales, Howell Harris originated the *seiat*, a kind of spiritual clinic which provided counselling support to backsliders: there were 428 *seidan* in Wales by 1750. Innovations of this kind, perhaps reflected also in the limited gestures of ecumenism made by Wesley in Ireland in the 1740s, helped create a dynamic spiritual and organizational force, which demonstrated a distinct cast of spiritual renewal in the areas in which it succeeded. Accused of Jacobitism (perhaps because of its undermining effect on Anglicanism as much as anything else), Methodism seems rather the token of a new phase of spiritual development.[42]

NOTES

1.   J. A. Sharpe, *Crime and the Law in English Satirical Prints 1600–1832* (Cambridge, 1986), p. 20; Nicholas Rogers, *Whigs and Cities* (Oxford, 1989), p. 366.

2.   H. T. Dickinson, 'The Jacobite Challenge', in Michael Lynch (ed.), *Jacobitism and the 45* (London, 1995), pp. 7–22 (11); Rogers (1989), pp. 315, 363, 380; Geoffrey Holmes, *The Trial of Doctor Sacheverell*

(London, 1973), pp. 263, 266, 274; Linda Colley, *In Defiance of Oligarchy: The Tory Party 1714–1760* (Cambridge, 1982), p. 105.

3. Isaac Kramnick, *Bolingbroke and his Circle* (Cambridge, MA, 1968), p. 114.

4. Paul Langford, *Walpole and the Robinocracy* (Cambridge, 1986), pp. 16–17; Frank McLynn, *Crime and Punishment in Eighteenth-Century England* (London, 1989), p. 96; Peter Burke, *Culture in Early Modern Europe* (Aldershot, 1988 (1978)), p. 270; Malcolm R. Zirkes, Jr., *Fielding's Socal Pamphlets* (Berkeley, CA, 1966), p. 55.

5. Paul Langford, *Public Life and the Propertied Englishman* (Oxford, 1991), p. v; Colley (1982), pp. 147, 286 ff.

6. Alexander, Lord Forbes of Pitsligo, *Essays Moral and Philosophical* (London, 1734), p. 161; Aberdeen University MSS 2740/4/18/1; Eveline Cruickshanks, 'The Political Management of Sir Robert Walpole, 1720–42', in Jeremy Black (ed.), *Britain in the Age of Walpole* (Basingstoke, 1984), pp. 23–43 (29). Cf. also Murray G. H. Pittock, 'The Political Thought of Lord Forbes of Pitsligo', *Northern Scotland* (1996), 73–86.

7. Beverley Taylor and Elizabeth Brewer, *The Return of King Arthur* (Cambridge, 1983), pp. 34–5.

8. Murray G. H. Pittock, *Poetry and Jacobite Politics in Eighteenth-Century Britain and Ireland* (Cambridge, 1994), p. 178 ff.; Murray G. H. Pittock, 'Forging North Britain in the Age of Macpherson', *Edinburgh Review* 93 (1995), 125–39; Connolly (1992), p. 122; Geraint Jenkins, *The Foundations of Modern Wales: Wales 1642–1780* (Oxford, 1987), p. 215; Prys T. J. Morgan, 'The Clouds of Witnesses: The Welsh Historical Tradition', in R. Bruley Jones (ed.), *Anatomy of Wales* (Glamorgan, 1972), pp. 17–42 (31).

9. Cf. Christine Gerrard, *The Patriot Opposition to Walpole* (Oxford, 1994).

10. Rogers (1989), p. 379.

11. John Cannon, *Samuel Johnson and the Politics of Hanoverian England* (Oxford, 1994), pp. 25–33 ff.

12. Gerrard (1994), pp. viii, 3, 108 ff., 145, 150 ff., 186, 194 ff., 215.

13. Frank McLynn, *Charles Edward Stuart: A Tragedy in Many Acts* (London, 1988), p. 149.

14. William Donaldson, *The Jacobite Song* (Aberdeen, 1988), p. ix; National Library of Scotland MS 17505; Pittock (1994), pp. 201–2; G. Jenkins (1987), pp. 150, 151, 294; Philip Jenkins, *A History of Modern Wales 1536–1990* (London, 1992), pp. 70, 73; James Hogg, *The Jacobite Relics*, First Series, (Paisley, 1874), pp. 121–6.

15. Daniel Corkery, *The Hidden Ireland: A Study of Gaelic Munster in the Eighteenth Century*, 2nd edn., (Dublin, 1925), pp. 132, 136, 140; Vivian Mercer, 'Swift and the Gaelic Tradition', *Review of English Literature* 3 (1962), 69–79; David Launey, 'The Free Trade Crisis: a Reappraisal' in Gerard O'Brien (ed.), *Parliament, Politics and People* (Dublin 1989), pp. 69–92 (72); Sean Murphy, 'The Dublin Anti-Union Riot of 3 December 1759', ibid., pp. 49–68 (50); Connolly (1992), pp. 238–9.

16. Cf. Murray G. H. Pittock, 'Jacobite Culture', in R. Woosnam-Savage (ed.), *1745: Charles Edward Stuart and the Jacobites* (Edinburgh, 1995), pp. 72–86.

17. Cf. Pittock (1994).

18. E. P. Thompson, *Customs in Common* (London, 1991); Paul Monod, *Jacobitism and the English People* (Cambridge, 1989).

19. Tessa Watt, *Cheap Print and Popular Piety, 1550–1640* (Cambridge, 1991), pp. 11, 16, 81; Raphael Samuel, *Theatres of Memory I: Past and Present in Contemporary Culture* (London, 1994), p. 11.

20. Monod (1989); Bishop Robert Forbes, *The Lyon in Mourning*, ed. Henry Paton, 3 vols., (Edinburgh, 1895), II, p. 254.

21. Pittock (1994), ch. 1.

22. Pittock (1994), chs. 1, 2, 4, 5.

23. Monod, (1989); Murray G. H. Pittock, *The Myth of the Jacobite Clans* (Edinburgh, 1995), pp. 54–6; also in Woosnam-Savage (1995), pp. 82–4.

24. John Ashton, *Chap-Books of the Eighteenth Century* (London, 1882), p. v; Rogers (1989), p. 363; Pittock in Woosnam-Savage (1995), p. 84.

25. Watt (1991), p. 258.

26. Cf. Pittock (1994), ch. 4.

27. Burke, (1988 (1978)), p. 200; Paul Monod, 'Pierre's White Hat', in Eveline Cruickshanks (ed.), *By Force or By Default? The Revolution of 1688–1689* (Edinburgh, 1989), pp. 159–89; Owain T. Edwards, 'Music in Wales' in Jones (1972), pp. 207–26 (212).

28. Pittock (1994), pp. 213–15.

29. David Buchan, *The Ballad and the Folk* (London, 1972), pp. 4, 5, 41; David Buchan, *Scottish Tradition* (London, 1984), pp. 11–12; Gavin Greig, *Folk-Song in Buchan and Folk-Song of the North-East*, with a Foreword by Kenneth S. Goldstein and Arthur Argo, (Halboro, PA, 1963), p. 1; Rogers (1989), p. 373; Joy Cameron, *Prisons and Punishment in Scotland from the Middle Ages to the Present* (Edinburgh, 1983), p. 57; Rosalind Marshall, *Virgins and Viragos* (London, 1983), p. 188.

30. David Daiches, *Robert Fergusson* (Edinburgh, 1982), pp. 14, 40, 41; Douglas Duncan, *Thomas Ruddiman* (Edinburgh, 1965), p. 170; T. L. Kingston Oliphant, *The Jacobite Lairds of Gask* (London, 1870), p. 112; David Johnson, *Music and Society in Lowland Scotland in the Eighteenth Century* (Oxford, 1972), pp. 188, 196.

31. William Gillies, 'Gaelic Songs of the 'Forty-Five', *Scottish Studies* 30 (1991), 19–58 (20–21, 29); Leah Leneman, *Living in Atholl 1685–1785* (Edinburgh, 1986), p. 12.

32. Cf. Maud Gonne MacBride, *A Servant of the Queen* (London, 1937).

33. Cf. Pittock (1994).

34. Raphael Samuel (ed.), *Patriotism: The Making and Unmaking of British National Identity*, 3 vols., (London and New York, 1989), I: p. xv; III: pp. xi, 18; A. J. S. Gibson and T. C. Smout, *Prices, Food and Wages in Scotland 1550–1780* (Cambridge, 1995), pp. 275, 279; G. Jenkins (1987), p. 220; David Hempton, *Methodism and Politics in British Society 1750–1800* (London, 1984), p. 14.

35.   Samuel (1989), III:p. xxv; Ashton (1882), pp. 291, 437–8, 475–7.

36.   Monod (1989), pp. 270–1.

37.   Monod (1989), pp. 187, 204–6, 216, 219, 220, 229, 273 ff.; Philip Jenkins, 'Tory Industrialism and Town Politics: Swansea in the Eighteenth Century', *Historical Journal* (1985), 103–23 (122).

38.   D. G. D. Isaac, 'A Study of Popular Disturbances in Britain 1714–54', (unpublished Ph.D. thesis: Edinburgh, 1953), pp. 163, 165; Colley (1982), pp. 116, 155.

39.   Mrs Gaskell's *North and South* bears witness to the enduring quality of the rural Tory Anglican /urban Whig Nonconformist dichotomy in the structuring of English identity.

40.   E. D. Evans, *A History of Wales 1600–1815* (Cardiff, 1976), pp. 71, 72, 73; *Cassell's History of the British People V* (London, 1923), p. 1761; Rupert Davies, *Methodism* (Harmondsworth, 1963), pp. 44, 82, 128–9; Colley (1982), p. 114.

41.   G. Jenkins (1987), pp. 343, 346, 347; Morgan in Jones (1972), p. 32.

42.   Hempton (1984), pp. 27, 32–3, 35–6; John Davies, *A History of Wales* (London, 1993 (1990)), p. 310.

4 Enlightenment and Empire

One Society? Britain in 1760

Despite assertions of a unified Protestant identity, one feature which repeatedly recurs in the documentation of regional disturbances in England and Wales in the eighteenth century is the presence of religious tension, usually between Anglicans and Dissenters. Far from being settled in their hegemony, the Anglican Church's supporters continued to exhibit a degree of insecurity which could border on paranoia:

> The Church of England ... almost always felt itself in danger. In the early eighteenth century it feared the rising threat from Dissent. In the 1720s and 30s it was alarmed by the growth of the many-headed hydra of heterodoxy: Socinianism, Arianism, Deism, Freemasonry and even atheism. The mid-eighteenth century saw the Anglican clergy worried by the Methodist revival, while in the later eighteenth century they feared the activities of the Rational Dissenters, they found the Evangelicals uncomfortable bed-fellows and they saw an increasing percentage of the urban poor failing to attend their churches ... In religious terms, eighteenth-century Britain was already a pluralist society.

By 1760, the violence which had been expressive of these worries earlier in the century had eased somewhat, though Parliament was still passing discriminatory legislation, such as the 1753 Marriage Act which allowed only Anglican clergy to 'solemnize valid marriages' in England and Wales. Nevertheless, the position altered, with the decline of the Jacobite threat and the Anglicanization of the Lutheran Hanoverians. Rather than the Franco-Jacobite challenge, it may have been the Seven Years' War and still more the French Revolution which served to unite a Protestant Britain pursuing imperial aims, though tension between Anglicans and Nonconformists continued for a century more than this at least. In this developing unity, however, Ireland was conspicuously absent, not only through the continuing oppression of the Catholic community, but also by the growth of Protestant nationalism, which peaked towards the end of the century. It was rather Scotland which provided a strong impetus towards British identity from the late 1750s on: one which continued to be much resented in England for twenty years thereafter. Some Scots alienized the recent past (in, for example, consenting to and feeding the misrepresentation of the '45 and Jacobite activity generally as specifically Highland) in pursuit of a new identity for themselves, while the trend for the Scottish aristocracy to send their children to English public schools, already noticeable early in the century, consolidated and probably accelerated. At the beginning of the century, members of the family of the Dukes of Atholl were attending Perth Grammar School; by the 1740s, Lord George Murray's son was at Eton. In the mid-1750s, while there were still British Army garrisons in Angus and Perthshire, a new (and increasingly central belt) generation of Scots was striving to be accepted on equal terms in the British state:

> From an early stage in the war [1756–1763] it became clear that a new generation of articulate Scots had emerged which looked forward to a degree of integration with and participation in the British state well beyond that taken for granted by their elderly leaders ...

Despite (indeed it was partly caused by Scottish ambition) the extensive hostility offered to Scots in England (as opposed to those fighting abroad) in the 1760s and 1770s, which at one point led even a staunch unionist like Dundas to threaten separation, and which routinely divided Scots sentiment towards the imperial capital between admiration and resentment, Scots entered steadily upon the offices of state. Whereas there was 'one Scot in perhaps every 20 diplomatic posts under William and Mary', there were to be 'a proportion of one in seven under George III': though this was still less than Scotland's share of Anglo-Scottish population and far less than her share of educated men. The Scottish Enlightenment and the concern of Scots to eradicate the more obvious traces of their native speech (though this trend has possibly been overestimated) alike contributed to a powerful drive towards gaining an equal footing in British society and being at its intellectual forefront. The development of the New Town of Edinburgh from the 1750s took place within a British context, and yet was designed as a statement of Scottish patriotic achievement within what was becoming (from the Scottish, though not as yet the English point of view) an imperial partnership. Scotland's growing role within that partnership after the poverty of the late seventeenth and early eighteenth centuries was amply borne witness to in the fact that in the late 1760s the Scottish share of British tobacco trade briefly rose above 50 per cent. The opening of imperial markets, foreshadowed by the Union, was at last beginning to outpace the tax demands of a British state reliant on its credit with stockholders to finance its frequent, lengthy and expensive wars (though the beneficial effects of Scottish economic growth were blunted by inflation in its long-depressed economy in the last decades of the century). Although the long wave of Scottish emigration had already begun, in the central belt, rapidly developing its modern status as the essential powerhouse of Scottish opinion and identity, such changes were not at the heart of social concern – and this was to be true of attitudes towards the Highland Clearances. In the 1750s and 1760s the raising of Highland regiments to fight in the British Army served to give the tartan (elsewhere banned) a new dimension of British loyalty, while also creating a bifurcation of the Scottish imperial contribution between military Highlandism and commercial Lowlandism, a rather misleading cultural construct which was inappropriately projected back on to accounts of the 1745 Rising.[1]

Thus although English society was still distrustful of Scots, Scottish culture was increasingly conforming itself to participatory norms: the New Town, for example, was intended to provide town houses for the Scottish nobility and gentry on the English model, in place of the noisy and confined apartment life of Old Town Edinburgh, which nonetheless in its enforced intimacy probably provided the nursery for the achievements of the Scottish Enlightenment. Long after this, however, and indeed right down to our own time, Scottish society's greater outspokenness and egalitarianism, as well as the different social ethos promoted by its educational, legal, clerical and financial systems rendered it far from homogeneous with its English counterpart, except at the highest levels of society (the irony here being that a 'North British' aristocracy badges itself as Scottish, while an apparently indistinct British middle class has far more peculiarly Scottish elements). Returning to 1760, a distinction needs to be drawn between a newfound complicity in the imperial project and an unwillingness to enter into a homogenized identity in domestic rather than imperial terms. Many domestic peculiarities remained in Scottish society which are slurred over or ignored in 'British' accounts: for example, the status of women, and the country's relatively liberal divorce laws (discussed in Chapter 2). Women's domestic power in Scotland, remarked on by foreigners as early as the fifteenth century, did in fact have some implications at law: for example, 'when a wife was eventually granted a divorce, she was put in possession of her jointure lands and was free to marry again'. When the Anderson's University (now Strathclyde University) was founded in Glasgow in 1796 to educate those in work, women were permitted to attend its lectures. Scottish education and society similarly show many marked particularities. In the nineteenth and twentieth centuries, ample evidence exists for Scottish resistance to perceived encroachment on areas of domestic identity; and in the aftermath of empire, the development of a more aggressively differentiated Scottishness bears witness to the continuity of a society within Scotland which participated in, rather than surrendered to, the imperial mission. It should not be forgotten, either, that a very significant proportion of the Scottish population remained Gaelic-speaking in 1760; and that for what must have been the many monoglots among them, there was no question of a formed British identity.[2]

Tendentious it may be, but it is at least arguable that English identity accepted as 'British' only those who displayed no difference from Englishness, save in token areas: Burns' suppers are acceptable, but reminding people of the existence of separate Scottish and Irish practices when they generalize about 'Britain' is not, as anyone who has tried it knows. If this is the case, it enables one better to understand the Irish situation, where since the mid-eighteenth century at least, *both* traditions have made alienizing claims of difference. While the Catholic Old English and Irish were burdened in 1760 by a weight of oppressive legislation (the adoption of Irish in Old English Catholic writing in Ireland can be seen as a sign of protest against this), the Dissenters were often hostile to any prospect of union. Their quest to gain autonomy for the Irish Parliament displayed a sense of political difference and national priorities alien from the British political classes, whether Scottish or English. In this context it was unsurprising that they began to find themselves categorized as Irish, irrespective of their confessional position.[3]

Nonetheless, while it is right to establish the extent and variety of Irish difference in 1760, it is not thus appropriate to exclude Ireland from the status of being 'British', as some recent scholarship has sought to do. It is hard to conceive of Irish society and politics as completely separate from those of mainland Britain, as Linda Colley has done; nor is it truly convincing to characterize Ireland as purely a colony, in the same relationship to Britain as East Africa or Burma, as Edward Said seeks to do. Scotland is part of Britain, so there is a tendency to overemphasize its 'Britishness', and thus endorse the *status quo*; most of Ireland is independent, and so its British heritage is underestimated. The exclusion of defeated minority traditions by a Whiggish historiography has been applied significantly in the case of West Britishness. What Burmese writer could have the status in *English* literature that Swift, Goldsmith, Burke or even Sir John Denham possess? Were the noble families of Boyle or Ormond, or Wellesley and Wolseley among British commanding generals, regarded in the same light as Zulus or Maoris? The class that W. B. Yeats wrote of in *Purgatory* and elsewhere, who 'from London and from India' came home to the Irish west to 'look at the May blossom in the park', was not imaginary, nor were they merely colonists who happened to live in Ireland. Edmund Burke, supposedly a member of the Ascendancy, yet frequently caricatured as an alien Jesuit, had many close relatives (including his wife and possibly his father) in Catholic Ireland; and many from the non-Catholic communities (such as Wolfe Tone and Robert Emmet) are ranked in the roll-call of Irish 'Catholic' nationalism. The Catholic middle class were in fact by the late nineteenth century moving towards British norms (Catholic Unionism is by no means an eccentric tradition), and Ireland was better represented than Scotland in the British Parliament, where by the late nineteenth century its own political parties were making a major impact. Although Ireland's 'Britishness' was perhaps less well developed than Scotland's, and coalesced at a later date, to write Ireland out of Britain is to risk serious misrepresentation of the nature of Britain and its identities, not least the identities of its elites, right into the twentieth century. James Joyce's short masterpiece, 'The Dead', clearly indicates (as does the rest of the *Dubliners* collection in which it appears) that the paralysis of Dublin society to an extent derives from its role as a provincial British city racked by futile chauvinistic dreams of its own status as an Irish and Catholic metropolis, dreams which in their manifestation only confirm Dublin's provincialism: for to be provincial is to be chauvinistic about particularity without any wish to evaluate it through external reference. Where Catholicism was absent, anti-Irishness was muted: and, of course, Catholics were (at least in abstract) the objects of opprobrium irrespective of nationality.[4]

Wales in 1760 was still underdeveloped in British terms. A few hundred thousand people, nine-tenths of whom (including many monoglots) were still Welsh speakers, lived in a largely rural society, in which gentry behaviour strongly echoed the English model, except at the lower end of the landed income spectrum in north and west Wales, areas which remained 'fundamentally Welsh in their speech and outlook'. Elsewhere, as E. D. Evans argues:

> Some would attribute to the [Jacobite] Movement a nationalist character interpreting it as a protest against English oppression; this ignores the fact that at this period the Welsh gentry were more concerned with assimilation into the English social and political scene than otherwise.

In parts of Glamorgan,

> 'Welsh' was a synonym in fashionable gentry parlours for drunken, ignorant and superstitious. Children of gentry stock were sent to private schools in order to acquire a polished English accent ... Ancient baptismal names passed out of circulation among the gentry ... As a result, by the early eighteenth century, the language and culture of a small squire in the Welsh heartland were a world apart from those of an affluent Glamorgan gentleman.

The entry of Welsh Tories more strongly into the offices of local administration by the late 1740s helped to dilute political disaffection into insignificance, though at a lower level the continued resilience of the Welsh language militated against any unreserved incorporation into a larger British identity, especially in the north and west of the principality. Politically, the Welsh-speaking group was in 1760 of no particular significance, as the rather contemptuous policy of the hierarchy (as opposed to some of the parish clergy) of the Church in Wales towards the language indicated. As in Scotland, the introduction of taxes which appeared to discriminate against native industry (as was the case with the Cider Tax in the 1760s) created discontent in both Wales and the West of England, but the political focus of Welsh discontent was apparently without a domestic agenda save on the language question. Print culture helped to crystallize that question's significance: 'the great increase in Welsh book production between 1660 and 1730', for which Welsh clergymen were largely responsible, led to the development over the next century and a half of print culture as a manifestation of a central 'Welshness'. As in the case of Scotland, Welsh identity was domestic, but on a more limited set of fronts.[5]

Britain in 1760 was thus, while far from homogeneous, in a stage of identity formation which, though it continued to develop, never became even nearly complete. The patterns of Irish, Welsh and Scottish society all differed from the English model, and within England and all these other countries ancient social, regional and particularly confessional divisions continued to operate. But what surely was different in 1760 was that these divisions had (except possibly in Ireland) a lack of such impact on British foreign policy as they had once had; and this was particularly apparent in the Scottish commitment to British identity. Whereas throughout much of the seventeenth and early eighteenth centuries, internal political and religious differences had implied different outlooks on the role of Britain abroad (Jacobitism had of course enlisted a succession of foreign powers in its support), this was not nearly so clearly the case by the accession of George III (though both the American war and the aftermath of the French Revolution provided temporary occasions for the renewal of division). In this sense, English and a majority of Scottish society were homogenized through their pursuit of common external aims. This is conventional enough, but the differences between external purpose and domestic identity must be closely examined in order to establish the real extent of British homogeneity. In 1760, the conflict between Anglicanism and Dissent was still manifest; huge areas of the islands were cut off by language and/or social structure from the society of southern England and the south midlands, which is the imagined 'core' of Britain. Scottish society, apparently eager to participate in the growing power of Empire, nevertheless retained its own distinct qualities to which it occasionally resorted in times of tension (the 1826 banking crisis is one example). Externally more unified than it was internally homogeneous, Britain in 1760 was moving towards the Victorian duality of localist loyalties within an imperial community. The Empire was the key to British unity: moments of its crisis, attrition and final disappearance in the twentieth century have been marked with an emerging plurality of voices from a unity which is now mainly historic, though its history may (with the exception of Ireland) be enough to preserve it.[6]

The Scottish Enlightenment: Cultural Development

The Scottish Enlightenment was a concentrated outpouring of analytical, speculative and historical work, a disproportionate amount of which achieved classic status. Out of it came the beginnings of many of the social sciences, particularly economics, sociology, politics and anthropology. Out of it also came the beginnings of modern geology and significant developments in philosophy (a central subject in Scottish higher education), chemistry, architecture and history. Medicine and the natural sciences owe much to it; and in 1762 the first chair in English Literature anywhere in the world was founded at the University of Edinburgh. Concentrated for the most part in the three largest Scottish cities (Edinburgh, Glasgow and Aberdeen), the Enlightenment achievement is strongly localized: the sudden flowering of this 'hotbed of genius' (Tobias Smollett's phrase) has seemed to some to be at odds with the continuum of Scottish culture. There are three main explanations of the roots and reasons for the Scottish Enlightenment: first, that it was made possible by the opportunity for peace and civil development created by Union; secondly, that it grew from the Scottish humanist tradition reaching back to George Buchanan and beyond; and thirdly, that it developed more immediately from the Episcopal culture of Restoration Edinburgh. In recent years, the place of the Enlightenment in native tradition has emerged strongly.[7]

The mainstay of the Scottish Enlightenment's intellectual achievements can be said to rest on two premises: first, the application of reason to knowledge, and secondly the notion of progress, particularly social progress: 'the study of man as a social and a sociable being was a central interest of the philosophers of the Scottish Enlightenment'. The development of a civil society, and the notions of what makes society civilized, were key elements in its thought, as they were also by-products in the activities of improvement; these concerns were clear as early as Francis Hutcheson's inaugural lecture at Glasgow in 1730 on 'The Natural Sociability of Man'. In this context, the growing power of the so-called Moderate divines within the Church of Scotland was important, for this group, which included famous figures such as Principal William Robertson, believed in the centrality of social action to theological practice. Distrusting the enthusiasts of a former age, the Moderate party 'later came to support patronage', thus demonstrating its interest in the interweaving of secular society and religious purpose. At the same time, Adam Ferguson's *Essay on Civil Society* (1766), which has been taken as the foundation of sociology, displayed a concern with social development also found in David Hume's historiography and the implicit links between economic and social change evident in the work of Adam Smith.[8]

The application of reason to knowledge on a consistent basis could lead, as was the case with Hume's philosophy, to conflict with the Moderate party on religious grounds, but it often also complemented the idea of civil progress, since the notion of the application of reason spreading to more and more fields of human knowledge, observation and endeavour carried as its corollary the premise of social development, for a better understanding might be held to make a better society. The New Town of Edinburgh, the so-called 'heavenly city of the Enlightenment philosophers', expressed both key premises of Scottish Enlightenment thought, in manifesting the environment of a better society in an architecture intended to express the application of rational principles to the parameters of urban existence.[9]

The thinkers of this era participated fully in the British horizons and drive to politeness offered in the mid-eighteenth century to Scots of their background and generation: yet the ultimate location for Enlightenment achievement is rather to be found in the native continuities of Scottish society, and the social interchange of a small world in cheek-by-jowl living conditions. The nature, as well as the theory, of the Scottish Enlightenment was social: in the words of Hugh Blair, 'what we call human reason, is not the effort or ability of one, so much as it is the result of the reason of many, arising from lights mutually communicated'. Though it inherited many of the professional and intellectual structures developed in Scotland under the rule of the later Stuarts, the Scottish Enlightenment also (as Jonathan Clark has recently argued in a wider, British, context) superseded the patriotic Scoto-Latinist culture of an earlier generation of antiquarians, philosophers and classicists. This culture, based on the east coast and especially in the north-east of Scotland, was, in its emphasis on Scottish national difference, and the use of 'the Scots language as a means of asserting Scotland's identity' an unsuitable vehicle for the new role of Scotland outlined by Enlightenment, which drew on domestic intellectual strengths to express British and non-particularist paradigms. This symbolic shift between the old and the new can be conveniently (at least from the vantage of cultural hindsight) located at the point where David Hume succeeded the north-eastern Jacobite Thomas Ruddiman as 'Keeper of the Advocates' Library'.[10]

If historiography has, under the guise of emphasizing the British and international Enlightenment dimension, on occasion underestimated the distinctive features of the Scottish Enlightenment, it is of course still the case that England had its own powerful if more disparate tradition, represented by figures such as Newton and Gibbon, each in his *métier* more distinguished than his Scottish equivalent. England, too, had its strongly social intellectual tradition, which found its expression largely through Nonconformist writing and action, such as William Tuke's foundation of 'The Retreat' at York. Quaker concern with prison conditions, mental illness and medical care all made decided contributions to the development of enlightened practice in late eighteenth- and early nineteenth-century England. The full impact of this influence in society was perhaps not felt until later in the period, because of the continuing disadvantages under which Dissenters, Quakers in particular, still laboured. As Anand Chitnis notes in an Enlightenment context, the exclusion of non-Anglicans from Oxford and Cambridge led to a considerable enrichment of university recruitment in Scotland: this was still discernible at the end of the nineteenth century. After 1789, such Dissenters were joined at the Scottish universities by scions of the English gentry who found the Grand Tour blocked to them by continental war.[11]

The English Enlightenment was far more variegated and diffuse than was the case in Scotland, unlike the antiquarian tradition, which had strong similarities to its Scoto-Latinist equivalent. From it sprang literary interests which were the counterpart of the Scottish interest in literature, and these were at least in part epitomized in the tradition's colossus, Samuel Johnson. But elsewhere the Anglican-dominated universities and the already class-ridden school system helped to prevent the rise of an intellectual movement as cohesive as that in Scotland, where local authority control of institutions such as Aberdeen Grammar School and Edinburgh University was already centuries old. Combined with local control of such major educational institutions, the provision of parish education for the better-off middle classes, attempted throughout the seventeenth century and enshrined in the 1696 Education Act of the Scottish Parliament, marked strong differences between educational culture in the two countries. The Enlightenment in Scotland was thus not only the flowering of a native legacy expressed in terms of British application and consolidation, it was also an expression (whether or not intentional) of national difference.[12]

The Scottish Enlightenment: Cultural Impact

Although the Enlightenment in Scotland had a fairly narrow urban intellectual base, its cultural effect was much more marked than this might suggest, not only in terms of its great contribution to the foundation of disciplines and the spread of ideas, but also in the more immediate realm of Scottish society. Its strongly social emphasis had a legacy through the Moderates to Kirk social action in the nineteenth century, while in the eighteenth, the development of new kinds of university curricula and the close links between Enlightenment thinkers and the central professions of Church and Law placed the ideas of intellectuals in the hands of the leaders of their society. The growth of printing-houses in Edinburgh (from six in 1763 to 16 in 1790), combined with educational projects such as the *Encyclopaedia Britannica* (1768), spread ideas to a wider audience, the farthest extent of which had been enumerated in Webster's first census of Scotland in 1757. Encounters with the ideas of urban intellectuals occurred well outside the leading centres of Glasgow and Edinburgh (where the first circulating library in Scotland had opened in 1728). In 1758, a public library was founded at Montrose, in 1768 one at Duns in Berwickshire, and another was set up in Leadhills in Lanarkshire. Artisans in these and other small towns read the books the leading figures of the day produced. At a higher social level, the generosity felt towards Edinburgh's plans for civic renewal can perhaps be seen in the Convention of Royal Burghs' 1752 decision to support the building of the New Town. In the longer term, the Scottish generalist and those caricatures of the nineteenth and twentieth centuries, the Scottish doctor and scientist, can be held to spring from the intellectual changes which permeated a significant part of Scottish society in the later eighteenth century. If 'the desire to learn how to write and speak English, as well to behave like a proper English gentleman' animated the Scottish middle class in the eighteenth century, the country was also energized by more native ideas.[13]

The broader influence of Scottish discoveries and new intellectual models on the natural and social sciences was also considerable. Although it was not until the late nineteenth century that many of the social science disciplines mapped out in the Enlightenment took root, the new spirit of intellectual endeavour made as strong a showing in Britain as did the more material aggrandizements of the Scot on the make identified by English propaganda in the 1760s and 1770s. The *Dictionary of National Biography* indicates that between 1685 and 1785, of the 2500 entries who attended a university, 1619 went to Oxford or Cambridge, but over 500 (343 at Edinburgh alone) attended Scottish universities, compared with 170 who received their higher education in Ireland. Given that England's population was five times Scotland's, but less than twice Ireland's, these are impressive figures: their specifically

Enlightenment characteristics are perhaps indicated in the fact that of 680 scientists, 126 attended Cambridge, 116 Oxford and 85 Edinburgh: again, a high score from a university in a country still regularly scorned as backward and indigent.[14]

The idea that scientific and social progress can be at odds (one familiar ever since) was also to be found in Scotland, by the early nineteenth century at the latest. Its most celebrated episode was perhaps the bodysnatching and murdering racket of William Burke and William Hare, which ended with the former being hanged in 1829: Hare turned King's Evidence. Robert Knox, the medical academic who, as keeper of the Anatomy Museum at Edinburgh from 1825, was the receiver of Burke and Hare's graverobbed and later murdered goods, symbolized the dark world of a science prepared to progress at all costs. This duality between socio-moral and technological concepts of progress was perhaps one of the key components in the quality of doubleness in Scottish life, character and fiction which has been remarked on by so many. If Knox was Dr Jekyll, Burke and Hare were Mr Hyde: the fear, as with *Frankenstein*, was that science would commit crimes in secret in order to prosper openly. Thus, arguably, a tension developed between the pure rationalism of the Enlightenment and the aims of its social science.[15]

The Idea of History

Enlightenment social thinking in Scotland took particular root in the shape of a historiography of progress, one which was also a historiography of accommodation with Britain. The historiographical developments of the Enlightenment did much to overshadow accounts of the construction of both British and Scottish history for two centuries, for

> The new philosophical historians, such as David Hume and William Robertson, saw history as the charting of human development through a number of stages, from barbarity to refinement.

This 'charting' borrowed much from the preconceptions of such writers about the nature of political development in their own century. As Marinell Ash and more recently Colin Kidd have demonstrated, the development of Scottish Whig historiography owed a great deal to the process of cultural embritishing after 1707. The pamphlet wars of the turn of the century had largely pitted patriotic Scottish history against the suzerainty claims of its Anglophile opponents in debates which were closely tied to historical precedent and still deeply interfused with the legendary or half-legendary matter of the Scottish and English foundation myths. As the century progressed, Scottish readings of history in a British context became more and more interlinked with English ideas of Germanic progress towards liberty, the Norman yoke and the overthrow of absolutism in 1688. By the 1790s, even Scottish radicals were appealing to notions of liberty claimed to be derived from King Alfred. Scottish Whig (and by this token overwhelmingly Presbyterian) historiography built itself up through growing identity with English models, and from this growing identity derived an increasing use of English examples. These were integrative developments, and were also well suited to the embarrassment (so strong a word is not unjust) with which at least some Presbyterian intellectuals viewed the dark night of the pre-Reformation Scottish state. As writing from this school occasionally makes clear, Scottish heroes such as Wallace and Bruce (not to mention the patriot bishops who aided them in the struggle for native independence) were weakened as role models by their religion and that of their society. Already used to regarding the Reformation as marking a clean break with a spiritually discreditable past, Scottish writers of this stamp probably had little trouble in regarding the Union as a similar watershed for good: the mental pattern which rejected vast swathes of the Scottish past was already formed. The cultural discontinuity of the Scottish Reformation (as opposed to its English counterpart) can be seen as central to the structural weakening of a continuing and unified sense of Scottish identity. Throughout the eighteenth century, this problem was intensified both by the drift towards English historical models and its counterpart, the increasing alienizing of pre-Union Scotland as a dark age by the Whig historical narrative. By the late eighteenth century, this process was so thoroughly accomplished that the very foundation of a Scottish Society of Antiquaries, when it was proposed in 1780, was challenged on the grounds that as we were cordially united to England not in government only, but in loyalty and affection and to a common Sovereign it was not, perhaps, altogether consistent with political union, to call the attention of the Scots to the ancient honours and constitution of their independent monarchy.

Such fears proved groundless. Scottish patriotism was not reignited in any significant way by such initiatives: rather they provided a basis only for 'outbursts of pedantic antiquarianism', with virtually no political content. Antiquarianism often lacked structure, and even when this was not the case, it was prone to portray the Scottish past as benighted and divided, or at best sterile: a 'canon of patriotic landmarks', fossilized into heritage. Indeed, when the heroism of the Scottish past proved unequivocal, it could be presented as a valiant but perhaps in the long term misguided attempt to resist progress, as well as itself being a sign of the Anglo-Germanism of Lowland Scots identity: Bruce and Wallace as 'mighty northern Englishmen', to quote one Scot of this persuasion. It has only been in this century that the very strong foundations of both the dismissive and antiquarian versions of the Scottish past laid down in the eighteenth century have been shaken, and on occasion undermined.[16]

The ethnic myth or at best half-truth of the Germanic origins of Lowland Scots was also developed in the eighteenth century. The strong Germanic emphasis in English readings of identity on the ineluctable march to freedom of the Saxon people was matched in eighteenth-century Scotland by an increasing emphasis on the idea (one which seriously misrepresented the facts of historical and linguistic development) that Lowland Scotland shared ethnicity and thus common purpose with Anglo-Saxon England. This view helped to alienize the Highlander as Celt: indeed, certain historical narratives, such as the account of the Jacobite Risings as affairs of the Celtic fringe, were at least in part generated by this construction of a Germanic identity among Lowland Scots who wished to distance their part of the country (and with it sometimes themselves) from suspicions of disloyalty and insurrection. At the same time, the exploits of Highland troops in the later eighteenth and early nineteenth centuries provided the seedcorn for a resuscitation of the Jacobite 'Patriot Highlander' motif in the guise of the adoption of tartan by Lowland Scots who would have despised it and its wearers 50 years earlier. This was an example of the antiquarian outbursts through which Scotland maintained a local identity within the framework of imperial purpose: like many of its kind, it was unstructured and historically flawed.[17]

It was not possible for Scottish Whig history to develop fully until its major adversary, the patriotic history of Episcopal (and occasionally Catholic) Scots writers had been consigned to defeat by the decline of Scoto-Latinate culture and the end of Jacobite aspirations. Although Episcopalian historians continued to write, the live controversy over the future of the Scottish nation which their views had expressed vanished with the hopes of the Stuarts. What such history did have to offer, though, was a much more comfortable encounter with Scotland's past than its Presbyterian equivalent (though that could use *very early* Scottish history, such as that of the Culdee church, for its purposes). As Colin Kidd notes, 'Jacobites were in fact better able to exploit the history of Scotland's imperial crown than Whigs'. But although the adversarial threat of Jacobitism kept 'whig historiography in a thriving condition', the final result of the struggle between rival histories was to be a breaking of 'the connections between the history of liberty and an ancient constitution', a cleavage which did not occur in English historiography, and perhaps more importantly as far as future national reawakening was concerned, in that of Ireland either. In the end, then, despite the preservation of a more native Whig tradition in the narratives of Presbyterian church history, the mission of the mainstream in eighteenth-century Scottish historiography was largely exemplified in 'the Scottish construction of Anglo-British identity', which viewed 'political union' as the means which 'had allowed Scotland to leap centuries of national historical development ... England represented modernity rather than a dominant core'. Scotland was, on this account, less a nation absorbed by a powerful neighbour than an 'area of backwardness fortunate enough to be undergoing assimilation and accelerated progress'. David Hume among others moved away from the history of Britain to the history of England as the central exemplar because 'the history of England is the history of liberty'. Thus England was placed at the unassailable centre of British history, and indeed sometimes acted as its sole narrative. It was not until the twentieth century that the conflation of England with Britain for ideological reasons connected to this central tenet began to subside. Hume appears to have endorsed this view despite challenging English Whig historiography in other areas, for 'North Britishness was a Scottish version of English whig identity, based on a commitment to English constitutional history': in other words, a Whig approach to historiography on the Scottish plane was fundamental for supporters of the Union.[18]

The idea of history as (Anglocentric) progress in this broad vein marched very well with the central concerns of rationalism and society which presided in the intellectual orbit of the Scottish Enlightenment. Thus it was that the Enlightenment era set the seal on the direction of Scots history, Lord Kames's *Essay upon British Antiquities* (1747) being a work which exemplified this general trend of accepting 'the idea of history as progress'. Despite native refinements such as 'Celtic Whiggism', the establishment of this history, in partnership with the assumption of English superiority, led towards an incorporation of Scottish experience under Anglocentric norms. It was Scottish writers who tacitly confirmed the English suzerainty arguments of the Union pamphlet wars in their implicit acceptance of the history of their larger sister-nation as a normative model for their own:

> It actually felt liberating to close the door on Scotland's dark and cobwebbed past: 'The Reformation was freedom, the Union was freedom, the Disruption was freedom, the death of Scottish history was freedom'. As her sons fell in with the onward march of history, Scotland moved out of it. She was locked for safekeeping in the kailyard.

Such was the crowning achievement of eighteenth-century Scottish Whig historiography. Ironically, in taking this course, such Scots echoed their arch-critic, John Wilkes, whose Whig history of English liberty was manifested in *The History of England from the Revolution to the Accession of the Brunswick Line* (1768). In Wilkes's view, England, like Rome, 'became the slaves of one family from generation to generation', but entered, like the Romans after Tarquin, 'the great aera of English liberty' after 'the flight of their last tyrant'. With the defeat of the 'one family' of the Stuarts, Scottish history prepared to enter on a road to freedom mapped out in the words of that family's bitterest critic. By the submerging of Scottish difference, the criticisms of Wilkes and others were at last stilled, in the joint venture of the British state.[19]

Exploring Empire

It was perhaps not until the full imperial flowering of the late nineteenth century that Empire and its images imposed themselves deeply on the cultures of Britain; but the speed of changing relationships with the colonies in the eighteenth century also had significant socio-cultural effects. In particular, the 1756–63 Seven Years' 'contest with France ... for world dominion' proved a turning-point. Together with the acquisition of vast tracts of land in Canada and India, the British state had to come to terms with the cultural pluralities which accompanied them: the recognition in the Quebec Act (1774) of French law and the Roman Catholic religion (on the principle that in Quebec it was the majority faith) was a bitter pill for xenophobic anti-Papists to swallow, while the place of Indian culture proved an arena of controversy at times hardly less fraught. Some statesmen, such as Edmund Burke (who himself came from a religiously plural background), were far-sighted in such matters. Writing of British India, he said:

My next enquiry ... is the quality and description of the inhabitants. This multitude of men does not consist of an abject and barbarous populace ... but a people for ages civilized and cultivated ... There have been (and still the skeletons remain) princes once of great dignity, authority, and opulence. There, are to be found the chiefs of tribes and nations. There is to be found an antient and venerable priesthood, the depository of their laws, learning, and history, the guides of the people whilst living, and their consolation in death; a nobility of antiquity and renown; a multitude of cities, not exceeded in population and trade by those of the first class in Europe ... our entrance into the dominion of that country was ... by various frauds and delusions ... Our conquest there, after twenty years, is as crude as it was the first day ... Were we to be driven out of India ... nothing would remain, to tell that it had been possessed, during the inglorious period of our dominion, by any thing better than the ouran-outang or the tiger.

Such impressive multiculturalism (though perhaps influential in the nineteenth-century debate on the subject-matter appropriate to Indian education) was not common, and the military games played out in India showed it too clearly to be becoming the instrument of the major European powers' historic quarrels. At Wandiwash on 22 January 1760, one of the last acts in the Jacobite legacy was played out when Count Lally's Irish-French force (there were also still many Scottish troops in the service of France, and these continued to be recruited up to 1789) was defeated by the British: but if the result of the Seven Years' War was beneficial to Britain in India, this was not so clearly so in North America, where the defeat of the French threat developed the conditions necessary for American secession. Irritated as the colonists were by the Stamp and Declaratory Acts, it was the removal of French power in North America which abrogated the need for British protection and in the end British involvement in the affairs of what became the United States.[20]

The American war was severely disruptive to Britain and British power, which was already having to deal with extensive changes triggered by imperial expansion. In 1773, the Regulatory Act 'first brought India under the government of the crown': the 'first governor-general', Warren Hastings, was later to become a *cause célèbre* owing to his pursuit by Burke. British society had not fully come to terms with the differing mores and differing financial conditions of British India, though these had been having an impact for some fifteen years. In the 1761 election, nabobs (those newly enriched in India) 'greatly inflated the price of seats ... the borough of Sudbury openly advertised itself for sale'. Burke described the situation thus:

The natives scarcely know what it is to see the grey head of an Englishman. Young men (boys almost) govern there, without society, and without sympathy for the natives. They have no more social habits with the people, than if they still resided in England; nor indeed any species of intercourse but that which is necessary to make a sudden fortune, with a view to a remote settlement. Animated with all the avarice of age, and all the impetuosity of youth, they roll in one after another; wave after wave; and there is nothing before the eyes of the natives but an endless, hopeless prospect of new flights of birds of prey and passage, with appetites continually renewing for a food that is continually wasting. Every rupee of profit made by an Englishman is lost for ever to India.

Here one can hear Burke's subtextual references to the condition and treatment of Ireland, a sympathy which, together with those he held for the Catholics, lost him his seat at Bristol in the 1780 election, the year of the Gordon Riots. Further civil rights for Catholics could not be long delayed after the permitted establishment of a Roman Catholic hierarchy in Canada by the Quebec Act, but the measures for relief brought forward in England and Scotland in 1778 and 1779 led to a major backlash, the ugliest manifestation of which was the Gordon Riots. 'Lord George Gordon and the Protestant petition' led to savage mob rioting in London, with many deaths. It was the last major outburst of militant anti-Catholicism: in the struggle for emancipation which followed, Protestant protesters on the British mainland restricted themselves to petitions.[21]

The removal of certain disabilities in Britain went hand-in-hand with an easing of the situation in Ireland, where colonial trade was thrown open in 1779. But this took place in an atmosphere of increasing nationalism, with Grattan's demand for the repeal of Poyning's Act (whereby the Irish Parliament could not amend legislation) and a push towards complete legislative independence:

> The granting of free trade in 1779 and legislative independence in 1782–3 represented British retreats in the face of Irish demands for greater autonomy, and it could be argued that this process began in 1759. It was only after the suppression of the 1798 Rebellion, and the emergence of growing Protestant disenchantment with the concept of Irish separation, that the British government was able to regain the lost ground and abolish the Irish parliament by an act of union in 1800.

In the meantime, such circumstances further destabilized the British polity at the critical juncture of the American war: after the French Revolution, they assumed dangerous proportions.[22]

Incoming wealth from the nabob class of colonial businessmen continued to push up the price of land and further undermine the position of the small squire. The supply of land was finite (despite gains through drainage and other improvement), and the increasing number of those wishing to convert movable imperial wealth into heritable British property was a major factor in keeping demand buoyant. Of the major economists of the day, both Sir James Steuart (a Jacobite) in *Principles of Money Applied to the state of the Coin in Bengal* (1772) and Adam Smith in *The Wealth of Nations* (1776) attempted to deal with some of the questions raised by a growing Empire.[23]

Imperial development also brought certain moral questions to the fore – usually those connected with the multicultural nature of colonial expansion. In Canada, European settlers gained extensive civil rights; in India, there were some who argued for a recognition of the subcontinent's cultural status; the black African was yet less fortunate. In 1710, there were 46 vessels engaged in the slave trade at London, Bristol and Liverpool. Rising more than it fell on an irregular basis throughout the century, by the 1770s this figure had reached 161. Opposition to slavery was nonetheless growing. As Adam Smith stated:

> The experience of all ages and nations demonstrates that the work done by slaves, though it appears to cost only their maintenance, is in the end dearest of all.

The Scottish lawyer Lord Mansfield's 1771 judgement 'freed every slave in Britain', though it was many years before the trade itself came to an end. In this context, it is interesting to note that the supporters of Catholic emancipation in the late eighteenth and early nineteenth century used images intended to collocate the plight of black and Catholic alike in the public conscience, the state of the Catholics being visually depicted as enslavement. Indeed, the rights of Catholics *to* property and the right of blacks *not to be* property were thematically linked restitutions of participation in a society committed to property as a measure of political voice. Both at home and abroad, property was becoming increasingly linked to improvement, and given the adverse characterization of Highlanders popular in England and indeed throughout Britain, it would be possible to parallel the East India Company's actions in Bengal in the 1790s, which supported 'improvement and industry on the western model', with contemporary developments at home, including perhaps the Highland Clearances.[24]

Imperial development naturally had its price. The Seven Years' War, as well as being ferociously expensive, was only the latest in a series of conflicts by which Britain was wresting the leadership of the world from the grasp of France: 'for more than half of the years between 1689 and Waterloo … Britain was at war' (the 1756–63 conflict being the first since the Revolution which offered real opportunities to British Catholic soldiers). It was the National Debt which made such prolonged warfare possible, but at a price that many contemporaries felt Britain could not afford. The bare figures themselves suggest the scale of financial prestidigitation which was necessary:

> Borrowing financed 31 per cent of spending in the War of Spanish Succession (1702–13) and over 40 per cent of that in the American War (1776–83). In more than half the years between 1713 and 1785 debt service took up more than 40 per cent of total revenue. At the end of the American war it even reached 66 per cent.

In the context of such colossal levels of debt (though never more than 20 per cent of it was unfunded), there were equally colossal levels of military expenditure. In the War of the Austrian Succession (1739–48), the Seven Years' War and the American war, military expenditure 'was between 60 and 75 per cent of total expenditure'. By 1793, the National Debt stood at £243 million: a gigantic sum, almost £20 000 million in today's money and a great deal more in the context of national productivity at the time. Small wonder that doomsayers among the radicals predicted (as in fact had been predicted throughout the eighteenth century) national bankruptcy.[25]

Just as government borrowing and heavy reliance on indirect taxation were funding the battle for imperial expansion, so the heavy expenditure of private individuals on travel represented another kind of development, one to be linked to Empire through the cult of orientalism and the colonizing qualities of early archaeology. Tourism did not have its birth in the eighteenth century, but it expanded appreciably then, despite the fact that its costs were high owing to the bespoke nature of travel in an age without mass transit systems. Its resultant high cultural character, iconized in the Grand Tour, conferred on it a kudos which it still retains, despite its now being cheaper to spend a fortnight in Italy than in Ireland. Travel also formed part of high cultural representation of its own identity, both in practices such as the collection of artifacts, and in the new genre of travel writing, as well as in the custom of having one's picture painted abroad. Representations of both peaceful tourism and imperial expansion were important in defining the range of possibilities to which those with the money and background for broad horizons should aspire. The travel writer, orientalist or tourist might not be iconized in Roman form as a member of a 'British officer-class defying the world', in that series of paintings which began with Benjamin West's *The Death of Wolfe* (1771), but he nevertheless appropriated, through artifact, image or writing, the countries through which he passed. In addition, just as imperial arms were in the process of subduing the world, so the touring eye engaged in a more subtle form of colonization, as foreign nations coalesced into stereotype beneath its gaze. The courtesies of France were held to hide French insincerity; Italy was a country in sad decline from its glorious forebears (the declining and falling Roman Empire), and was now on the verge of barbarism. Deep xenophobia infected both English art and culture more generally, though arguably the most severe xenophobia of that century was reserved for the Scots and Irish.[26]

As with the reifications of an earlier stage of imperial expansion and trade in Pope's *Rape of the Lock*, material culture played a key role. This was to be the case right into the twentieth century, with its manifold productions of kitsch. But it was markedly so in the eighteenth, before Romanticism (and, to an extent, Primitivism) revalued the aspirational status of the countryside. The Grand Tourist travelled between cities, and the products of cities were material ones: therefore the culture which was experienced abroad was experienced, collected and communicated in material terms. The collecting of paintings, antiquities, coins and the objects of classical or oriental civilization developed as leisurely pursuits. In the Victorian period, the cultural anxiety produced by Darwinism and the *fin de siècle* led to fear of the Empire as evidenced through such collected objects (such as can be seen in the collectors of the Holmes stories, who are usually villains, or in the orientalist fears of Bram Stoker's *Jewel of Seven Stars* or Rider Haggard's *She*). In the eighteenth century, this process was still on a journey towards the apogee of its triumph and self-confidence. That journey was, as Jeremy Black has pointed out, bonded to an appreciation of the past: and as the social and industrial changes of the later eighteenth century grew more manifest, so did interest in one particular past – that characterized by Primitivism. The return to oral culture and primary epic in the work of James Macpherson, Thomas Gray and Percy among others, was one which took refuge in a cultural form which for at least a century had been becoming disassociated from the worlds of literature or administration, and was now coming under threat 'not from the revolutions in literature alone, but also those of society itself'.[27]

NOTES

1. H. T. Dickinson, *The Politics of the People in Eighteenth-Century Britain* (Basingstoke, 1995), p. 5; John Cannon, *Samuel Johnson and the Politics of Hanoverian England* (Oxford, 1994), p. 26; Bruce Lenman, *Integration, Industrialisation and Enlightenment: Scotland 1746–1832* (London, 1981), pp. 30, 40, 43; cf. Murray G. H. Pittock, *The Myth of the Jacobite Clans* (Edinburgh, 1995), Introduction and chapter 1.

2. Rosalind Marshall, *Virgins and Viragos* (London, 1983), pp. 102, 196, 315.

3. Nicholas Canny, 'The Formation of the Irish Mind: Religion, Politics and Gaelic Irish Literature, 1580–1750', in C. H. E. Philpin (ed.), *Nationalism and Popular Protest in Ireland* (Cambridge, 1987), pp. 50–79 (51); Sean Murphy, 'The Dublin Anti-Union Riot of 3 December 1759', in Gerard O'Brien (ed.), *Parliament, Politics and People* (Dublin, 1989), pp. 49–68.

4. Cf. Edward Said's *Culture and Imperialism* (London, 1993) for a colonial reading of Ireland.

5. E. D. Evans, *A History of Wales 1600–1815* (Cardiff, 1976), pp. 60–1, 71; Geraint Jenkins, *The Foundations of Modern Wales: Wales 1642–1780* (Oxford, 1987), pp. 219–20, 223.

6. In this context, the central argument of Linda Colley's *Britons* (New Haven, CT, 1992) becomes increasingly accurate after 1760.

7. Cf. for example David Allan, *Virtue, Learning and the Scottish Enlightenment* (Edinburgh, 1993).

8. Anand Chitnis, *The Scottish Enlightenment: A Social History* (London, 1976), p. 94.

9. Cf. Chitnis (1976), pp. 66–70.

10. Hugh Blair, cited in Thomas G. Addington, 'A Rhetorical Study of Student Notes of Lectures on Composition', in partial fulfilment for the

requirements of a Ph.D at Penn State (Ann Arbor, MI, 1989); Jonathan Clark, *Samuel Johnson* (Cambridge, 1994); David Daiches, *The Scottish Enlightenment* (Edinburgh, 1986), pp. 18, 19.

11.   Chitnis (1976), p. 134.

12.   Chitnis (1976), p. 12.

13.   Chitnis (1976), pp. 58–79; Peter Jones, 'The Polite Academy and the Presbyterians, 1720–1770', in John Dwyer, Roger Mason and Alexander Murdoch (eds.), *New Perspectives on the Politics and Culture of Early Modern Scotland* (Edinburgh, n.d. [c. 1983]), pp. 156–78 (158); Thomas P. Miller, 'C18 Scottish Rhetoric in its Socio-Cultural Context', unpublished thesis in partial requirement for the degree of Ph.D. (Austin, TX, 1984), p. 26; Michael Lynch, *Scotland: A New History* (London, 1991).

14.   Miller (1984), p. 112.

15.   The importance both of science *and* doubleness of identity in Scottish fiction such as James Hogg's *Confessions of a Justified Sinner* or R. L. Stevenson's *Dr Jekyll and Mr Hyde* should perhaps be emphasized in this context.

16.   Lynch (1991), p. 343; Colin Kidd, *Subverting Scotland's Past* (Cambridge, 1993); idem, 'The canon of patriotic landmarks in Scottish history', *Scotlands* (1994), 1–17; Marinell Ash, *The Strange Death of Scottish History* (Edinburgh, 1980), p. 34; Mitchison in Hepburn, p. 95; John Davidson, cited in Pittock (1995), p. 26.

17.   Cf. Pittock (1995), ch. 1.

18.   Kidd (1993), pp. 74, 78, 125–7, 128, 208, 210, 214.

19.   Ash (1980), p. 22, 148–50; Michael Fry, 'The Whig Interpretation of Scottish History' in Ian Donnachie and Christopher Whatley (eds.), *The Manufacture of Scottish History* (Edinburgh, 1992), pp. 72–89 (83); John Wilkes, *The History of England from the Revolution to the Accession of the Brunswick Line*, Volume I (London, 1768), pp. 5, 37, 38.

20.   *Cassell's History of the British People*, V, 7 vols., (London, 1923), pp. 1648, 1652, 1678–9, 1682–3, 1693; Conor Cruise O'Brien, *The Great Melody* (London, 1992), p. 322.

21.   Cassell (1923), pp. 1663, 1728n.

22.   Sean Murphy in O'Brien (1989), pp. 50, 68; Cassell (1923), p. 1736; O'Brien (1992), pp. 323–4.

23.   Cassell (1923), pp. 1749, 1751; Lenman (1981), p. 85.

24.   John Rule, *The Vital Century: England's Developing Economy 1714–1815* (London, 1992), p. 268; Lenman (1981), pp. 89, 93; Paul Langford, *Public Life and the Propertied Englishman* (Oxford, 1991), pp. 8, 34.

25.   Colley (1992), p. 326; Rule (1992), pp. 276, 277, 279.

26.   Cf. Jeremy Black, *The Grand Tour* (Oxford, 1992); Colley (1992), p. 179.

27.   The quotation is from the 1802 Preface to Wordsworth's *Lyrical Ballads*.

5 Orc and the Primitives

Primitivism: the Case of James Macpherson

Broadly speaking, Primitivism was a high cultural construction of positive response to an orally based folk culture which was beginning to suffer large-scale attrition through improved communications, migration to cities, clearances and war. It provided a cultural counterweight to the modernization and rationalization of society represented by Enlightenment, permitting an apparently live connection to the past from those who espoused in their daily round the ideas of the present. Primitivist writers and commentators turned their attention to margins and peripheries in the British Isles at the same time as the dominant culture of Britain was becoming more and more insistently metropolitan. The strong impulse towards the regionalization of literature in the nineteenth and twentieth centuries (as Seamus Heaney said in 1986, 'We are all regionalists now') can be held to derive from the marriage of Primitivist and Romantic agendas which glorified both the isolated individual and the marginal culture, the former being often seen to greatest advantage in the latter: Wordsworth was a prime exemplar of this pattern. Slightly earlier than this, works such as Goldsmith's 'Deserted Village' displayed anxiety over clearance and enclosure from the point of view of the social margin, while Thomas Gray's 'The Bard' praised the Welsh periphery. The growing practice of ballad-collecting, the preservation of oral literature in textualized form, attempted to save before it was too late a culture under threat from mobility and literacy. No one is more central to the first phase of this movement than James Macpherson.[1]

James Macpherson (1736/8–96) was brought up in Ruthven in Badenoch, 'deeply rooted in two kinds of Jacobite society'. As a boy, he saw both General Cope's advance against Charles Edward's army, and Major-General Gordon's attack on Ruthven

Barracks. At the end of the Rising, Macpherson may have joined his cousin in 'hurling stones at the troops who were setting fire to the Chief's house'. Later, as a student at King's College, Aberdeen, he came into contact with the Episcopalian culture of Scoto-Latinism in one of its last redoubts. His early poetry, such as 'On the Death of Marshal Keith' (1758) and 'The Hunter', shows a strong undertow of Jacobite feeling, but it was with the publication of *Fragments of Ancient Poetry Collected in the Highlands of Scotland* (1760), and still more with *Fingal* (1761) and *Temora* (1763), that Macpherson's career took off. In these poems, partly reconstructed from Gaelic orally transmitted originals, partly composed of bridging passages and all veneered with a lugubrious nostalgia for a vanished era, Macpherson purported to present to the world a primary epic, brought to birth no doubt in defence of the culture of the supposed 'savages' of the 'Forty-five, which indicated to a European-wide readership the true cultural status of the Homeric and mysterious Highlands.[2]

'Ossian', as the putative bard of these poems was known, was the son of Fionn MacCumhal, a central figure in Hiberno-Scottish mythology, and the resuscitation of Celtic mythic exploits with which the poems deal had an instant and massive effect on western European culture. To the state-of-the-art qualities in English society recognized in continental Anglomania could now be added nostalgia for a Scottish society of transcendently heroic primitivism. By 1763, the Ossian poetry had been translated into Italian, by 1764 into German; and in 1774 *Temora* appeared in French, 'translated by the Marquis de Saint-Simon'. What many English figures (including, famously, Samuel Johnson) 'resented as a piece of Scotch impertinence' had great appeal beyond Britain (though not in Ireland for a number of reasons, one of which may have been Macpherson's relocating the myths to Scotland). Influential on Madame de Staël and later Mendelssohn (cf. *Fingal's Cave*), Goethe was one of Ossian's chief protagonists in literature, as Napoleon was to be in the life of action:

It [Ossian] struck the most resounding note in European literature of the eighteenth century, and laid its spell on the greatest man of action and the greatest man of thought, Napoleon and Goethe.[3]

In England, despite the presence of many doubters, Macpherson's epic 'seems to have prompted Thomas Percy ... to publish the contents of a seventeenth century manuscript of English ballads he had acquired ... as the well-known *Reliques of Ancient English Poetry* in 1765'. In turn, Percy had been in correspondence with the Reverend Evan Evans, who as early as 1758 had been collecting Welsh poetry (which appeared in 1764 as *Specimens of the Poetry of the Ancient Welsh Bards*), while Charlotte Brooke's *Reliques of Irish Poetry* (1769), 'acknowledges its debt to Percy in its title'. Macpherson's work therefore stood at the determining point of a nexus of work devoted to rediscovering and rehabilitating the literature of a fading orality, especially when it bore a Celtic tinge. Oral tales and ballads, however, lacked the high cultural clout of the epic, to which Macpherson thus skilfully conformed them, with the result that his version of Primitivism reigned supreme in a Europe which was displaying anxiety 'that luxury and over-improvement were destroying essential human virtues'. Jefferson, Schubert, Brahms and Oscar I of Sweden all bear witness to the powerful appeal of Ossianic epic across frontiers, reflected in Napoleon's setting up of an Académie Celtique in Paris in 1807.[4]

Macpherson naturally gained wealth and power from his fame (or indeed notoriety). From his position as a poor parochial schoolmaster in Badenoch at the end of the 1750s, he rose to be a Highland laird and agent to the Nabob of Arcot: he was elected MP for Camelford in 1780. On the face of it, his career was based on a factitious presentation of Scottishness designed to gain him reputation and success, which, despite its undertones, was depoliticized enough to cause little trouble. But this would be at best a partial reading. Unlike Chatterton, with whom it is tempting to compare him, Macpherson was not a literary forger, but a writer who, like Burns, dressed up traditional and oral culture to their best advantage in order to forge (and not in the sense usually attributed to Macpherson) a tradition anew. Moreover, Macpherson had, at least obliquely, a political point to make. Both the early poetry and the 'Ossian' writings characterize the past in terms of Scottish heroism and independence: indeed, it has been argued that episodes from the recent Jacobite wars appear thinly disguised in the pages of Macpherson's epic. The longstanding scepticism concerning the 'authenticity' of his achievement has to some extent been fuelled by the cultural nationalism of his enterprise, which, while it detached the Scottish past from the present by locating it in the historyless zone of epic heritage, also promoted it as superior and heroic. In his own life as a Highland laird, Macpherson also displayed a strong inclination towards traditional values, being a benevolent and greatly loved landlord in an era when land use was on the brink of changing radically through the Clearances. Macpherson was instrumental in restoring the chief, Cluny's, estate to its historic owner in 1784, and was also reputed to have warned his tenants against the coming of a new generation of landlords who would abrogate their customary rights:

> a countryman of his, recalling his day a century later, wrote of 'poor kind James, of unhappy connections' warning his tenants and dependants on the Balavil estate with uncanny foreboding of the changes attendant on a new race of proprietors: *Mo thruaighe sibh dar thig an Sassunach* ('woe unto you for when the stranger comes'). A Gaelic elegy composed at the time of his death described how Macpherson brought prosperity and well-being to his people, and amongst his many virtues praised him as *ciobar a chinne*, 'shepherd of the clan'.

Macpherson, a complex man, was thus the defender of the traditions he exploited: though it might be claimed that he exploited them only to defend them. There was something 'destabilizing about his work and its claims' which fed into and to an extent denominated the cultural and political agenda of Primitivism as a whole: 'a passionate lament for the passing of an ancient civilization'.[5]

The Politics of Primitivism

Primitivism clearly displayed an interest in the past, albeit a frequently dehistoricized past: it was thus prey to that infection of all moral and social praise of vanished time, nostalgia. In this guise, Primitivism was boosted by the cult of sentiment: for Primitivist politics were often more concerned with feeling and emotion towards what was disappearing than they were concerned with any effort to retain it. A sentimental attitude, particularly a sentimental attitude towards the past, was one of the luxuries permitted by Enlightenment and improvement. As the countryside was altered and the mentalities of Europe shifted, while its empires consolidated or grew, it was increasingly easy to indulge a longing for an unreturning past which posed no threat. Such was, for example, to be the fate of Jacobitism in nineteenth- and twentieth-century Britain, celebrated in the reified charisma of kitsch. The collecting of ballads, like the collecting of artifacts, was a way of ordering an alien culture within the confines of one's own: and Primitivism grew in this ambience. By the late eighteenth century in Britain, there was little need for high culture to suppress disaffected folkways (at least until the 1790s), as it had so often tried to do in the previous 150 years. In similar vein, perhaps, a Europe that was once terrified of wolves presses for their preservation in our own day, and zoologists vie to proclaim the wolf's harmlessness, in the teeth of centuries of evidence. Affection for the wolf as some kind of primary fauna is the same phenomenon as that which 200 years ago kindled affection for a primary literature, long scorned and, when inconvenient, suppressed.[6]

Yet even at this stage it appears that the politics of certain kinds of oral culture were omitted, suppressed or edited out by collectors. Recent work on oral repertoires has suggested that middle-class figures from whom ballads were collected, such as Mrs Brown of Falkland, were more likely than 'authentic' representatives of demotic culture such as Agnes Lyle to bowdlerize and omit political or bawdy references. Agnes Lyle's repertoire, for example, frequently characterized the English monarchy as treacherous, alien and anti-Scottish in a way still politically sensitive in the west of Scotland in the radical period of the early nineteenth century.[7]

Most Primitivist representations of orality left out this aspect. Though Macpherson could skilfully conjoin a heritage-style presentation with a cultural nationalist undertone, other editors and collectors tended to deny even this power to the culture on which they drew. When James Hogg published his *Jacobite Relics* for the Highland Society of London in 1819–21, there was considerable criticism of their supposed barbarousness, even though Hogg had himself apparently gone to some lengths to water down the political significance of his material. Genteel society was criticizing the songs of a passionate political movement for not displaying the good-natured sentimental regret with which they now wanted to treat it. Primitivism of this kind sought to revitalize the past only in order to emphasize one particular dimension of the present. This was particularly useful in Lowland Scotland, which was, while pushing itself through Enlightenment ideas of civility and social progress towards the scale of London metropolitan value, equally desirous of maintaining a localized identity. This sense of difference was to be increasingly found in a conditional Highlandization of Lowland Scotland in militaristic and nostalgic terms. The Celtic heroism of Ossian's lays could be recaptured in the exploits of Scottish troops in the British Army, while images such as Alexander Runciman's *Hall of Ossian* (1772) lay 'stress upon the natural values of primitive, bardic poetry' in a context of self-congratulatory nostalgia:

> Runciman's ideas coincide, not only with those of James MacPherson, and of Hugh Blair ... but also very significantly with those of his friends among the pioneers of the vernacular revival in poetry and of the collectors of folk song, especially Robert Fergusson and David Herd.

In this dual dimension of military celebration and Primitivist antiquarianism, it was no surprise that the former triumphed. The Highand Clearances, in many respects the ultimate challenge to the way of life Primitivism celebrated, were unchallenged (and indeed conducted) by those who liked to celebrate the glorious past of Highland heroism. Those remaining in the Highlands were, like noble savages elsewhere, 'the indispensable atavistic natives in the Victorian triumph of peace and progress'. Macpherson's sophisticated ambivalence was rapidly overtaken by a more nerveless sentimentality: the journey from heroism to atavism took no more than 60 years.[8]

There were exceptions of course, among them men like Joseph Ritson, who maintained a combination of Jacobin and Jacobite political beliefs, while being an avid song-collector: his *Scottish Songs* (1794) confirms that, 'member of Godwin's circle' as he was, he had a strong commitment to both political views arising out of their opposition to tyranny. Of Robin Hood he wrote in 1795 that he was 'a man who, in a barbarous age, and under a complicated tyranny ... display'd a spirit of freedom and independence': in other words, Ritson, like Burns, was one of the few folklorists of his generation to read a political message from the struggles of the past forward into the present. Within a high cultural milieu, Ritson was something of a crank, but there is considerable evidence that within the continuing folk culture itself, political oppositionalism was a live issue, not only in the radicalism of such as Agnes Lyle in Scotland, but in the survival and nationalist metempsychosis of forms such as the Irish *aisling*.[9]

Nevertheless, times had altered. The Romantic and pre-Romantic interest in ballads brought them forward as vehicles of cultural or national identity, but not in a manner that could remotely threaten the ruling order in the sense Fletcher of Saltoun had once implied. Predominantly, that was not its purpose. In the case of Sir Walter Scott (whose *Minstrelsy of the Scottish Border* appeared in three volumes in 1802–3),

> when he died in 1832, the year of reform, his fictionalized version of Scots history based on unassimilated antiquarian interests and sentimentality for lost causes was already part of the cultural support for the violent reaction against radicalism.

Unfair to Scott's masterly conceptualizations as the above may be, it is accurate as to their influence. The politics of Primitivism, despite exceptions, found their major role in the nostalgic pageantry of Victorian popular historicism. In the colonially imagined world of the Highlands, the heroes of the Fianna (also known as Victorian sportsmen) could engage in the primitive hunt. History was on the journey to becoming a commodity, and the 'Celtic fringes' and some of the remoter parts of England (e.g. the Lake District) traded on their culture and landscape to enter the world of the imagined other as surely as did the Orient which British arms were conquering abroad. Wales and Ireland were partial exceptions to this process. In Wales, for example, the literary revival heralded at the beginning of the eighteenth century by Edward Lhuyd's *Archaeologica Britannica* (1707) was, although it contained antiquarian elements, also a means of creating a contemporary milieu for Welsh writing (and a patriotic one: Lhuyd himself stated that 'I don't profess to be an Englishman, but an old Briton').[10]

Revolution in Writing I

In the eighteenth century, writing was of course the major means
of reaching large audiences on the controversial issues of the day.
The faultlines in British politics after 1689 had not only produced
a swarm of pamphlets and broadsides: their presence had also
served to expand the newspaper industry. Although, in the age of
compositors and hand-made paper, books were usually only
printed in runs of around 1000 copies, some of the key texts of
eighteenth-century controversy sold far more than this (as indeed
did some other books, such as Bishop Sherlock's apocalyptic pastoral letter of 1750, which may have sold up to 105 000). The
American Revolution significantly revived the practice of controversy, itself largely dormant since the abatement of the Jacobite
threat. Sales of controversial works once again reached very high
levels: Thomas Paine's *Common Sense* (1775) sold 150 000 in the
American colonies, while in the aftermath of the French
Revolution the same author's *Rights of Man* (1791) may have sold
over 200 000 copies. The former book, which may have reached
between a quarter and two-fifths of the entire population of the
future United States, gave voice to what are still some of the
enduring political prejudices of American society, particularly its
distrust of big government, with Paine arguing that 'Society is produced by our wants and government by our wickedness'. *Rights of
Man* appealed to a rather different audience than that of the
partial democracy of the new United States, being read very
widely in working men's groups and societies: it was composed in
a deliberately plain style designed for a general readership among
the skilled workmen and artisanal/lower-middle classes (to which
Paine himself, originally a staymaker, belonged). In the aftermath
of the French Revolution, the book had a profound effect on the
thinking of radical groups, and some of Paine's ideas (for
example, on welfare benefits) entered the realm of political discourse on a much longer-term basis.[11]

   Edmund Burke's *Reflections on the Revolution in France* (1790), in
reply to which *Rights of Man* and many other books, including
Mackintosh's *Vindicae Gallicae*, were written, did not sell so well
(around 30 000): but then its target market ('the cause of the
gentlemen', as George III put it) was not nearly so big. Burke's
attack on the French Revolution has the merits of predicting the

Terror before it took place, and also (as Conor Cruise O'Brien argues) identifying in the French Revolution the likeness of a new totalizing kind of political change, more like the Communism that was to come than the relatively limited political nationalism of the American Revolution. The fact that many of Burke's contemporaries saw the French and American Revolutions in a similar light damaged his reputation for consistency, and he is by and large misrepresented to his posthumous readership as an unthinking reactionary, rather than one of the most progressive and alert minds of his day.[12]

Religion was still a powerful motivating force in the controversial writing of the period, and both Burke and Paine used it innovatively. Paine's benevolent Deism forms the unchallenged premiss upon which much of his superstructure of societal cooperation and goodwill rests. Burke was innovative in placing faith and religious conviction in its essence ahead of any particular forms, though without being a deist: his defence of the antiquity and seriousness of the Hindu religion is in this context even more remarkable than his defence of the French Church (and this at a time when some in Parliament sympathized with the early stages of the French Revolution on account of its perceived anti-Catholicism). Both these writers had thus, in their different ways, less of a party attitude to religion than their predecessors, to some extent no doubt on account of the ideas of the Enlightenment.[13]

John Cannon has recently argued for Samuel Johnson's status as an Enlightenment thinker, and in his political pamphlets too can be found examples of questions and attitudes which seem more our contemporaries than those of Sacheverell or the 'good old cause' Presbyterians. Although *Taxation no Tyranny* (1775) was written against the American cause, the dilemmas it raises, such as 'what is a nation?' and 'what places/cultures are entitled to national identity?' are very much with us still: Johnson in fact pursues the example of Cornish independence as a comparator to the American situation, an interesting and by no means ridiculous example in the light of today's (albeit limited) Cornish nationalism. *Taxation no Tyranny* also advances an argument which it shared with some of the Moderate divines in Scotland who through pulpit and print pointed out the hypocrisy of American claims for independence while that country was so infected by the institution of slavery: Johnson conjures up an image of a man calling for independence from tyranny while poised to flog a black slave as an emblem of the absurdity of American pretensions. The notions of nationality and liberty were both being challenged and defined.[14]

Domestic slavery was also a subject of the debate which grew out of the revolutionary era. After publishing her own *Rights of Man*, Mary Wollstonecraft, a determined feminist nourished in the Dissenting tradition, published *A Vindication of the Rights of Woman* (1793), a book which argued for parity of esteem and provision in female education, and was possibly the first to advance the nature/nurture argument in its assertion that no girl would play with a doll were there a 'better' toy to hand. Just as Mary Astell had effectively outlined the lineaments of a separatist feminist case at the beginning of the eighteenth century, so at its end Mary Wollstonecraft outlined the social case, which concentrates more on parity of esteem, education and socio-political rights. Although Wollstonecraft overtly favoured female education so that the newly indolent wives of the growing urban bourgeoisie could talk to their husbands on interesting subjects without boring them, the basis nonetheless exists in her argument for the entry of educated women to the professions and other occupations then barred to them.

It has been argued that Wollstonecraft was responding, not just to the climate of the French Revolution (in which she is an independent voice: for example, she lambasts Rousseau for his patronizing attitude towards women), but also to a social revolution nearer home, which, as it drew families into the cities, withdrew women from their partnership role in rural occupations into a new position of leisured segregation from male employment. In the context of this new group, *A Vindication of the Rights of Woman* can be read as a call to arms, directed at those sinking into an unaccustomed torpor brought about by social change, no longer able to participate in their husbands' employment, and too badly educated to provide cultural and intellectual diversion and development at home.

Wollstonecraft's attack on 'the *divine right* of husbands, like the divine right of kings' is an early identification of what today would be called patriarchy. In her own day, its borrowing of revolutionary rhetoric was an attempt on her part to partake of that 'stream of popular opinion that has carried all before it' in 'every age'.

This proved to be too optimistic: her search for a place for women in the radical bandwagon by and large fell on deaf ears (Paine was himself, after all, only in favour of universal *male* suffrage). Even among the feminist community, Wollstonecraft was a figure to be avoided for much of the nineteenth century: she was seen as an extremist, and her lifestyle as a threat to the family values they did not wish to be seen undermining. Nonetheless, she too was a prescient figure. Some of her ideas surface, thinly disguised, not only in the writing of George Eliot (Dorothea in *Middlemarch*), but, more surprisingly, in the novels of Wollstonecraft's close contemporary, Jane Austen, who appears on the surface to have a Burkean commitment to stable order, and displays an antipathy to French and perceivedly French values of insincerity and persiflage which must have gladdened the heart of many a reader in the age of the Napoleonic Wars. Yet although women never discuss politics in Austen's novels (Henry Tilney stops when he comes to the subject in Catherine Morland's company in *Northanger Abbey*), they nonetheless appear, not only in the idealized Tory landlordism of Darcy or Knightley, but also in the characterization of women. Catherine Morland herself presents to the world a new Wollstonecraftian heroine of action, freed of gender stereotyping, and a great contrast with the passive female victims of the Gothic novel which at the beginning of the story she so mistakenly admires:

> Her father was a clergyman ... and he was not in the least addicted to locking up his daughters ... Catherine ... was fond of all boys' plays, and greatly preferred cricket not merely to dolls, but to the more heroic enjoyments of infancy, nursing a dormouse, feeding a canary-bird, or watering a rose-bush ... She was moreover noisy and wild, hated confinement and cleanliness, and loved nothing so well in the world as rolling down the green slope at the back of the house.

Austen is moving the heroine away from her traditional employments towards (in however limited a sphere) an enterprise of sense, not merely tomboyism, but the beginning of something more: pluck and the ability to discriminate. At the same time, a semantic shift accompanies that of character: the traditional employments of the 'heroine' are ironized (as later in nineteenth-century literature when 'nursing a dormouse' reappears in *The Mill on the Floss* in Maggie Tulliver's defiance of her brother's expectation that she would remember to feed his rabbits). Nor is this the only sign of a link between Austen and Wollstonecraft: the latter's assertion of the stagnation and folly bred by the idleness of rich women being amply borne out in the characterization of Lady Bertram in *Mansfield Park* (the very title of which quite possibly reflects Lord Mansfield's anti-slavery judgement of 1771: Austen's family disliked slavery) and Mrs Bennet in *Pride and Prejudice.* These elements of contemporary feminism in Austen's writing have their own part to play in the disruptive irony which erupts through the social values she cherishes.[15]

William Godwin, Wollstonecraft's husband (she died in giving birth to their daughter, later Mary Shelley), was also an important radical writer, and influential on the young Wordsworth. Godwin was among the first to be a serious anarchist: he appeared to believe that wherever the rules of a society operated, the lineaments of social power would tend to engender corruption. His political views were expressed not only in his lengthy *Political Justice,* but also in a novel, *Caleb Williams,* which was written in the context of the radical trials of the early 1790s, in particular that of Joseph Gerrald of the London Corresponding Society, sentenced to fourteen years' transportation for sedition on 10 March 1794. In his novel, subtitled *Things as They Are,* Godwin uses the conventions of Gothic fiction in order to allegorize the secrecy of the state and the ultimately terrifying nature of what it conceals (tyrannical power and the old crimes of which it is guilty). The oppressive power of the squirearchy to manipulate law through reputation and the Justice of the Peace system is savagely attacked; even Squire Falkland, the Burkean beau ideal, has deliberately allowed a poor tenant farmer and his son to hang for a murder he himself committed, driven in his turn by the pride and rage attendant on his social niche and reputation. Godwin's Falkland is the dark side of Austen's Darcy: any power has too many temptations for even benevolence to use it well.

In a different form, but just as effectively as the Anglican establishment had once feared, the Dissenting conscience played a powerful role in undermining the state in the French Revolutionary period. Godwin had been a Dissenting minister; Wollstonecraft had kept a Dissenting school in the early 1780s,

and Paine's Deism was a more extreme form of the same movement. When in *Mansfield Park* Mary Crawford mocks Edmund
Bertram's desire to become a priest in the Church of England,
she is not mainly making an economic point (by 1837, the average
living was £500 p.a., and probably well clear of that for the sort of
living bestowed on a baronet's son): she represents the anticlericalism of revolutionary France (her persiflage is stressed),
and its friends among the Dissenters, deists and rationalists of
Britain.[16]

Revolution in Writing II

Such anticlericalism can also be found in the imaginative fantasy
of a writer such as William Blake, who in his pre- and post-
Revolutionary *Songs of Innocence* and *Songs of Experience* arraigns the
Church as an institution which sides with the political
establishment in the constraint of human potential:

> A little black thing among the snow:
> Crying weep, weep in notes of woe!
> Where are thy father & mother? say?
> They are both gone up to the church to pray.
>
> Because I was happy upon the heath
> And smil'd among the winters snow:
> They clothed me in the clothes of death
> And taught me to sing the notes of woe.
>
> And because I am happy & dance & sing
> They think they have done me no injury:
> And are gone to praise God & his Priest & King
> Who make up a heaven of our misery.

> 'The Chimney Sweeper' (*Songs of Experience*)

The 'black thing', here a chimney sweeper, elsewhere the child of
'the southern wild', who is 'black, but O! my soul is white', are
among those oppressed not only by slavery and the prospect of an
early demise (forced on them by secular authority), but also by

the inner corruption of the spirit, the 'mind-forg'd manacles' of the implanted conscience, which (and here Blake is close to Godwin) corrupts even attempts at social reform, where these fall short of the full liberation of the imagination represented by the revolutionary spirit, Orc. Blake's idea of the inward self-oppression created by tyrannical power structures is an early version of what a later revolutionary era might characterize as 'false consciousness'. Although hardly himself of a practical turn of mind, Blake's identification of the internalization of tyranny by its victims displayed understanding of a more sophisticated stamp than the rather facile revolutionism of Shelley's *The Mask of Anarchy*. In 'The Little Black Boy', Blake's boy looks forward to heaven, but only in terms of a continuing servitude to the white boy and 'white' consciousness: the black boy's hope is to 'be like him and he will then love me'. In 'The Chimney Sweeper' poem in *Songs of Innocence*, the child's misery is again relieved by a dream of paradise, the rule of entrance to which is the tyrannical premiss 'if all do their duty, they need not fear harm'. 'The Garden of Love' is filled with 'Priests in black gowns ... binding with briars, my joys & desires', while 'The Human Abstract' sums up social Christianity's correlative need for continuing injustice about which to be indignant:

> Pity would be no more,
> If we did not make somebody Poor:
> And Mercy no more could be,
> If all were as happy as we ...

In these songs, which bear a close affinity of form to eighteenth-century hymns, Blake undermines the social rigour and moral smugness which could be identified as being bound up with the form he uses: the hymn is recast. His Prophetic Books take the whole process further, though in a less accessible form. In them, the spirit of revolution, Orc, linked to both France and America (France 'reciev'd the Demons light' from the American Revolution), symbolizes the energies of Prometheus, puberty and political change alike:

> The shadowy daughter of Urthona stood before red Orc.
> When fourteen suns had faintly journeyed o'er his dark abode;

His food she brought in iron baskets, his drink in cups of iron;
Crown'd with a helmet & dark hair the nameless female stood;
A quiver with its burning staves, a bow like that of night,
When pestilence is shot from heaven; no other arms she need:
Invulnerable tho' naked, save where clouds roll round her
　　loins,
Their awful folds in the dark air; silent she stood as night;
For never from her iron tongue could voice or sound arise;
But dumb till that dread day when Orc assay'd his fierce
　　embrace.

America, Plate 16

In his combination of eerie visual and stridently symbolic political change, Blake transformed the sublimity of Ossian from the zone of nostalgia to that of revolution, in terms which would be of use to Yeats in an Irish nationalist context a century later. In keeping with the universalism of revolution however, Blake invokes pan-British involvement with little sign of the recognition of specific place or circumstances.[17]

Despite his opposition to slavery and trial for sedition (1803: the poet threw a dragoon out of his garden), Blake, like Wordsworth and Burns, had little practical effect on the developments of the Revolutionary period. Yet all of these writers in their different ways provided rhetorics of change: so much is made explicit by Wordsworth in his Preface to the *Lyrical Ballads* of 1802, where he speaks of the need to create a poetic language suitable not 'for the revolutions of literature alone, but also those of society itself'. Involved as a spectator and sympathizer in French revolutionary activity of the early 1790s, by the appearance of the first volume of *Lyrical Ballads* (1798), Wordsworth had developed a poetic rhetoric which combined an exaltation of the manners and customs of the provincial rural poor with nostalgia for vanishing folkways already substituting itself for his earlier desire for major political change. Wordsworth's combination of Romantic manifesto with the incipiently heritage quality of Primitivism, gave his poetry a 'bias to the poor' which evaded radical commitment. Although poems such as 'The Idiot Boy' defend disability as appropriate subject-matter for poetry, and though 'Michael' suggests that even the smallest smallholder feels as passionate about his land and inheritance as the greatest squirearch, such democratic sentiments are entirely compatible with a benign rural conservatism. Wordsworth's solitaries are several degrees down the social scale from Pope's Man of Ross, but they would have been comfortable with each other: Wordsworth's own family were of minor gentry status, and better off than Kyrle had been. The poetry of rural solitaries both developed the cult of the countryside, and enabled localized radicalism on single issues which affected a community, while having no bearing on core political change.[18]

Burns is the only major writer to deal with the national dimension of change in the 1790s. Radicalism was widespread throughout the British Isles, and many of its views were homogeneous wherever they were to be found; but there was an undoubted nationalist edge to revolutionary activity in Ireland, and to a lesser extent in Scotland. In Ireland, such unrest formed part of the dissolution of political authority which culminated in the 1798 rising, sponsored by Revolutionary France, though vitiated by divisions between the middle-class and relatively secular United Irishmen and the 'surging Catholic nationalism' of the Defenders, a division complicated by the emergence of the Orange Order on the Ulster scene in the mid-1790s. The United Irishmen were, however, very successful organizers (they had 'a genius for mass mobilization'), and drew on folk and popular culture, such as the ballads, to spread their views, as the Jacobites had done before them and the IRA were to do after them. It does not seem, however, that the use of the Irish language alone could any longer guarantee concealment: evidence exists that 'by the end of the eighteenth century some knowledge of Irish appears to have been common enough among the Protestant middle and upper classes'. In Scotland, where, despite widespread opposition to the American War of Independence, 'Scots emerged from the war in a mood to demand reform' though 'not their own revolution', radicalism had a nationalist tinge. Jacobin radical activity in Scotland included the singing of Jacobite songs, such as 'The Sow's Tail to Geordie', and radicals such as the 'violently Anglophobic' Thomas Muir (1765–99) tried to interest France in sponsoring 'an independent Scottish republic', apparently promising that such an attempt would meet with support from a general Highland rising! An address of 23 November 1792, probably influenced by Muir, clearly indicated the continuing presence of nationalism in Scotland:

> We rejoice that you do not consider yourselves as merged and melted down in another country, but that in tis [*sic*] great national question you are still – Scotland: the land where Buchanan wrote, and Fletcher spoke, and Wallace fought!

Indeed, links between Jacobin areas and those that had once been Jacobite were marked not only in Scotland, but in the industrial towns of South Wales and elsewhere. The national dimension was not, however, present in Wales, though after the French invasion of Pembrokeshire in 1797 damped down Revolutionary sympathies, the Romantic rehabilitation of Owain Glyndwr remained as an oblique testimony to Welsh national feeling. Scots besides Muir on the other hand 'were ... unequivocally in favour of the recovery of Scottish national sovereignty', while Scotland's representation in the British Parliament was mocked by James Thomson Callendar in words which anticipate some of the more conspiratorial language of twentieth-century nationalism. Having 'claimed that Scottish MPs behaved ... as the servile tools of English misgovernment', Callendar went on to say that

> It is true, that we have very near a twelfth part of the British House of Commons; but our representatives have no title to vote, or act in a separate body.

In 1796, the emissary of the French Committee of Public Safety to Scotland reported 'that the Scots were much disposed to revolution and that "This feeling had existed since the Union of England and Scotland"'. Contacts between the United Irishmen, the Defenders (who were active in the west of Scotland) and Scottish revolutionaries also stressed the national dimension, though by no means always in purely nationalist terms. It remains true, however, that the problems caused by Union and a lack of representation for Scottish interests ('the day which set upon your independence, and blotted your name from among the nations of the earth') were part of the United Scotsmen's critique of what would nowadays be called the democratic deficit between Scotland and England.[19]

While such views were in a minority (though strong enough to persuade the French in 1798 to plan for separate republics in England, Scotland and Ireland – as indeed they had been prepared to do fifty years before), there was clearly a surviving strain of anti-Union feeling in Scotland. This later became manifest both in the rhetoric surrounding the 1843 Disruption and the subsequent development of the National Society for the Vindication of Scottish Rights, and also in the 1820 general strike and radical insurrection, elements of which used the slogan 'Scotland Free or a Desert', still found in nationalist graffiti today. This year of 1820 was also the last known occasion on which the Fiery Cross or Crostarie, ancient emblem of clan militarism, was used in Scotland. It was an expression of serious radical discontent which gained serious support in the west of the country:

> on 2 April [1820], manifestos posted throughout the west called for a strike the next day in support of the formation of a Provisional Government ... The breadth of support ... is indicated by the 60 000 who obeyed the strike call. Glasgow, Paisley and other centres were immobilised, as weavers, factory workers, miners and other workmen took part.

Though only a tiny minority of these rose in arms, the Insurrection of 1820 was still arguably the most serious radical challenge faced by the government in mainland Britain.[20]

Burns's politics, though of themselves complex and quite possibly inconsistent, developed a poetic rhetoric which melded Jacobin, Jacobite and nationalist elements. His concept of 'Liberty' (as in 'Bruce's Address to his Army before Bannockburn' and 'the Tree of Liberty') can be seen as a jacobinized version of the concept of 'fredome' in Barbour's epic poem, the *Bruce* (that the War of Independence was still very important in Scottish popular culture in the eighteenth century is borne out not only by earlier patriotic publishing, but also in John Brim's verdict that 'Blind Hary's *Wallace* ... was ... the favourite book of "the vulgar" in late eighteenth-century Scotland'). Burns's practice of collecting and altering folk songs was one which operated more closely to the sources whence he drew than was the case with Wordsworth: the Scottish poet's work is largely free of the intellectual tourism characteristic of Primitivism. In 'A Man's a Man for a That', which has been called 'The Marseillaise of Equality', embodying 'even the very words of Paine', Burns creates a universal radical manifesto out of the unique qualities of Scottish history's struggle for liberty against a larger neighbour, not only through the linguistic tensions of the poem, but also by rooting it in the famous Jacobite song 'Tho Georthie reigns in Jamie's stead'. Likewise, Scottish 'common sense' philosophy is transmuted into Burns's vision of a time when 'Sense and Worth, o'er a the earth/Shall bear the gree, and a that'. Elements of high culture are melded with the Scottish folk tradition to provide a vision of national identity at once proletarian and universal: a vision which endures to this day.[21]

In 'The Tree of Liberty' (probably by the poet), Burns seems to be offering a warning to his fellow Scots that England is not ready for universal revolution: the Tree of Liberty cannot be found ''twixt London and the Tweed'. A phrase from this poem, 'common cause' ('Like brethren in a common cause/We'd on each other smile, man') continues in rhetorical use as the name adopted by one of the contemporary groups pressing for Scottish Home Rule. The poet would no doubt have welcomed this, for it is characteristic of his *oeuvre*

> that the perpetual struggle of Scottish history is the same whenever it takes place: history has modality, but liberty does not. The language speaks beyond situation to the essential struggle for freedom and national resistance, which, in the light of developments in Scotland's ancient ally, is in the process of acquiring universal meaning through space as well as across time.

Burns's achievement in releasing a political language of universal claims out of the particularities of the Scottish folk tradition has provided his poetic rhetoric with a more lasting political appeal than any of the other Romantics. 'Bruce's Address' is the national anthem of Scotland recognized by the Scottish National Party, while 'A Man's a Man' has widespread radical connotations: Burns's high degree of popularity in the Soviet Union testified to the success of his universalism. By an ironic contrast, Blake's well-known 'Jerusalem' has become an unofficial anthem in the Conservative Party.[22]

One Nation?

'Nations do not grow like a tree, they are manufactured,' observes Gwyn A. Williams in *When Was Wales?*, thus summing up the contemporary habit of seeking to construct an identity, rather than accepting a traditional and less variable organicism. Is the nation then – was Britain in 1789 – an 'imagined community' in Benedict Anderson's phrase, or an organic one, as Burke was to proclaim it the very next year?[23]

In some ways the difference between these two positions (which is admittedly sometimes one of emphasis, rather than absolute distinction) can be seen as crucial: the organicists should reject separatist irredentism before it tears up a community they regard as partaking of the sacred quality of life, while those who see identity as a construct should at least in theory be just as ready to deconstruct it. Many of today's nationalist tensions in the UK and elsewhere derive from the partial supersession of an organic notion of identity by a constructive one: in Scotland, for example, there is much talk of making a new polity, but the rhetoric of this is not on the whole of one with deep roots in the Scottish past, or at least few much older than 1960s corporate welfarism. The organicist position is the more traditional one, and the one adopted in the self-definition of major states: by British Unionism, in the American Civil War, in Canadian belief in the integral status of Quebec and in many other cases. It tends still to be the view of those defending power, because organicist readings of identity (as Burke saw) entrench existing structures of authority through a historical hallowing. When in the 1992 General Election campaign, Douglas Hurd proclaimed that any breach in the Anglo-Scottish Union would be 'a betrayal of ancestors', he was alluding to the Burkean social contract between the dead, the living and those yet to be born, an organicism which empowers its roots.[24]

Burke's *Reflections on the Revolution in France* (1790) thus appears to provide a perfect moment of closure for the period covered by this book: a powerful organicist defence of the British state, and an attack on the deconstruction of the organic state of France by overtheorized revolutionaries. And yet Edmund Burke can be read as as much of a perfect figure of disturbance in this tableau of British unity. One of the many paradoxes in the life and beliefs

of this great thinker was that the recognition of national particularism, which accompanied his organicist beliefs, led him to recognize differences and difficulties in the British polity and its
Empire, which those who prefer a constructive model of identity
have sometimes since smoothed over. The trouble with theorizing
the imagined community, or the account given by such scholars as
Ernest Gellner of nationalism, is the underlying assumption that
the theory operates independently of particular circumstance, the
same problem as is found in Said's postcolonial account of
Ireland, discussed in Chapter 4. 'Circumstances', Burke famously
proclaimed, 'in reality lend their colour to every human action.'
Burke's opposition to theory was itself truly theoretical: it insisted
on taking account of all factors, and not simply glossing over differences between Ireland, Wales, France, America and India.

In her acclaimed *Britons* (1992), Linda Colley offered a vision of
British unity in the eighteenth century based on Protestantism
and economic self-interest: a codification and revision of a very
traditional position. This book has not endorsed her views as concerns the earlier part of the century, but by 1789, and especially in
the years following, it has increasing validity. British unity was conditionally achieved in the face not so much of a Catholic, as a deist
and revolutionary France. The crises of prolonged war, and the
huge disturbances provoked by Napoleon in Europe, helped to
close many of the remaining gaps in belief and practice through
an implementation of counter-revolutionary Tory values: though
particularist practices still remained as important local loyalties
within the imperial framework. When Ireland, in armed rebellion
in 1798, was joined to Britain by the 1801 Union, the process
might have seemed complete.

Much continued to depend, however, on the strength of
English identity and power in the age of Empire, when many
Scots, Welsh and even Irish were willing to identify themselves as
'English', at least abroad. This strength and this willingness were
the cement of the imperial age, but the absence of one or both
was to prove trying in a context where Britain as a whole still
retained strong localist particularism bound to languages, culture
or institutions. Hegel wrote 'that the development or attainment
of values in the state takes place in a concrete medium of laws,
customs, and, in general, institutions', thus implicitly endorsing
Burke's stress on particularism. Britain did not, in 1789, and does

not today, satisfy these conditions, being more akin to Hegel's
definition of a 'civil society', when the state is not 'an actual, historical event ... the *living will* of its people'. Despite John
Redwood's recent assertion (remarkable from a former Welsh
Secretary) that Britain had spoken 'a common language for a
thousand years', differing language groups were, and to some
extent still are, important denominators of difference. Moreover,
Irish, Scottish and northern English society were and are viewed
as to different degrees distinct from British behavioural norms.
Institutions and religious practice which reflected this were still
strong in 1789 and continue today, while the disestablishment of
Anglicanism in Ireland and Wales in the nineteenth and early
twentieth centuries can be seen as further breaches of institutional unity in historical time. Scotland's separate legal system,
widely regarded as a potential bar to Union at the time, denominated and denominates a complex series of differing values on
issues as diverse as house purchase, sheriffdoms and the procura-
tor fiscal service (now partly copied in the Crown Prosecution
Service), while Scotland's other domestic institutions have always,
at least in part, followed a separate agenda, as Lindsay Paterson
argues in *The Autonomy of Modern Scotland*. Most important
perhaps is the fact that British identity and history, whether portrayed in history, journalism, cultural studies, social sciences or
now through the electronic media, has historically tended to
present a view both of its past and present which minimizes
internal difference to an absurd degree, promoting ignorance of
British diversity at the heart of Britain and irritation with multiple
examples of petty misunderstanding at the margin. There is a gulf
in communication here which bears witness to the distinction
between what Peter Heeks has identified as the 'logos' ('demonstrable truth') and the 'mythos ('authoritative pronouncement')
of history. In short, British history has often neglected logos for
mythos. As I suggested at the beginning of Chapter 1, in constantly reiterating a central narrative, a mythos has been constructed and immeasurably strengthened: what Heeks calls the
'authoritative normativity of a tradition ... the *doxa*, a common ...
assumption rooted ... in the prevailing political or social order'
has prevailed, and if there are unusual or unfamiliar details in this
book, this is because it has sought to uncover areas of the logos, of
'demonstrable truth', often passed over.[25]

During the Napoleonic Wars and the heyday of industrialization and Empire, British difference was enshrined in local patriotisms which themselves were often strong commercially, and could express themselves in domestic space. But at no time were these differences eradicated, and sometimes they grew wider. The study of the eighteenth century is very important because this is the period out of which, to choose an organic reading, Britain was engendered. It was a state which achieved great success in foreign policy in that century, but it was still a divided state (even if French proposals to split Britain into three republics were unworkable, the very fact that they repeatedly got as far as government consideration was interesting). Britain did not think of resurrecting Burgundy or Aquitaine in the event of a French defeat; but Britain was divisible along legal, institutional and national lines in a way France was not. Britain consolidated and triumphed; but internal differences were in the end submerged only to return in the prolonged, bloody and incompetent loss of Ireland at what was supposed to be the zenith of Empire: and the fact that the rhetoric of the Irish struggle on both sides reached back to the Jacobite era is important. No other internal difference has reached this magnitude since Culloden: but the lack of parity of esteem for institutional and cultural diversity within Britain, the price once paid for imperial solidarity under the banner of Englishness, now provides, in the absence of discrete domestic and imperial space, a persisting irritation, though as yet no more than that, even if the sounds of identities being constructed mar the slumbers of the British lion, from whose strength such sweet triumphs once flowed.

NOTES

1. Seamus Heaney's address to the first Region and Nation conference at the University of Aberdeen in 1986.
2. Murray G. H. Pittock, 'Forging North Britain in the Age of Macpherson', *Edinburgh Review* 93 (1995), 125–39 (125); Fiona Stafford, *The Sublime Savage* (Edinburgh, 1988), pp. 18, 46.
3. Bailey Saunders, *The Life and Letters of James Macpherson* (London, 1894), pp. 20, 183, 236n.; Stafford (1988), p. 2; P. Hume Brown, cited in R. A. Jamieson and Murdo Macdonald, 'An Ossianic Miscellany', *Edinburgh Review* 93 (1995), 91–124 (116).

4. Jamieson and Macdonald (1995), 115–16; George Pratt Insh, *The Scottish Jacobite Movement* (Edinburgh and London, 1952), p. 183.

5. Cf. Kenneth G. Simpson, *The Protean Scot* (Aberdeen, 1988); Murray G. H. Pittock, *The Invention of Scotland: the Stuart Myth and the Scottish Identity, 1638 to the Present* (London and New York, 1991), ch. 3; Jamieson and Macdonald (1995), 105; Pittock, *Edinburgh Review* (1995), p. 136; Pratt Insh (1952), p. 175.

6. Cf. Murray G. H. Pittock, *The Myth of the Jacobite Clans* (Edinburgh, 1995), ch. 4.

7. William Bernard McCarthy, *The Ballad Matrix* (Bloomington, IN, 1990) for a discussion of Agnes Lyle and the politics of repertoire (cf. p. 143 in particular).

8. Duncan Macmillan, writing in *Cencrastus* 17 (1984), 25–29 (28); Peter Womack, *Improvement and Romance: Constructing the Myth of the Highlands* (Basingstoke, 1989), p. 66.

9. Arthur Johnston, *Enchanted Ground: The Study of Medieval Romance in the Eighteenth Century* (London, 1964), p. 120n; Joseph Ritson, *Scottish Songs*, 2 vols., (London, 1794), II: p. 79n.; Dave Harker, *Fakesong* (Milton Keynes, 1985), p. 18.

10. Harker (1985), pp. 8, 40, 41, 48; Prys T. J. Morgan, 'The Clouds of Witnesses: The Welsh Historical Tradition', in R. Bruley Jones (ed.), *Anatomy of Wales* (Glamorgan, 1972), pp. 17–42 (30); Geraint Jenkins, *The Foundations of Modern Wales: Wales 1642–1780* (Oxford, 1987), p. 224.

11. There is a good discussion of the effect of Paine's ideas in H. T. Dickinson, *Liberty and Property* (London, 1977); John Cannon, *Samuel Johnson and the Politics of Hanoverian England* (Oxford, 1994), p. 204.

12. Cf. Conor Cruise O'Brien, *The Great Melody* (London, 1992).

13. For Paine's beliefs, see Mark Philp, *Paine* (Oxford, 1989).

14. Cannon (1994).

15. Mary Wollstonecraft, *A Vindication of the Rights of Woman* (Penguin edition), pp. 102, 128; Jane Austen, *Northanger Abbey* (Penguin edition), pp. 37–8.

16. Robert Towler and A. P. M. Coxon, *The Fate of the Anglican Clergy: A Sociological Study* (London and Basingstoke, 1979) charts the living standards of the Anglican priesthood.

17. William Blake, *The Poems* (Penguin edition), pp. 106, 107, 108, 123, 127, 128, 221 ff.

18. The very title of Wordsworth and Coleridge's *Lyrical Ballads* is indicative of the hybridity between high and oral culture which they sought.

19. D. B. Swinfen, 'The American Revolution in the Scottish Press', in Owen Dudley Edwards and George Shepperson (eds.), *Scotland, Europe and the American Revolution* (Edinburgh, 1976), pp. 66–74 (73); George Pratt Insh, 'Thomas Muir of Huntershill', National Library of Scotland Advocates MS 23.3.30 (Eaglescarnie Papers Deposit 344 Box 1), pp. 61, 166–7; Henry Meikle, *Scotland and the French Revolution* (Glasgow, 1912), pp. 67, 147; John Brims in Roger Mason (ed.), *Scotland and England 1286–1815* (Edinburgh, 1987), pp. 247–65 (247, 253, 261); Morgan in

Jones (1972), p. 34; Peter Berresford Ellis, *The Celtic Revolution* (Talybont, 1993 (1985)), p. 44; E. W. McFarland, *Ireland and Scotland in the Age of Revolution* (Edinburgh, 1994), pp. 235, 248 ff., 255; Nancy J. Curtin, *The United Irishmen: Popular Politics in Ulster and Dublin 1791–1798* (Oxford, 1994), pp. 4, 11, 201; S. J. Connolly, *Religion, Law and Power: The Making of Protestant Ireland 1650–1760* (Oxford, 1992), p. 131; Oliver Rafferty, *Catholicism in Ulster 1603–1983* (London, 1994), p. 91; John Brims, 'Scottish Radicalism and the United Irishmen', in David Dickson, Daire Keogh and Kevin Whelan (eds.), *The United Irishmen: Republicanism, Radicalism and Rebellion* (Dublin, 1993), pp. 151–61 (156, 157); for earlier French plans to break Britain up into separate republics, see Frank McLynn, 'An Eighteenth-Century Scots Republic: An Unlikely Project from Absolutist France', *Scottish Historical Review* 59 (1980), 177–81.

20.   McFarland (1994), p. 240; Murray G. H. Pittock, *The Invention of Scotland,* (London and New York, 1991), chs. 3, 4.

21.   Brims, in Mason (1987), p. 254; Meikle (1912), p. 122; *The Poems and Songs of Robert Burns*, ed. James Kinsley, Volume 2 (Oxford, 1968).

22.   Murray G. H. Pittock, *Poetry and Jacobite Politics in Eighteenth-Century Britain and Ireland* (Cambridge, 1994), p. 219.

23.   Gwyn A. Williams, *When Was Wales?* (London, 1979), p. 6; Benedict Anderson, *Imagined Communities: Reflections on the Origin and Spread of Nationalism* (London, 1983).

24.   Cf. Pittock (1995), Introduction and chapter 1.

25.   Gerald Newman, *The Rise of English Nationalism: A Cultural History 1740–1830* (London, 1987), p. 242; Michael H. Mitias, *Moral Foundations of the State in Hegel's 'Philosophy of Right'* (Amsterdam, 1984), p. 33; Peter Heeks, 'Myth, History and Theory', in *History and Theory* 33:1 (1994), 1–19 (1, 3); Lindsay Paterson, *The Autonomy of Modern Scotland* (Edinburgh, 1994).

Select Bibliography

Burnett, John, *A History of the Cost of Living*, Harmondsworth, 1969.
    Good overview; now appears a little out of date.
Cannon, John, *Samuel Johnson and the Politics of Hanoverian England*, Oxford, 1994.
    A close study of the interrelationship of history and literature in the life of one of the century's foremost figures.
Chitnis, Anand, *The Scottish Enlightenment: A Social History*, London, 1976.
    Wide-ranging and fair account of the Scottish Enlightenment in context.
Clark, Jonathan, *English Society 1688–1832*, Cambridge, 1985.
    The definitive revisionist study of the period.
——, *Samuel Johnson*, Cambridge, 1994.
    A bid to revise the literary history of the eighteenth century.
Colley, Linda, *Britons: Forging the Nation 1707–1837*, New Haven, CT, 1992.
    Highly acclaimed study which makes the case for a common British religious and economic identity at a fairly early date.
Connolly, S. J., *Religion, Law and Power: The Making of Protestant Ireland 1650–1760*, Oxford, 1992.
    Outstanding and provocative revisionist study.
Cruickshanks, Eveline, ed., *Ideology and Conspiracy: Aspects of Jacobitism 1689–1759*, Edinburgh, 1982.
Cruickshanks, Eveline and Black, Jeremy, eds., *The Jacobite Challenge*, Edinburgh, 1988.
    Good general collections of essays on the subject.
Dickinson, H. T., *Liberty and Property*, London, 1977.
    Excellent and clear account of the major ideological shifts in the century.
——, *Caricatures and the Constitution*, Cambridge, 1986. A rewardingly close look at the political print in the French Revolutionary period.
——, *The Politics of the People in Eighteenth-Century Britain*, Basingstoke, 1995.
    Scholarly and detailed; heavily focused on England.
Dickson, David, Keogh, Daire and Whelan, Kevin, eds., *The United Irishmen: Republicanism, Radicalism and Rebellion*, Dublin, 1993.
    Good modern collection of essays on the subject.

Dwyer, John, Mason, Roger A. and Murdoch, Alexander, eds., *New Perspectives on the Politics and Culture of Early Modern Scotland*, Edinburgh, n.d. [1983].
> A detailed and varied collection, with many outstanding essays.

Ellis, Peter Berresford, *The Celtic Revolution: A Study in Anti-Imperialism*, Ceredigion, 1993 (1985).
> A decided *parti pris* with many interesting suggestions and anecdotes.

Holmes, Geoffrey, *The Trial of Doctor Sacheverell*, London, 1973.
> The most thorough account available of the Sacheverell phenomenon.

Holmes, Geoffrey and Szechi, Daniel, *The Age of Oligarchy: Pre-industrial Britain 1722–1783*, London, 1993.
> Wide-ranging and sensitive account.

Jenkins, Geraint H., *The Foundations of Modern Wales: Wales 1642–1780*, Oxford, 1987.
> Detailed examination of Wales in the period.

Jones, Clyve, ed., *Britain in the First Age of Party 1680–1750: Essays Presented to Geoffrey Holmes*, London, 1987.
> Good coverage of Scotland and Ireland.

Langford, Paul, *Public Life and the Propertied Englishman 1689–1798*, Oxford, 1991.
> An exhaustive account of the importance of property.

Lawson, Philip, *The East India Company: A History*, London, 1993.
> Good general survey of one of the major motors of Empire.

Lenman, Bruce, *Integration, Enlightenment and Industrialisation: Scotland 1746–1832*, London, 1981.
> Precise, scholarly and readable account.

Lynch, Michael, ed., *Jacobitism and the '45*. London, 1995.
> Opinions on the 250th anniversary of the 1745 Rising.

McFarland, E. W., *Ireland and Scotland in the Age of Revolution*, Edinburgh, 1994.
> One of the very few books on this important subject.

McLynn, Frank, *Crime and Punishment in Eighteenth-Century England*, London, 1989.
> A highly politically aware account of its subject.

Marshall, Rosalind K., *Virgins and Viragos*, London, 1983.
> An excellent and underrated history of women in Scotland.

Mason, Roger A. (ed.), *Scotland and England 1286–1815*, Edinburgh, 1987.
> Particularly good coverage of the debate in the seventeenth and eighteenth centuries.

Monod, Paul, *Jacobitism and the English People, 1688–1788*, Cambridge, 1989.
> The standard account of English Jacobitism.

Moody, T. W. and Vaughan, W. E., eds., *A New History of Ireland Vol. 4: Eighteenth-Century Ireland 1691–1800*, Oxford, 1986.
> Coverage of Ireland during the period.

Newman, Gerald, *The Rise of English Nationalism: A Cultural History 1740–1830*, London, 1987.
Alert and reflective study.

O'Brien, Conor Cruise, *The Great Melody*, London, 1992.
An extraordinarily powerful study of Edmund Burke and his whole milieu: good on the question of dual British and Irish identity in the eighteenth century.

O'Callaghan, J. C., *The Irish Brigades in the Service of France*, Glasgow, 1870.
Still unrivalled in many respects.

Philpin, C. H. E., ed., *Nationalism and Popular Protest in Ireland*, Cambridge, 1987.
Good contemporary opinions on the subject.

Pittock, Murray G. H., *Poetry and Jacobite Politics in Eighteenth-Century Britain and Ireland*, Cambridge, 1994.
A 'four nations' literary history of the 1688–1832 period.

——, *The Myth of the Jacobite Clans*, Edinburgh, 1995.
An examination of the means whereby British history is constructed, focusing in particular on misrepresentations of the '45.

Rogers, Katharine, *Feminism in Eighteenth-Century England*, Brighton, 1982.
Good examination of the topic.

Rule, John, *The Vital Century: England's Developing Economy 1714–1815*, London, 1992.
Good for economic change and development.

Samuel, Raphael, ed., *Patriotism: The Making and Unmaking of British National Identity*, 3 vols., London and New York, 1989.
One of the most variegated and sensitive examinations of the question.

Schwoerer, Lois G., ed., *The Revolution of 1688–1689: Changing Perspectives*, Cambridge, 1992.
A cultural examination of the Revolutions of 1688–9.

Szechi, Daniel, *The Jacobites*, Manchester, 1994.
Short, stimulating and original study.

Trevelyan, G. M., *English Social History: A Survey of Six Centuries Chaucer to Queen Victoria*, London, 1945 (1942).
Still very interesting, diverse and detailed. More about the periphery than one might expect.

Womack, Peter, *Improvement and Romance: Constructing the Myth of the Highlands*, Basingstoke, 1989.
Interesting and suggestive but rather overtheoretical.

Index

Defoe, Daniel, 21, 31, 58, 66, 70
  women in his work, 90
Deism, 128
Denham, Sir John, 88, 132
Derry, 109
Devonshire, 24
Disruption (1843), 170
Dissent, 5, 40
  strength of, 45–6
  threat to Anglicanism, 128
Dissenters, 15
  strength of, 45
  penalties on, 80–1, 122
  persecution of, 104–5
  riots against, 121
  economic success of, 122
  at Scottish universities, 138
Dissenting conscience, 164–5
Douglas, Gavin (Bishop of
    Dunkeld), 117
Druidism, 36, 104, 107, 112
Dryden, John, 4, 8, 23, 33, 34–5, 37,
    88
  and popular culture, 22
Dublin, 45, 81, 108, 109, 118, 133
Dunblane, 19
Dundee (town), 78
Dundee, John Graham, Viscount of,
    27, 106, 109
Dunfermline, Earl of, 53
Duns, 139
Durham, 58

East India Company (Scottish), 26
  (English), 70
Edinburgh, 7, 78, 118, 119, 135,
    139
  population of, 9, 71
  in 1685, 9
  New Town, 130, 136
  university, 135, 138, 139–40
Education Act (1696), 85, 138
Edward I, 29
Eliot, George, 163
Elizabeth I of England, 3
  and Wales, 14
  royal symbolism of, 34
  and Essex's rebellion, 39

Emmet, Robert, 132
enclosure movement, 77–8
England, 1
  nationality and identity of, 54
  in 1685, 2, 6
  claims to suzerainty over
    Scotland, 29–30, 37
  view of Anglo-Scottish Union,
    58–9
Episcopalians, 102
  and historiography, 143
  culture of, 154
Episcopal Church
  strength of, 10, 18, 41, 45
  royalism of, 20
  toleration of (1712), 27
  and Catholicism, 43–4, 53
  and the Union, 44
  and the Episcopal Church of
    America, 44
  persecution of, 81
Eton, 129
Essex, 98
Etherege, George, 38
Evans, Evan, 155
Exclusion Crisis, 3, 8, 53
Exeter, 24, 119

famine
  in Scotland, 26
Ferguson, Adam, 136
Fergusson, Robert, 19, 78, 117,
    158
Fielding, Henry, 21, 38, 74, 93,
    101
Financial Revolution, 66–8, 70–84
Fire of London (1666), 4, 9
Fletcher, Andrew of Saltoun, 25, 32,
    115
Flint, George, 43
Flintshire, 13, 14, 15
folk culture, 114–18
Forbes, Lord Alexander of Pitsligo,
    101–2
Ford, John, 39
Foundation myths
  of England and Scotland, 28–9,
    35, 37, 112

Index

Lightning Source UK Ltd.
Milton Keynes UK
UKHW012152200820
368567UK00003B/757